Classic American Cooking

PEARL BYRD FOSTER

Drawings by SUSAN GABER

SIMON AND SCHUSTER
NEW YORK

MANUFACTURED IN THE UNITED STATES OF AMERICA
1   3   5   7   9   10   8   6   4   2
LIBRARY OF CONGRESS CATALOGING IN PUBLICATION DATA

FOSTER, PEARL BYRD.
CLASSIC AMERICAN COOKING.

INCLUDES INDEX.
1. COOKERY, AMERICAN.   I. TITLE.
TX715.F754   1983   641.5973   83-14946
ISBN 0–671–44303–8

ACKNOWLEDGMENTS

I am most grateful to Evelyn Connell for her tremendous dedication and assistance in the painstaking transcription of the recipes and uncountable hours of testing them; to Kim Honig, my editor, for her patience in transforming hundreds of recipes into a book; and, of course, to Jim Villas, for his unwavering support of my work throughout the years.

And thanks to the countless others, too numerous to name here, who have been helpful to me all along the way.

CONTENTS

CONTENTS

CONTENTS

INTRODUCTION

by James Villas

Before Pearl Byrd Foster retired from the restaurant business in New York to devote all her attention to this long-awaited book, guests arrived at the front door of Mr. & Mrs. Foster's Place in proper attire, having been informed while making a reservation on the phone that it was jacket and tie for the gentlemen. You were also told politely by that soft Virginia voice not to be late and not to have much for lunch. You knocked just as you would at a private home, the locked doors opened, and there stood the elegant Mrs. Foster swathed in dark Ultrasuede and hardly the image of one who had been cooking since noon. The place was minuscule, and the decor could have been described as austere had it not been for the exquisite floral arrangements. No menu, no fancy china or flatware, a limited but intelligent wine list with the finest American labels—no nonsense. You were there to see Mrs. Foster and taste her innovative American food, and, like the other sybarites waiting to be served, you knew this was serious business.

To suggest that this lady has become a legend in her own time is not hyperbole, and to insinuate that she is one of the pioneers of what is now being called the New American Cuisine is a triumph of understatement. Professional gastronomes, journalists, luminaries and ordinary lovers of great food the world over showed up repeatedly on East Eighty-first Street, not only to savor Pearl's inimitable creations but, without fail, to make one more futile attempt to discover the secrets of her duck pâté, hot lemon soup, Bourbon beef and oyster pot, and snow cream. As for myself, I came to cherish this place as a sort of culinary shrine, just as I've come to cherish my close friendship with Pearl more than that with anyone else in the profession. The truth is that whether the subject be the biblical origins of carob, the gustatory merits of mutton, the medicinal qualities of garlic, the intricate seasoning of pâtés or the boning of a gigantic goose, she is a veritable encyclopedia of knowledge. Most food enthusiasts flock to their vast culinary libraries when in need of inspiration and information; I pick up the phone and call Pearl Foster.

"Exactly who is Mrs. Foster and what is she really like?" were the questions most frequently asked by those who visited the restaurant, watched her ring the small silver bell that preluded the description of her famous soups and desserts, and listened to her informal table discourses on food and wine punctuated throughout by her very Southern "honey" this and "darling" that. Well, I suppose I could go into biographical detail about how, as a child, she crossed the Oklahoma prairie in a covered wagon, foraged for wild persimmons and Jerusalem artichokes (which she crunched raw), cultivated her own quarter-acre of tomatoes and, by the age of twelve, was creating and preparing dishes for the family meals; or how she played the New York stage before meeting her late husband; or why she turned over the opportunity to be the first passenger to fly the Atlantic to a girl named Amelia Earhart ("I was frightened, let's face it, and she was brave"); or why she used to meet her celebrated cousin, Admiral Richard E. Byrd, under the clock at the Biltmore ("Don't forget, honey, I'm a Byrd on both sides of the family"). Over the years her pink cloche hats and smart white turbans contributed much to the orchidaceous July transatlantic sailings of her beloved *France* and *Queen Elizabeth II*, and Pearl thought nothing of boarding those ships bearing such staples as almonds, carob powder and raw sugar, as precautions against the possibility that she might be asked by somebody in England or France to prepare her carob almond torte. Summers in Europe found her rambling about the kitchen of some Scottish castle, talking food with Waverly Root in Paris, learning to skin eels in Brussels, grilling *loup au fenouil* in an apartment in southern France, observing the subtleties of pasta making at the Gritti Palace in Venice or savoring the glories of Alsatian cuisine at her beloved Auberge de l'Ill in Illhaeusern. When there was something new to learn about food, no place was too distant for Pearl, and when she found a dish she truly loved, she wasted no time transforming it into something with distinct American character.

"Oh, darling, why must you go on about those aspects of my life?" she's forever chiding. And indeed, the only topic that really sustains Pearl's interest at any given time is the dish or dinner on which she currently happens to be working. Most customers at the restaurant were content enough just to hear her discuss the luscious creations served on a regular basis as part of the six-course, fixed-price dinner: tiny chicken livers in Madeira; a wedge of feathery quiche (the recipe for which even I was never able to obtain); a choice of homemade soups (Virginia peanut, hot lemon, mushroom consommé, cold apple) with fresh corn sticks "for dunkin'"; salad with red-wine dressing; such main courses (ordered in advance on the phone) as trout with macadamia nut butter, Bourbon beef and oyster pot, and boned duck with apple and wild rice; and for dessert, pecan pie, carob cheesecake, snow cream, frosty lime pie and any other delicacy Pearl might have whipped up.

But Pearl's inventive mind has always been in search of new flavors, different textures, and new combinations that might contribute to her lifelong campaign to elevate the spirit of American cookery from the banal to the sublime. When someone once sent her a case of California walnuts, she set out to create both a new pâté that had crunch and a plantation molasses-and-walnut pie; when a twelve-pound country ham arrived from an admirer in Kentucky, she first tested it in her jambalaya, found the cured flavor too assertive, then incorporated it successfully into Texas wheat puffs; and no sooner had she received a freshly killed goose from Long Island than she devised an apple, prune and walnut stuffing for the goose, which was served with port gravy. Yogurt pie enriched with pure clover honey, Brussels sprouts sautéed with peanuts, squash soup spiked with apple, shrimp and corn chowder, roast boned chicken with curried chutney glaze, potato salad with hot Creole mustard, lemon soufflé pudding—Pearl's creations go on and on, year after year. And after begging so long for recipes, we now finally have this magnificent collection of her prized recipes.

No one who knows Pearl can be unaware of her short temper in the face of phoniness and pretension, and nothing incurs her wrath faster than any suggestion that Paul Bocuse, Michel Guérard, and other famous French chefs have brought about a radical change in the food world by insisting that the freshest ingredients be prepared in the simplest manner possible. "Baloney!" she retorts. "I've personally done the Lyons markets with Bocuse—at a date, that is, when he actually shopped himself—and what I saw him doing was no different from what I've been doing for decades with my American food. No doubt Paul is a very fine chef during those increasingly rare moments he's actually in the kitchen, but as for creating a new approach to ingredients and cooking, well, it's just not so. Darling, if you want to see a couple of truly serious chefs in France who share many of my own views, either make your way into Paul Haeberlin's kitchen at the Auberge de l'Ill or visit Richard Olney at his villa near Toulon."

Unlike the many other restaurant chefs of whom she doesn't exactly approve, Pearl has always done her rounds of the markets every working day of the week, and at the restaurant she did stay in her kitchen from exactly twelve noon till the last order was served late in the evening. Having picked up a few kiwi fruit (years before the item became so fashionable), salad greens and fresh vegetables, dairy products from a health-food store, perhaps an especially handsome chicken or slab of calf's liver, and heaven knows what other ingredients intended for heaven knows what dishes to be either tested or served that evening, she prepared herself for deliveries of meat and seafood in much the same way Henri Soulé used to await his caviar merchants. "Honey, those lobsters had better be kicking!" I once heard her say to a terrified delivery boy, "and if there's one whiff of odor to that backfin crab meat, you'll be making a trip back here within the hour." "You see, honey," she continued, turning to me while grabbing for the crab meat, "the question you must always ask is 'How fresh is fresh?' Sure, they'll tell you that the shrimp and pompano are fresh, but what I want to know is how long did it take that shrimp to arrive in New York from the Carolinas, and how long did it sit there on ice before reaching my front door? You just never know, not till you smell it and check the texture."

Although a lady of a certain age (a subject one would be well advised not to pursue in her presence), Pearl has always been viewed as a cyclone of energy, determination, and self-confidence, the type of dynamic individual who has tremendous faith in her own instincts and abilities and little respect for those who don't strive to realize their full potential. If some might accuse her of *amour-propre* when it comes to the way she enjoys talking about her food, it's only because they don't quite understand her overall sense of mission and profound devotion to American cooking and eating well. "My taste buds are alive and I have a lot of energy," she once wrote me from France. "My vitality seems endless, and my desire to learn is so deep it burns inside me. Change my style of American food? No—no—a thousand times no! But I must learn more about French foods—the uses of butter and other fats, the fascinating ways of preparing vegetables, the different cuts of meat, the sauces." People who mistake this sort of enthusiasm and dedication for egoism had best indeed stay clear of Pearl Byrd Foster.

Over the years I must have exchanged with Pearl literally hundreds of notes, letters, and spur-of-the-moment memos resulting from our mutual obsession with the gustatory experience, but I treasure none of her astute communications more than the one she was once inspired to write during a night of insomnia. Scrawled, as always, on sheets of personalized Tiffany stationery, the rambling missive not only sums up much of her gastronomic philosophy but also identifies her, like M.F.K. Fisher, as a female Brillat-Savarin of the twentieth century. I doubt that Pearl will mind my sharing a few random examples:

"Purity and simplicity: the keys to great cooking."

"Food must be beautiful in the cooking pan, on the serving platter, and on the dinner plate. This is a big order—but an important one."

"Nature's own earthy ingredients are mouthwatering, and the flavors must be maintained by not overcooking."

"Clear consommé should be a must at any great dinner."

"Plates should be spare—never overloaded."

"Fullness and richness of flavor must not be lost in a blanket of sauce."

"When invited to a dinner, punctuality is the loftiest virtue."

"With food there must always be a rhythm of design. Color effects a delight to the eye. Harmony is the key."

"Like life, food must not become routine. There are many things to do just ahead in a full life—so with food—many new experiences of taste. So one must work with great zest coupled with the desire for achievement. And there must be a bit of glory about it all."

—James Villas, Food and Wine Editor of *Town & Country* and author of *American Taste: A Celebration of Gastronomy Coast to Coast,* June 1982

FOREWORD

Another cookbook? Yes, another cookbook! Why, then, with the shelves in the bookstores stacked with cookery books, do I assemble a book and finally have it published, drawing from literally thousands of my recipes, some traditional American, some purely Southern and mainly my own taste combinations that have evolved over the thirty years I have been cooking and teaching and serving the public?

Because so many of you have asked for it. However, I warn those of you who are not familiar with the apron, the boning knife and the stove that cooking is hard work. To be a truly good cook you must *love* it, and there should be a bit of glory in the results.

Also, more of you than I can count have asked me *where, when* and *how* I learned to cook—so be patient with me for a moment and I will go back through the years and tell you briefly how it all started.

My *very first* memory of food was gathering and eating the sweet wild persimmon. To quiet my incessant begging for this precious sweet, my Uncle Willard Byrd hoisted me high onto his shoulder, carried me out into a heavy snowstorm, with a basket clutched in my mittened hands, to a wild persimmon tree. I picked and filled the basket with the icy fruit, which we took back to the fireside where everyone participated and enjoyed the icy sweet goodness of the wild persimmon from which we often made a cream pie.

My father, a teacher—adventurous and restless to see and live in an undeveloped area of our land—decided to lift our deep Southern roots and take us to southwestern Oklahoma, where the people and the prairie land were so different from the lush green beauty of the South; almost everything that grew was so different from that of our beloved South. However, in no time I learned to gather wild edible greens in spring and to help my mother with her garden. All this was very important because my father's salary was small and times were indeed hard.

One year I was permitted to have one-quarter of an acre of land to use as my very own in any way I desired. I planted tomatoes in what was virgin soil. The harvest—after many hours of digging soil, pulling weeds, removing the long green worms that ate the green tomato leaves—was bountiful. It was there at an early age I began to love and respect the soil.

I learned to can, to preserve, to make catsup, chili sauce, piccalilli, and to develop—with Mother's guidance—various recipes with the tomatoes. Also, I participated in all the other food preparations, in the making of apple butter, pumpkin soup, pumpkin butter and numerous canned and preserved fruits and vegetables. It gave me a sense of accomplishment to learn to make buttery hot biscuits and delicious corn pone; to fry chicken; to help in making sausage and hogsheads cheese; to cure the hams; to make lard; to cook black-eyed peas topped with pods of okra; etc., etc. I always found a beauty in food—the colors, flavors, shapes all fascinated me. I sought books that explored the origins of various foods.

Also during the school vacation months I cooked the main noontime meal (dinner) for the family and several farm workers. That is where, at the eager age of twelve, I started to create my own recipes—surprising my family (and, of course, I do believe now, in order to hear their praise) with dishes like Creamed Leeks on Crusty Corn Bread Squares. A large clump of leeks grew in a field at least a half-mile from the house. Day after day I jumped the furrowed ridges of upturned soil with a basket slung over my arm to gather leeks. I pulled them up, sometimes breaking them off at the top of the soil. Fresh Corn Pudding and a Salad of Mustard Greens smothered with crushed crisp bacon and hard-boiled egg with a hot vinegar topping were also some of my creations.

When the crops were "laid by," the land did not need us, so it became vacation time away from the farm. We packed up, hitched up our horses—old Beck and George—to a covered wagon and drove far over the praries, cooking our meals using dry mesquite wood for fire—a crude procedure indeed. Mother let me help her prepare our favorite stews on these trips—such as Red River Stew and—most popular of all—the Covered Wagon Stew. The food for stews on a covered wagon trip would keep without *refrigeration*—an almost unknown prairie word in those days.

The years slipped by and the time came to go away to school. Even though my love for cooking was very deep, I decided after a visit to the circus with all the beautiful horses, the dancing and the clowns that I wanted to be a performer on the stage.

My parents sent me to New York, where I lived with Uncle Thomas Byrd's family and attended private school. From there I went to the university, where I studied and worked toward a career in the theater. After a brief fling on the stage, I realized that since I could not reach the top in my chosen field, it would be wise to change careers, so I left the theater.

I returned to my first love—cooking, and learning and living with food. I took a position as a hostess in one of New York's famous restaurants hoping to learn more about food and restaurant management.

However, after a few months, my independent, creative spirit (I was bold—made recommendations from the very start and was ignored) was smothered and I left, seeking a place where my ideas and respect for food would be accepted.

All through these months I was tempted to return to the theater. Once I even tried to attract attention by a publicity campaign: glamorous photos of me were disseminated, clothes specially designed, and even a news release was printed up revealing that I'd be the first woman passenger to fly the Atlantic. After a couple of weeks, however, I became overwhelmed with fear (a premonition perhaps?) and I turned this much-publicized trip over to a fabulous and courageous young woman, far better equipped emotionally than I was for the flight—Amelia Earhart.

So I gladly went back to the kitchen and spent long hours cooking, tasting and trying to do an outstanding job. Having a sensitive taste for flavors, I determined never to present a dish to anyone that I did not like—would not eat myself. This policy has prevailed over the thirty-odd years that I served the public.

After some attempts to locate just the right job so that I could preserve my own food ideas, I found a position in a little restaurant then named "Foster." This evolved into four restaurants and a commissary employing over two hundred staff members. My late husband, an advertising man, turned over the entire operation to me. Later when these restaurants were sold, I opened the Schooner, where my own test kitchen was built and where I worked for two years as a chef under the direction of the famous Louis Diat—learning the many basics of French cuisine. This restaurant was sold after two years. From the Schooner I went to a large national company for eleven years where I created recipes, taught, and gave large-scale food promotions. I was then asked to take the food editor's job for two magazines published for the restaurant trade. This lasted for several years until the magazines were sold. I then opened up another restaurant, Mr. & Mrs. Foster's Place, in New York City, where I was chef-owner. This was a successful operation for many years until I closed the restaurant and retired a few years ago—which enabled me to devote my time and energy to this book.

PEARL BYRD FOSTER

PART I

RECIPES

CHAPTER ONE

APPETIZERS

MOUSSE OF AVOCADO WITH
HERBED TOAST

½ *pound fresh spinach (for*
  concentrate)
2 *ripe avocados, peeled*
juice of 1 small lemon, strained
salt and freshly ground black pepper
few drops Tabasco sauce
  1 *to 2 tablespoons minced green*
    pepper
  2 *teaspoons unflavored gelatin*
  ¼ *cup water*
  1 *cup heavy cream, whipped*

FOR THE HERBED TOAST:
  6 *slices white bread*
  6 *tablespoons (¾ stick) unsalted*
    butter, melted
approximately 1 teaspoon mixed
  herbs (to taste)

  3 *cups shredded lettuce*
  2 *large ripe tomatoes, skins*
    removed and cut into wedges
    and 24 large capers, drained
    for garnish

METHOD:

1. To make spinach concentrate: Wash the fresh spinach, place in a heavy pot with a tight fitting cover and steam until wilted. Puree in blender and then push through a sieve. (This concentrate can be used in other recipes to color soups, vegetables, etc.)

2. Place avocado and lemon juice in blender and puree. Add salt, pepper, minced green pepper and Tabasco to taste.

3. Add gelatin to water and let stand for 5 minutes, then set bowl in pan of hot water to dissolve the gelatin. Add gelatin to avocado mixture.

4. Stir 1 tablespoon of the spinach concentrate into avocado mixture, then fold in the whipped cream and taste for seasoning, adding more salt and pepper if necessary.

5. Fill 6 well-buttered heart-shaped molds with mixture and chill for several hours.

6. *To make Herbed Toast:* Mix herbs of your choice with melted butter. Toast the bread lightly, cut off crusts and then, cutting on the diagonal, divide each slice into four pieces. Dip each piece into the herbed butter and place in hot oven to crisp.

7. To serve, place a warm towel around mold and turn out onto a bed of shredded lettuce, garnish with tomato wedges and capers and serve with the hot herbed toast.

CARROT BLINI WITH RED CAVIAR

SERVES 6
(Makes 20–24 blinis)

3 *eggs*
3 *cups coarsely grated carrots*
1 *cup all-purpose flour, sifted*
1 *teaspoon salt*
⅛ *teaspoon freshly ground black pepper*

1 *cup milk (approximately)*
unsalted butter for frying
1 *cup red caviar*
1 *cup sour cream*

METHOD:

1. Beat eggs slightly and add grated carrots.

2. Mix flour, salt and pepper together in a large bowl. Blend carrot mixture and milk alternately into seasoned flour until a thick batter is formed.

3. Melt butter in a sauté pan. When hot, spoon batter into pan to make small, thin individual cakes. Cook over moderate heat until golden brown underneath, turn with spatula and brown other side. The blini should be thin and crisp. Serve hot with caviar and sour cream on the side.

CHERRY TOMATOES WITH SOUR CREAM DIP

SERVES 6–8

1 *pint cherry tomatoes*
1 *cup sour cream*
1 *tablespoon chopped fresh dill or ½ teaspoon dried dill weed*
1 *teaspoon fresh or frozen chopped chives*

1 *tablespoon chopped fresh parsley or ½ teaspoon parsley flakes*
lettuce leaves

METHOD:

1. Wash tomatoes, leaving stems on. Drain on paper towels. Refrigerate.

2. In a small serving bowl, combine sour cream with rest of ingredients.

3. Refrigerate sauce, covered, about 1 hour, or until chilled.

4. Place dip in a bowl in center of a large serving tray. Arrange lettuce leaves around, placing cherry tomatoes on top of the lettuce.

BUTTON MUSHROOMS ON TOAST SQUARES BLANKETED WITH DILLED SOUR CREAM

SERVES 6

1 *pound fresh, firm button mushrooms*
juice of half a lemon
4 *tablespoons butter*
sweet paprika to taste

FOR THE DILLED SOUR CREAM:
½ *cup chopped fresh dill or 1 teaspoon crushed dill weed*

1 *tablespoon onion juice*
1 *pint sour cream*
salt, freshly ground black pepper and cayenne to taste

FOR THE TOAST SQUARES:
6 *slices white or whole wheat bread*
8 *tablespoons (1 stick) butter*

METHOD:

1. Wash mushrooms in a sieve or colander under running water, shake well and dry with paper towels. Remove stems and discard, or use in another dish if desired. Squeeze lemon juice over mushrooms, turning to coat.

2. Melt the 4 tablespoons butter in sauté pan, add mushrooms and toss to coat evenly with butter. Heat just *one* minute—they should remain firm and crunchy.

3. *To prepare dilled sour cream:* Stir dill and onion juice into the sour cream. Add salt, freshly ground black pepper and cayenne to taste and mix well.

4. *Prepare the toast squares:* Preheat oven to 350°F. Cut crust from bread and brush both sides of the bread slices liberally with the melted butter, then lay on cookie sheet and toast in oven until golden on both sides.

5. Place toast squares on serving plates, spoon mushrooms over the toast and cover with a blanket of dilled sour cream. Dust lightly with paprika and set under the broiler for about a minute to heat. Serve immediately.

CHEESE STRAWS

MAKES 30 STRAWS

½ cup all-purpose flour
½ cup grated Cheddar cheese,
  firmly packed
¼ teaspoon salt

⅛ teaspoon cayenne pepper
4 tablespoons butter
1 small egg, beaten

METHOD:

1. Preheat oven to 425°F.

2. Mix together the flour, cheese, salt and pepper. Cut butter into the flour mixture (as when making pastry) with pastry blender or tips of fingers until it is the same size grain as cornmeal and then add the beaten egg. If more liquid is needed to hold ingredients together, add a few drops water—the consistency should be similar to that of pastry dough. Once the dough can be gathered into a ball, stop handling it.

3. Roll dough thin (about ¼ inch thick), cut into strips and bake on ungreased baking sheet in hot oven until lightly brown—about 15 to 20 minutes.

CHEESE BALLS

MAKES APPROXIMATELY 5 DOZEN

1 pound Cheddar cheese, grated
¼ cup all-purpose flour
½ teaspoon salt
cayenne pepper
4 egg whites
2 whole eggs

⅓ cup milk
¾ cup cornflake crumbs (or more
  if necessary)
vegetable oil or shortening for
  frying

METHOD:

1. Mix cheese, flour, salt and cayenne.

2. Beat egg whites until stiff but not dry. Carefully fold into cheese mixture. Chill thoroughly.

3. Beat whole eggs, add milk and beat well.

4. Remove cheese mixture from refrigerator. With a teaspoon, scoop up small portions and shape into balls with hands.

5. Dip into egg mixture, then into cornflake crumbs. Fry in deep hot fat (350°F) for about 2 minutes. Drain on paper towels. Serve hot.

CHEESE-ANCHOVY SPREAD

SERVES 6

2 *three-ounce packages cream cheese*
½ *tube (approximately 2 ounces) anchovy paste*
1 *tablespoon lemon juice*

1 *teaspoon Worcestershire sauce*
1 *teaspoon minced onion*
crackers, potato or corn chips or bread (for canapés)

METHOD:

Mix first 5 ingredients together; chill to blend flavors. Use as a spread for crackers, potato or corn chips or on bread as a canapé topping.

CUCUMBER AND CHEESE CANAPÉ

MAKES 12 CANAPÉS

3 *ounces cream cheese, slightly softened*
2 *teaspoons chili sauce*

2 *teaspoons rum*
12 *small toast squares*
12 *cucumber slices, salted*

METHOD:

1. Blend cheese, chili sauce and rum together.
2. Spread squares of toast with mixture.
3. Place a slice of cucumber on top. Refrigerate until ready to serve.

CHICKEN LIVER AND CALIFORNIA WALNUT PÂTÉ

SERVES 6

½ pound fresh chicken livers
2 tablespoons melted butter
1 medium onion, chopped
(approximately ½ cup)
salt, freshly ground black pepper,
and paprika
6 ounces California walnuts,
chopped (approximately
1½ cups)
2 ounces (4 tablespoons) dry
sherry

2 ounces (4 tablespoons) Madeira
8 tablespoons (1 stick) unsalted
butter at room temperature
¼ teaspoon mace
½ teaspoon powdered thyme
(optional)
pinch of cayenne
lettuce leaves, thinly sliced
cucumber and freshly ground
black pepper for garnish

METHOD:

1. Cut membranes, fat and any green spots from livers. Dice and place in a broiler pan. Add the 2 tablespoons melted butter and the onion, season lightly with salt and pepper, and dust with paprika. Toss to coat livers and onion with butter. Spread liver-onion mixture thinly over pan bottom.

2. Broil close to high heat until lightly crisped. Turn with a spatula and broil other side. Remove from heat.

3. Prepare pâté: Mix the sherry and Madeira together and pour half of wine mixture into a blender (or food processor). Add walnuts a few at a time and blend after each addition until smooth. Add remaining wine and the livers and blend until all ingredients are incorporated, using a rubber spatula to scrape down the sides of the blender.

4. Add the 8 tablespoons butter, blend well, then mix in mace, thyme (if using it) and cayenne. Spoon into a serving bowl and chill thoroughly.

5. Serve on crisp leaves of lettuce surrounded by thin slices of cucumber dusted liberally with freshly ground pepper.

DUCK LIVER PÂTÉ WITH PISTACHIO NUTS

SERVES 6

1 cup (2 sticks) unsalted butter
¼ pound rendered goose fat or
other poultry fat
2 medium onions, peeled and
thinly sliced
6 large duck livers, washed and
trimmed, cut into small pieces
½ cup fine Madeira
salt and freshly ground pepper to
taste

⅛ teaspoon mace (or more if
desired)
2 drops Tabasco sauce
4 ounces toasted pistachio nuts
small crisp toast points (cut crusts
off slices of toast and slice
diagonally into 4 triangles each)
watercress for garnish

METHOD:

1. Melt butter and goose fat in a large sauté pan.

2. Toss sliced onions in melted fat to coat, then add livers. Stir-cook on low heat until livers and onions are done and onions are a light golden color. *Do not burn.*

3. Place Madeira in blender (or food processor), add livers, onions (along with fat they were fried in) and seasonings. Blend until creamy smooth, scraping from bottom once (if using a blender). Taste and correct seasonings if necessary.

4. Put half the nuts in blender, blend just to crush slightly and stir into pâté mixture.

5. Spoon pâté into mold. Smooth top. Sprinkle remaining nuts over top and refrigerate until ready to serve.

6. Serve pâté directly from mold or turn out onto a chilled plate. Garnish with watercress. Place toast points around the mold or dish.

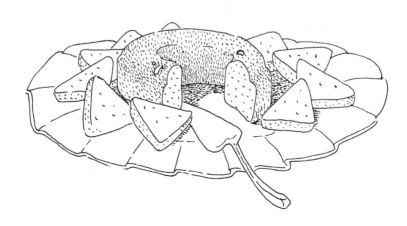

BAKED IMPERIAL CRAB SNUG HARBOR

SERVES 8

This dish also makes a wonderful luncheon entree (just increase the amounts).

3 tablespoons butter, softened
¾ cup soft bread crumbs
1½ pounds Maryland lump crab meat, shell pieces and cartilage removed
1½ tablespoons lemon juice
3 tablespoons butter
3 tablespoons all-purpose flour
1½ cups milk, warmed
3 tablespoons finely chopped green pepper
3 tablespoons minced shallots or onion

3 tablespoons small capers, well drained
¼ teaspoon Worcestershire sauce or to taste
¾ teaspoon dry mustard
salt, freshly ground black pepper and Tabasco to taste
¼ cup mayonnaise, preferably homemade
parsley
2 hard-boiled eggs, sieved
8 strips pimento for garnish

METHOD:

1. Preheat oven to 350°F.

2. Grease the bottom and sides of a baking pan with the 3 table-spoons softened butter and sprinkle crumbs over butter.

3. Sprinkle lemon juice over crab meat and lay it (without breaking the lumps) over crumbs.

4. Prepare a cream sauce: Melt the 3 tablespoons additional butter in the top of a double boiler over boiling water, then blend in flour until smooth. Add warm milk gradually, stirring constantly, and cook until thick and smooth.

5. Add green pepper, shallots or onion, capers and seasoning to cream sauce and heat it slowly for 2 to 3 minutes to cook pepper and onion. Remove from heat, fold in mayonnaise and spoon mixture over crab meat, pushing it down into the crab meat.

6. Mix parsley and sieved egg together and sprinkle over top. Place in oven and bake 15 minutes.

7. To serve: Place pimento strips over top, serving from baking pan onto hot plates.

SHREDDED CRAB BAKE

SERVES 12

This is a favorite with those who like mildly seasoned foods cooked with wine. Tomato aspic, spiced peaches and ripe olives make excellent accompaniments for a light luncheon.

2 pounds lump crab meat, shell
  pieces and cartilage removed
4 large eggs
2 tablespoons chopped parsley
2 tablespoons fresh lemon juice
1 small green pepper, minced
2 teaspoons minced onion

½ cup mayonnaise, preferably
  homemade
2 tablespoons dry sherry
1 teaspoon Worcestershire sauce
⅛ teaspoon cayenne pepper
3 to 4 cups soft bread crumbs,
  tossed in ¼ cup butter

METHOD:

1. Preheat oven to 400°F.

2. Mix all ingredients except crab meat (reserving half of the buttered crumbs for topping), then fold in crab meat, being careful not to break lumps.

3. Spoon into 12 buttered baking shells; top with remaining crumbs. Bake for 15 minutes. Serve hot.

POTTED DEVILED CRAB

SERVES 8

3 tablespoons butter
3 tablespoons all-purpose flour
1½ cups light cream
1½ teaspoons Dijon or Creole
  mustard
2 tablespoons grated onions
salt to taste
1 tablespoon lemon juice
⅛ teaspoon cayenne pepper
2 tablespoons mayonnaise,
  preferably homemade

1 tablespoon chopped fresh parsley
1 tablespoon minced green pepper
4 egg yolks, beaten
2 cups cooked lump crab meat,
  bits of shell and cartilage
  removed
1 cup soft bread crumbs
lime slices and fresh parsley sprigs
  for garnish

METHOD:

1. Preheat oven to 350°F.

2. Melt butter, mix in flour and, over medium heat, stir to a smooth paste. Then add cream, blend well and cook for a few minutes until sauce thickens.

3. Remove from heat and add mustard, grated onion, salt, lemon juice, cayenne, mayonnaise, parsley, green pepper and beaten egg yolks to mixture and blend well.

4. Add crab meat, trying not to break up the lumps.

5. Toss all ingredients lightly. Place mixture in a buttered bake-and-serve dish. Sprinkle the top with soft bread crumbs.

6. Bake for 15 to 20 minutes.

7. Serve from the baking dish, garnished with slices of lime and sprigs of parsley.

CRAB MEAT DEWEY

SERVES 8

1½ *pounds lump crab meat*
2 *shallots, chopped*
1 *cup dry white wine*
1 *cup (2 sticks) unsalted butter*
½ *pound mushrooms (stems removed), thinly sliced*
2 *tablespoons all-purpose flour*

¼ *cup heavy cream, scalded*
1 *tablespoon sliced black truffles (optional)*
salt and freshly ground black pepper to taste
8 *slices white bread*

METHOD:

1. Preheat oven to 350°F.

2. Remove shell pieces and cartilage from crab meat, and simmer for 5 minutes in its own juice.

3. Add shallots and half of the wine. Set aside.

4. Brown mushrooms in half the butter and set aside.

5. Melt remaining butter, blend in flour and mix until smooth. Add cream, remaining wine, truffles (if you are using them), mushrooms and salt and pepper to taste. Stir constantly until mixture is well-blended and has thickened. Add crab mixture.

6. Turn into a buttered baking dish and bake for 15 to 20 minutes. This may also be cooked under broiler flame. In that case, broil for 7–9 minutes, being careful that it does not burn.

7. To prepare toast points, remove the crusts from the bread slices, then toast the bread and cut diagonally into four triangles each. Serve hot with the toast points.

MARYLAND CRAB AND GRAPEFRUIT COCKTAIL WITH WHITE WINE DRESSING

SERVES 6

6 *cups finely shredded lettuce*
1 *pound cooked Maryland lump crab meat, bits of shell and cartilage removed*
2 *large grapefruits, cut into sections*
6 *large ripe strawberries, stems on, or 1 cup seedless green grapes*

FOR THE WHITE WINE DRESSING:
1 *teaspoon salt*
1 *teaspoon dry mustard*
½ *teaspoon white pepper*
½ *teaspoon sugar or honey*
¼ *cup dry white wine*
3 *drops Tabasco sauce*
2 *tablespoons fresh lemon juice, strained*
¾ *cup olive, peanut or safflower oil*

METHOD:

1. Place 1 cup shredded lettuce in each of 6 large glass goblets or glass bowls.

2. Lay the crab meat on top of the lettuce and place grapefruit sections around it.

3. *Prepare the White Wine Dressing:* Mix salt, mustard, white pepper and sugar or honey together, then add to wine and mix. Add the Tabasco and lemon juice, then the oil, a little at a time, beating after each addition until creamy smooth.

4. Spoon 2 tablespoons dressing on each serving of crab meat and place a strawberry or a few grapes on top. Serve either at room temperature or chilled, with extra dressing on the side.

MEDALLION (ROCK LOBSTER TAIL) COCKTAIL

SERVES 6

This delicious low-fat, low-calorie cocktail is suitable for almost any diet. An easy-to-prepare appetizer, it may also be made ahead of time. This recipe was developed to use frozen South African rock lobster tails. These lobsters are caught in the cold turbulent waters off the Cape of Good Hope. They go directly from those icy waters into the deep-freeze holds of ships which bring them 6,700-odd miles to our markets. Only the tails containing the tender succulent meat are shipped.

6 (*about 4½ ounces each*) *rock lobster tails*
2 *cups water*
8 *tablespoons dry vermouth*
2 *garlic cloves, crushed*
1¼ *teaspoons salt*

FOR THE COCKTAIL SAUCE:
7 *tablespoons catsup*
4 *tablespoons fresh lemon juice*
3 *tablespoons minced parsley*

lettuce leaves and watercress for garnish

METHOD:

1. Defrost and wash the lobster tails.

2. Combine water, vermouth, garlic and salt in large pan. Add tails.

3. Bring to a boil, cover and let simmer 10 minutes.

4. Remove tails, reserving liquid. Rinse the tails under cold running water, then let cool.

5. With shears, cut away thin underside membranes. Remove tail meat from shell in one piece, reserving shells. Chill the tails.

6. *Prepare a cocktail sauce* by adding catsup and lemon juice to reserved cooking water. Cook over high heat until liquid is reduced and thickened. Strain and add minced parsley. Chill.

7. To serve: Cut chilled tails into thin medallions. Replace slices in empty shells so red markings show. Place tails on chilled plates garnished with crisp lettuce leaves and springs of watercress. Spoon the cocktail sauce over each tail.

LOBSTER SARAMBA

SERVES 2

6 *tablespoons butter*
3 *tablespoons chopped green pepper*
½ *cup diced mushrooms*
salt and freshly ground black pepper to taste
2 *tablespoons all-purpose flour*
2½ *cups heavy cream*
3 *egg yolks*
¾ *cup dry sherry*

1½- to 2-*pound lobster, boiled, meat removed from shell*

FOR THE FLAVORED CRUMBS:
4 *tablespoons butter*
½ *teaspoon sweet paprika*
¾ *cup cracker crumbs*
1 *tablespoon grated Parmesan cheese*
¼ *cup dry sherry*
salt and freshly ground black pepper to taste

METHOD:

1. Melt 3 tablespoons butter in a sauté pan and sauté the green pepper and mushrooms until soft. Season with salt and pepper.

2. Blend in flour, add 1½ cups cream and, stirring constantly, gently cook over low heat for 5 minutes until smooth and moderately thick. Remove from heat.

3. Beat egg yolks and remaining cream together and slowly add to the green pepper-mushroom mixture. Again over low heat, stir until sauce thickens; do not allow it to boil.

4. Melt the remaining 3 tablespoons butter in the top part of a double boiler over hot water and add sherry and lobster meat. Heat gently.

5. Add the pepper-mushroom cream sauce to the lobster mixture, mix lightly and let stand over simmering water for about 10 minutes to blend flavors. Remove from heat.

6. *Meanwhile, prepare the flavored crumbs:* Melt the 4 tablespoons butter, add the crumbs, sauté until crumbs are golden, then add other ingredients, blending well.

7. Put the lobster mixture in a serving dish or casserole, sprinkle with the flavored crumbs and serve. For a browned, crusty top, place the dish or casserole under the broiler for a few minutes (be careful it doesn't burn).

DEVILED OYSTERS

SERVES 6

24 *large shucked oysters, drained, all pieces of shell removed*
¾ *cup Creole mustard (can be purchased in most gourmet food stores)*
2 *cups bread crumbs, seasoned*

with salt and freshly ground black pepper
vegetable oil and melted butter for frying

FOR THE CREOLE MUSTARD BUTTER:
1 *cup (2 sticks) butter*
½ *cup Creole mustard*

METHOD:

1. Warm the ¾ cup mustard and dip oysters in it, letting excess drain off. Place on a sheet of wax paper or aluminum foil.

2. *Prepare the Creole Mustard Butter:* Warm butter slightly to soften (*do not let it melt*) and add the ½ cup of mustard, stirring until smooth. Refrigerate until ready to use.

3. Dip oysters in crumbs and fry until golden in a large skillet ¼ full of vegetable oil and melted butter. Serve piping hot with the Creole Mustard Butter on the side.

CHAFING DISH OYSTERS

SERVES 12

3 *quarts shucked oysters in their liquor*
6 *tablespoons butter*
3 *tablespoons all-purpose flour*
3 *teaspoons lemon juice*

pinch of nutmeg
salt and cayenne pepper to taste
6 *egg yolks, beaten*
toast
fresh parsley for garnish

METHOD:

1. Heat oysters in their liquor until plump and edges curl.

2. Drain oysters, reserving liquor.

3. Melt butter in a chafing dish, and blend in flour, lemon juice and nutmeg, mixing until smooth.

4. Add 1 cup of oyster liquor and season with salt and cayenne to taste.

5. Remove from heat, and add egg yolks, beating well until mixture thickens. Add oysters. Return to heat for a moment until oysters are heated through. Serve on toast garnished with parsley.

OYSTERS PROVENÇALE

SERVES 6

24 oysters
1 cup olive oil
1 cup chopped onion
1 garlic clove, chopped very fine
½ cup chopped celery
½ cup chopped fresh parsley

2 cups tomato paste
4 teaspoons lime juice
2 cups oyster juice
salt and cayenne pepper to taste
slices of lime and fresh parsley
    sprigs for garnish

METHOD:

1. Remove oysters from shells. Reserve shells. Strain liquor and set that aside as well.

2. Place oysters in a bowl and pour olive oil over them.

3. Mix together chopped onion, garlic, celery and parsley and sprinkle over oysters, then toss lightly.

4. Blend tomato paste with oyster liquor and lime juice. Season with salt and cayenne pepper.

5. Combine liquid mixture with oysters, cover and refrigerate until ready to serve. Place in halved oyster shells. Serve garnished with slices of lime and parsley sprigs.

PICKLED OYSTERS

SERVES 6

24 oysters in their shells
2 cups vinegar
1 tablespoon whole allspice
few blades of mace
salt and freshly ground black
    pepper

handful of black peppercorns
peel from one small orange
1 lemon, sliced
1 sweet red pepper, chopped

METHOD:

1. Remove oysters from shells, straining and reserving the liquor.
2. Cook oysters in liquor until they curl.
3. Strain off liquor and return it to pot, keeping it hot. Put oysters in ice water, changing water twice, then drain well and place in a well-washed jar large enough to contain oysters and liquor.
4. Add vinegar, allspice, mace, salt, pepper, peppercorns and orange peel to hot oyster liquor and bring to boil. Simmer 5 minutes.
5. Add lemon slices and chopped red pepper. Cool and pour over oysters.
6. Cover jar and refrigerate for 36 hours. Serve cold.

SAVORY SCALLOPS

SERVES 12

1 cup (2 sticks) butter	3½ pounds bay scallops
1 cup minced onion	1 cup dry white wine
3 teaspoons Worcestershire sauce	

METHOD:

1. Preheat oven to 375°F.
2. Melt butter in small frying pan. Add onion and sauté until golden brown. Stir in Worcestershire sauce.
3. Pick over and rinse scallops. Divide among 12 large scallop shells or individual baking dishes. Divide butter-onion mixture evenly over scallops. Add about 1 tablespoon of wine to each portion and bake for 10 minutes. Serve at once.

SCALLOPS WITH CHAMPAGNE

SERVES 6

36 bay scallops (or 12–15 sea scallops)	1 cup champagne
salt and freshly ground black pepper	6 large scallop shells
8 tablespoons (1 stick) butter	1½ ounces fine fresh bread crumbs, preferably toasted

METHOD:

1. Preheat broiler to high.

2. Wash scallops well, and pat dry with paper towels. (If using sea scallops, cut each into 2 or 3 slices.) Season scallops lightly with salt and pepper.

3. Melt half the butter in a frying pan, add scallops and sauté briefly.

4. Add the champagne and cook gently no longer than 5 minutes. Taste for seasoning and remove the pan from heat.

5. Grease the scallop shells with the remaining butter and place a portion of the scallop mixture in each shell; dust lightly with bread crumbs.

6. Heat under broiler until the top is lightly brown, adding a bit more butter if the mixture seems too dry.

FRIED FROG'S LEGS

SERVES 6

Crisp frog's legs are an unusual food for crunching, and in this recipe they taste like Southern fried chicken.

2 pounds frogs' legs, skinned and
ready to use
fine bread crumbs (enough to cover
frog's legs—about 2 cups)
¼ teaspoon grated nutmeg
¼ teaspoon cayenne pepper
salt and freshly ground black
pepper
2 to 3 eggs, beaten
oil or fat for deep-frying

FOR THE PARSLEY BUTTER:
1 cup (2 sticks) unsalted butter,
softened slightly
2 tablespoons chopped fresh
parsley
2 tablespoons lemon juice

lemon wedges and parsley for
garnish
hot rolls

METHOD:

1. Soak frog's legs 15 to 20 minutes in salt water. Drain and dry well on paper towels.

2. Season the bread crumbs with nutmeg, cayenne and salt and pepper.

3. Roll the frog's legs in seasoned bread crumbs, then dip into beaten

eggs, and again in the bread crumbs. Shake lightly to remove excess crumbs.

4. Heat oil or shortening in a deep saucepan or kettle (a 3- or 4-quart pan will need 6 cups of oil or 3 pounds of fat to deep-fry properly) until hot. Place the frog's legs in a wire basket and dip into the hot fat. Fry until golden brown. Drain on paper towels and place on a hot platter.

5. *Prepare the Parsley Butter:* Thoroughly blend the softened butter, parsley and lemon juice.

6. Serve the frogs' legs hot, garnished with parsley and lemon wedges and accompanied by a dish of the Parsley Butter and hot rolls of your choice.

CHAPTER TWO
SOUPS

CHILLED APPLE SOUP

SERVES 8–10

4 *tablespoons unsalted butter*
3 *cups finely chopped leeks, white*
   part only (about 4 large or
   5 small)

9 *large apples, peeled, cored and*
   chopped
2 *tablespoons curry powder*
4½ *cups buttermilk*
chopped fresh parsley for garnish

METHOD:

1. Melt butter in large soup kettle. Add leeks, apples and curry powder. Sauté lightly for approximately 4 minutes. Remove from stove and cool.

2. Add buttermilk and stir well. Puree in batches in blender or food processor to a smooth texture. Chill for 1 hour and serve garnished with parsley.

GOLDEN APPLE SOUP

SERVES 4–6

3 *large tart apples (or 4 medium),*
   unpeeled
4 *cups chicken stock (very strong*
   and well seasoned)

salt and freshly ground pepper to
   taste
¼ *cup dry sherry*
3 *tablespoons unsalted butter*
1 *cup heavy cream, whipped*

METHOD:

1. Cut unpeeled apples into quarters and remove seeds. Put into a soup kettle with the chicken stock. Bring to boil, then lower heat and simmer for 20 minutes. Remove from heat and cool to room temperature.

2. Place the apple mixture into a blender and puree. Strain through a sieve.

3. Return the puree to the soup kettle and bring to a boil. Season with salt and pepper, add sherry and butter, then simmer for about 10 minutes; taste and correct seasoning if necessary.

4. Serve hot in bowls, topped with a tablespoon of whipped cream added at the last minute.

Note: In order to remove the fat from the chicken stock, it can be prepared the night before and placed in the refrigerator. Next day remove the fat before using.

KIWI FRUIT SOUP

SERVES 6–8

The kiwi has gained in popularity recently in this country and elsewhere and is used in a multitude of ways in the nouvelle cuisine. I have used this fruit, which is imported from New Zealand, for years.

5 cups (about 2 pounds) peeled
   and diced kiwi fruit (9 to 10
   large fruits)
4 cups sauterne
2 cups water
½ cup sugar

pinch salt
2 tablespoons cornstarch
2 cups melon balls
unsweetened whipped cream
   (optional)

METHOD:

1. In a medium saucepan, combine kiwi fruit, 1 cup of sauterne, water, sugar and salt. Bring to a boil and cook over medium heat for 5 minutes.

2. Dissolve cornstarch in ¼ cup of sauterne. Stir cornstarch mixture into soup and boil 1 minute, stirring constantly.

3. Remove from heat, and stir in remaining sauterne. Put half the kiwi fruit soup into blender container. Cover and blend at low speed until pureed. Stir into remaining soup.

4. Add melon balls and chill. Serve with whipped cream if desired.

CONSOMMÉ OF FRESH LEMON SOUP

SERVES 10–12

1 *small onion, sliced*
1 *cup chopped fresh parsley,*
   stems included
6 *garlic cloves, peeled and cut*
   in half
1½ *tablespoons grated lemon peel*
2 *tablespoons vegetable oil*

12 *cups good, rich chicken broth*
½ *cup fresh lemon juice, strained*
salt, freshly ground black pepper
   and Tabasco or other hot sauce
1 *large or 2 small egg yolks,*
   beaten
½ *cup heavy cream, whipped*
chopped fresh parsley for garnish

METHOD:

1. Place onion, parsley, garlic, lemon peel and 1 tablespoon vegetable oil in a large stainless-steel pot with a cover. Add chicken broth, bring to a boil, cover and simmer 20 minutes.

2. Strain and discard the solids. Add the ½ cup (or to taste) lemon juice. Heat. Season to taste with salt, pepper and 1 or 2 drops of hot sauce. Remove from heat until ready to serve.

3. When almost ready to serve, beat the egg yolks and then add the remaining tablespoon of oil to the yolks, a drop at a time, beating continually until creamy. Reheat consommé. Again turn off heat and add egg mixture, beating to prevent curdling.

4. Pour consommé into hot cups. Float a teaspoon of the whipped cream over top of each and garnish with chopped parsley.

Note: This soup will freeze well if the eggs and cream are not added beforehand.

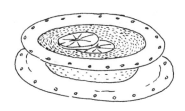

LIME GLACÉ

6 *cups chicken stock*
1 *medium onion, sliced*
5 *large cloves garlic, crushed*
2 *small stalks celery, leaves*
  included, chopped
4 *sprigs parsley*
1 *tablespoon (1 envelope)*
  unflavored gelatin
⅓ *cup cold water*

½ *cup fresh lime juice, strained*
4 *drops Tabasco sauce or to taste*
1 *cup (½ pint) heavy cream,*
  whipped
2 *tablespoons chopped candied*
  ginger
juice of 1 lime
6 *very thin slices of lime, twisted,*
  for garnish

METHOD:

1. Put onion, garlic, celery and chicken stock in covered pot and simmer until vegetables are very tender.

2. Drop the parsley into the hot stock to wilt; remove parsley with 1 cup of stock and puree in blender. Return mixture to the still-simmering soup and bring to a full boil. Pour soup through a fine sieve into a large bowl, pressing the vegetables with the back of a spoon to remove all the liquid. Discard the vegetables.

3. Dissolve gelatin in the cold water for 5 minutes. Add to the hot strained stock, stirring to dissolve gelatin.

4. Cool to room temperature. Stir in the ½ cup of lime juice and the Tabasco. Chill to thicken.

5. Serve in ice-cold goblets each topped with a generous dollop of the whipped cream, and 1 teaspoon of candied ginger on top. Sprinkle the additional lime juice over the soup and garnish with the twisted lime slices.

CHILLED ORANGE SOUP

SERVES 6

Fruit soup must never be overchilled: if too cold, the subtle fruit flavors are lost. The jellied soups, however—madrilenes, consommés and various others—should be served quite cold. This basic recipe may be used for most fruit soups.

3 tablespoons quick-cooking
   tapioca
3 cups water
½ tablespoon clover honey
few grains salt
1 cup frozen orange juice
   concentrate

2 cups diced fresh orange sections
1 ripe banana
½ cup seedless green grapes
6 large ripe strawberries, stems
   on, for garnish

METHOD:

1. Place tapioca and water in saucepan. Bring to a boil, stirring constantly. Remove from heat.

2. Add honey, salt and orange juice concentrate. Cool, stirring once after 20 minutes. Cover and refrigerate.

3. When ready to serve, fold in the orange sections, banana and grapes (if a thinner soup is desired add less fruit). Serve in cups and top each with a strawberry.

ORANGE CARROT SOUP

SERVES 6

4 tablespoons butter
½ cup chopped onion
4½ cups chicken broth
2 cups cooked, sliced carrots,
   drained
2 tablespoons all-purpose flour
1 can (6 ounces) frozen orange
   juice, undiluted, thawed

½ teaspoon salt
⅛ teaspoon freshly ground black
   pepper
1 cup heavy cream
1½ teaspoons chopped chives
orange slices for garnish

METHOD:

1. In a small skillet, melt 2 tablespoons butter. Add onion and sauté until tender.

2. Puree onion mixture, 2 cups of chicken broth and carrots in an electric blender until smooth.

3. In a large saucepan, melt remaining 2 tablespoons butter. Blend in flour, and cook until smooth and bubbly, stirring occasionally. Add remaining broth to flour-butter mixture and cook until slightly thickened.

4. Add orange juice concentrate, salt, pepper, heavy cream, chives and pureed carrot mixture to saucepan and stir until blended. Keep heat low and be careful not to let the soup boil. Taste for seasoning. Serve hot, or refrigerate until well chilled. Garnish with orange slices.

STRAWBERRY SOUP

SERVES 6

4 cups (3 pints) fresh strawberries, washed, stems removed
½ cup sugar or 4 tablespoons honey
2 teaspoons arrowroot

1 cup orange juice
1 cup Bordeaux
1 cup sour cream
6 strawberries for garnish

METHOD:

1. Place berries and sugar or honey in blender and puree.

2. Dissolve arrowroot in 2 tablespoons of the orange juice and add to strawberry puree with the remaining orange juice. Place in saucepan and cook over low heat, stirring constantly, until the arrowroot has cooked and soup thickens. Remove from heat and add wine.

3. Refrigerate soup. Serve it chilled, topped with sour cream and a strawberry for garnish.

ALMOND SOUP

SERVES 6

6 cups chicken broth
1 pound chicken giblets
12 peppercorns
1 onion, sliced
1 stalk celery with leaves,
   coarsely chopped
1 carrot, coarsely chopped
½ teaspoon dried thyme
½ bay leaf

¼ teaspoon mace
3 whole cloves
⅔ cup blanched almonds
2 tablespoons olive oil
1 tablespoon unsalted butter
3 tablespoons dry sherry
salt to taste
3 slices white bread

METHOD:

1. Put the chicken broth in a large saucepan and add giblets, peppercorns, onion, celery, carrot, thyme, bay leaf, mace and cloves.

2. Bring the broth to a boil, reduce heat, cover and simmer from 30 to 45 minutes.

3. While the stock is simmering, pulverize ½ cup of the almonds in a blender or food processor. Then rub the pureed almonds through a sieve, discarding any large pieces. Add olive oil and mix together to form a paste. Set aside. Cut the remaining almonds into slivers and sauté them in butter until browned, which will take about 5 minutes. Set aside.

4. Preheat the oven to 375°F. Trim the crusts from the bread and cut slices diagonally in half to form six triangles. Place them on a cookie sheet and toast in oven for about 15 minutes, or until they are crisp and lightly browned; or toast them in a toaster.

5. After the soup is done strain it through a sieve lined with cheesecloth, again into the saucepan, or into a flameproof casserole which can be brought to the table. Discard giblets or save for another use. Set the pan or casserole over low heat and add the almond paste, stirring well until incorporated. Add sherry and salt to taste.

6. Pour the soup into bowls, float a toast triangle on top of each, sprinkle with sautéed almond slivers and serve.

VIRGINIA PEANUT SOUP

SERVES 6

I remember the peanut patch at our home. In the early autumn we gathered the large raw "green" peanuts from the roots of the vines. We washed them free of the rich Virginia soil still clinging to them, placed them in a large roasting pan, and roasted the nuts in a hot oven to a tender juicy texture.

2 cups dry-roasted, unsalted
   Virginia peanuts
6 cups chicken stock
2 tablespoons unsalted butter or
   peanut oil
2 large garlic cloves, cut in
   quarters
1 medium onion, sliced

2 stalks celery, cut in 1-inch
   pieces, leaves included
2 tablespoons arrowroot
1 tablespoon tomato sauce
5 drops Tabasco sauce
½ teaspoon Worcestershire sauce
salt and freshly ground black
   pepper to taste
1 cup heavy cream, whipped

METHOD:

1. Place 1 cup of the peanuts in blender with 1 cup chicken stock. Blend at low speed, push nuts down with spatula, then blend on high speed until pureed. Add another cup of stock and remaining nuts; blend again until very smooth. Strain peanut mixture through fine sieve.

2. Sauté garlic, onion and celery together in butter for 2 minutes. Puree in blender with 1 more cup of stock. Put pureed mixture into a saucepan.

3. Dissolve arrowroot in a little water, add to pureed vegetables and cook over medium heat for 5 minutes. Add remaining 3 cups of stock, strained peanut mixture, tomato sauce, Tabasco, Worcestershire sauce, salt and pepper to taste. Continue to cook for 5 minutes longer. Serve soup hot, each serving topped with a spoonful of whipped cream.

CHILLED ARTICHOKE SOUP

SERVES 6

8 *small artichokes*	3 *cups water*
1½ *lemons* (3 *halves*)	3 *cups thickly sliced potatoes*
8 *tablespoons* (1 *stick*) *unsalted*	*salt and freshly ground black*
butter	*pepper*
8 *cups chicken broth*	

METHOD:

1. Wash the artichokes well. Cut in half vertically. With a small sharp knife, remove the chokes, and rub cut surfaces liberally with lemon.

2. Melt the butter in a heavy kettle. Add the artichokes and turn to coat with the hot butter.

3. Heat 5 cups of the broth to boiling and add to the kettle (reserve and refrigerate the remaining broth). Add the water, bring to a boil, cover and simmer 20 minutes.

4. Add the potatoes, salt and pepper to taste, and cook about 20 minutes longer. With a slotted spoon remove the artichokes to one bowl and pieces of potato to another. Strain and reserve the cooking liquid.

5. Cut the artichokes across where the leaves are attached to the base to separate them from the bottoms. Using a silver spoon, scrape all the edible material from each artichoke leaf, adding it to the potatoes. Add the artichoke bottoms, diced, to the potato mixture.

6. Puree the artichoke-and-potato mixture in a blender (or food processor) in batches, using the reserved liquid as needed to assist the blending if it is too thick. Add any leftover reserved liquid and pass the mixture through a fine mesh strainer.

7. Chill mixture several hours or overnight. Whisk enough of the remaining chicken broth into the chilled puree to make desired consistency. Check the seasoning and add more salt and pepper if needed. Serve in chilled bowls.

COLD CREAM OF ARTICHOKE SOUP

SERVES 8

4 tablespoons unsalted butter
two 9-ounce packages frozen artichoke hearts, thawed and
 coarsely chopped
2 medium-size white onions,
 chopped

2 potatoes, peeled and diced
6 cups chicken stock
2 cups heavy cream
2 tablespoons chopped fresh
 parsley and fresh basil leaves,
 for garnish

METHOD:

1. Melt the butter in a heavy saucepan, then sauté chopped artichokes in the butter with the onions and potatoes.

2. Add stock, cover and simmer 40 minutes.

3. Puree the soup in a blender or food processor. Strain through a
fine sieve and refrigerate at least 3 hours.

4. When ready to serve, beat in the cream. Garnish with the chopped
herbs.

CREAM OF ASPARAGUS SOUP

SERVES 8

1½ pounds asparagus
3 tablespoons unsalted butter
¼ cup minced shallots or onions
1 clove garlic, minced
6 cups chicken stock
1 cup heavy cream

2–3 tablespoons arrowroot
 (optional)
salt and cayenne pepper to taste
Cheese Biscuits or rye crisps
 (optional)

METHOD:

1. Snap off the tough bottoms of the asparagus and discard. Wash
the asparagus well to remove sand or grit. Cut off the tips in 2-inch
lengths and reserve. Dice the remainder of the stalks.

2. Melt butter in a skillet and sauté diced stalks with shallots and
garlic until the latter are limp.

3. Simmer the tips for 3 minutes in 1 cup of the chicken stock, strain
stock into sautéed asparagus mixture and set tips aside. Add remaining
stock to sautéed asparagus and simmer 8 to 10 minutes.

4. Puree sautéed asparagus in blender or food processor and then strain through a fine sieve. Add cream and arrowroot (if used), stir and heat, but do not boil.

5. Add asparagus tips, season to taste with salt and cayenne and serve in hot tureens with Cheese Biscuits or rye crisps, if desired.

CHILLED AVOCADO CREAM SOUP

SERVES 6

2 cups mashed ripe avocado (2
　 small avocados, approximately
　 1½ pounds)
1½ cups hot chicken broth
1 cup dry white wine

2 cups light cream
2 teaspoons lemon juice
salt to taste
chopped fresh dill for garnish

METHOD:

1. Mash avocado, add to hot broth and strain through fine sieve.

2. Stir in white wine, cream and lemon juice, season with salt and refrigerate until chilled.

3. Garnish with chopped dill and serve in chilled bowls.

CREAM OF BLACK BEAN SOUP

SERVES 8–10

Beans Get Around. They grow like mad, are cheap and are just about indestructible when dried. In their many varieties, they play hitching post for everyday dishes all over the world. But their travels abroad are recent history. Except for a couple of European strays, the common bean family, more than 500 varieties strong, sprouted first in the Americas, where its offspring were (and still are) raised by Indians.

Franklin D. Roosevelt's first Vice-president, John Nance Garner, once griped that his job didn't amount to "a hill of beans," which points up one thing this vegetable lacks—status. The basic black bean used in the following two recipes is routine stuff in Latin America, the Caribbean islands and our own South.

A good dollop of sherry adds pizzaz to black bean soup. Possible garnish: crisp bacon bits, sliced lemon, hard-cooked eggs, curry-flavored croutons, chopped watercress or sour cream.

2½ cups dried black beans, picked
   over and washed
10 cups water (for soaking)
7 cups water (for cooking)
1 cup (8 ounces) chopped ham
½ cup chopped celery

1 cup chopped onion
2 tablespoons bacon fat
3 cups heavy cream, warmed
salt and freshly ground black
   pepper

METHOD:

1. Cover the beans with 10 cups water and refrigerate overnight.

2. The following day drain off the water and add the drained beans to 7 cups water along with the chopped ham, celery, onion and bacon fat. Simmer, covered, 4 to 4½ hours, stirring occasionally, until the beans are soft. (If beans are not covered completely add a little more water as they cook.)

3. Push mixture through strainer or food mill (not too fine), then add the warm cream and season with salt and pepper to taste.

4. Reheat before serving.

PUREE OF BLACK BEAN SOUP

SERVES 12

1 pound dried black beans, picked
   over and washed
6 cups cold water
1 large unpeeled potato, scrubbed
   and cut in half
1 large, highly seasoned pork
   sausage (1½–2 pounds), thinly
   sliced
1 carrot, peeled, cut in half
1 large onion, stuck with 1 clove
2 stalks celery, cut in half

9 cups beef stock
4 garlic cloves
2 tablespoons arrowroot or
   cornstarch
2 tablespoons chili sauce
2 tablespoons Burgundy
salt, freshly ground black pepper,
   Tabasco sauce
8 ounces (½ pint) sour cream
12 thin slices lemon for garnish

METHOD:

1. Cover beans with the cold water and refrigerate overnight.

2. Next day strain, discarding soaking water, and put beans into a 6-quart heavy-bottomed pot with a cover. Add potato, sausage, carrot, onion, celery and 6 cups of the beef stock. Bring to a boil, cover and simmer 3 to 4 hours, stirring often, until beans are tender. If liquid cooks down, add cold water so that beans remain covered.

3. When beans are done, pour the remaining beef stock into blender,

add garlic and arrowroot and puree. Add puree to beans and simmer to thicken. Puree the mixture in blender, in batches, and then strain through a fine sieve. Return mixture to pot, bring just to a boil and season with chili sauce, wine, salt, pepper and Tabasco to taste.

4. Serve soup hot in bowls, from a tureen if desired. Add a tablespoon of sour cream and a slice of lemon to each bowl.

Note: Leftovers may be frozen; this soup freezes well.

PROVENÇALE BEAN SOUP

SERVES 8

1 pound (2 cups) dried navy beans
12 cups cold water
1 cup chopped onions
2 cups sliced carrots
3 leeks, white part only, cleaned, washed and sliced
2 garlic cloves, minced
2 tablespoons vegetable oil
2 pounds smoked pork butt
½ cup chopped fresh parsley

salt and freshly ground black pepper
1 teaspoon dried thyme
2 bay leaves
4 whole cloves
2 cups (¾ pound) pared, cubed sweet potatoes
2 cups (6 medium) pared, cubed turnips
2 cups shredded green cabbage

METHOD:

1. Place beans in a large saucepan with 6 cups water, bring to a boil and cook 2 minutes. Remove from heat and allow to stand 1 hour.

2. In soup kettle sauté onion, carrots, leeks and garlic in oil until wilted.

3. Place pork butt on sautéed vegetables; add beans with cooking liquid. Stir in remaining water, parsley, salt, pepper, thyme, bay leaves and cloves, cover and cook 1½ hours on low heat.

4. Then stir in remaining vegetables, bring to a boil, cover, and cook 1 hour longer, or until tender. Remove pork, cut into small pieces and return to soup. Serve hot.

QUICK BEET CONSOMMÉ

SERVES 10–12

*two 1-pound cans julienned beets,
    with juice
four 10½-ounce cans condensed
    beef consommé*

*4 cups water
salt and freshly ground black
    pepper to taste
1 cup sour cream*

METHOD:

1. Drain the beets, reserving the juice.

2. Combine juice, beef consommé and water in saucepan. Bring to boiling point.

3. Add beets and return just to boiling. Season with salt and pepper to taste. Serve in heated soup cups with a dollop of sour cream on top.

CELERY ROOT SOUP

SERVES 12

The celery root, also called celeriac, is not the root of a celery plant but rather a special variety of celery with an enlarged root. This vegetable has no stalks or leaves and its taste is slightly bitter. Bitterness can be eliminated by blanching the celery root in salted boiling water with 2 tablespoons of lemon juice, or marinating it in salted lemon juice.

*4 celery roots (approximately 4
    pounds), blanched (see above),
    peeled and chopped
14 cups (3½ quarts) chicken stock
4 garlic cloves, pierced
2 small onions
1 tablespoon chopped fresh basil
    leaves, or ½ teaspoon dried,
    crushed basil leaves*

*1 large carrot, diced
salt and freshly ground black
    pepper
2 cups (1 pint) heavy cream
3 tablespoons butter
3 tablespoons chopped fresh
    parsley*

METHOD:

1. Place chopped, blanched celery roots in a large soup kettle with the chicken stock, garlic cloves, onions, basil and carrot. Bring to a boil

and simmer for 30 minutes or until celery root is very tender. Remove from heat, let cool slightly, then puree in blender until smooth.

2. Add salt and pepper to taste, return to heat and add cream, butter and parsley. Simmer until very hot but do not boil. Serve hot.

CHILLED CUCUMBER SOUP

SERVES 6–8

7 cucumbers
2½ tablespoons butter
1 small Bermuda onion, diced
3 bay leaves
2½ tablespoons all-purpose flour
6 cups water
6 chicken bouillon cubes

3 cups light cream (or half-and-half)
1½ tablespoons lemon juice
1 tablespoon (or more if desired) chopped fresh dill
salt and freshly ground black pepper

METHOD:

1. Peel 5 cucumbers, cut in half lengthwise, scoop out the seeds and dice.

2. Melt butter in a 4-quart saucepan. Sauté diced cucumber, onion and bay leaves until vegetables are tender, about 5 to 10 minutes. Add flour, water and bouillon cubes. Bring to a boil, stirring until blended, lower heat at once and simmer about 15 minutes. Let cool.

3. When mixture is cool, remove bay leaves and discard. Puree soup in blender or food processor.

4. Peel remaining 2 cucumbers and halve lengthwise. Remove seeds. Grate cucumbers with a fine grater.

5. Add grated cucumbers, light cream (or half-and-half), lemon juice, dill, salt and pepper to puree. Refrigerate and serve chilled.

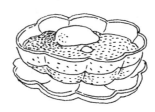

GARDEN SOUP

SERVES 6

1½ bunches watercress, stems
  removed
1 medium head lettuce or other
  greens such as escarole
4 small green onions
4 cabbage leaves
6 celery stalks with leaves
1 teaspoon chopped fresh thyme or
  marjoram leaves

few sprigs parsley, chopped
3–4 cups chicken or beef broth
salt and freshly ground black
  pepper
3 tablespoons butter
2 egg yolks
⅔ cup heavy cream

METHOD:

1. Wash the lettuce, onions, cabbage and celery, then chop by hand, or briefly grind in blender or food processor.

2. Place chopped vegetables, with the thyme and parsley, in a soup pot with the stock, cover, and simmer slowly for 40 minutes.

3. Add salt and pepper to taste and swirl in the butter. Remove from heat.

4. Beat egg yolks, add cream and stir into soup. Reheat over low flame, if necessary. Sprinkle with freshly ground black pepper. Serve hot from a heated tureen.

JERUSALEM ARTICHOKE AND CELERY SOUP

SERVES 4–6

The Jerusalem artichoke grows wild along the Atlantic coast from Georgia to Nova Scotia. It is a gnarled root vegetable not related to the artichoke at all, but the tuber of a plant in the sunflower family.

1 pound Jerusalem artichokes
water to cover
1 teaspoon salt
1 cup chopped celery
1 tablespoon chopped onion
2 tablespoons butter
1 tablespoon all-purpose flour

3 cups milk
salt and freshly ground black
  pepper
½ cup light cream
2 egg yolks
chopped fresh parsley for garnish

METHOD:

1. Scrub artichokes well, removing any bruised or darkened spots, and cut into small chunks. Bring a pot of water to a boil and add salt. Add artichoke pieces and simmer until tender. Drain well and set aside.

2. Sauté celery and onion in butter over medium heat until limp, stirring occasionally. Stir in flour and cook 5 minutes more until smooth and thick. Place celery-onion mixture and artichokes in blender or food processor with 1 cup milk and blend until smooth. Strain if desired.

3. Pour mixture into a saucepan, add remaining milk and heat gently. Season to taste with salt and pepper. Just before serving, beat egg yolks into cream with fork and gradually stir into soup. Be careful to keep on a low flame or the mixture will curdle. Serve hot with parsley as a garnish.

CREAM OF LEEK SOUP WITH PUFFED POTATO SKINS AND ROASTED PEANUTS

SERVES 12

Leeks, one of mankind's oldest cultivated vegetables, have not declined in popularity over the centuries. They grow well in most countries. The French use them generously in soup making; they are also excellent stuffed or creamed. The tops, if young and tender, add to their flavor. Leeks are milder in flavor than onions and stay fresh in the ground longer than most other vegetables without loss of flavor. To purchase, bottoms should be white and leaves green, with no yellow color on the green tops or white bottoms.

The soup that follows may be served hot or cold.

10 *large leeks*	*salt, freshly ground black pepper*
1 *small celery root (celeriac)*	*and few drops Tabasco sauce*
4 *tablespoons butter or vegetable*	2 *cups heavy cream*
oil	2 *egg yolks (optional)*
3 *large potatoes*	*a bowl of roasted fresh peanuts*
8 *cups chicken stock*	

METHOD:

1. Wash leeks well, pulling them apart to remove all the sand. Cut off tops, including about 1½ inches of the tender green, and cut into 1-inch pieces. Wash, peel and cut celery root into 1-inch pieces. Sauté leeks and celery root in butter or oil until translucent. Do not brown.

2. Scrub potatoes. Peel ¼-inch-thick strips for the Puffed Potato Skins, dry them well, and place skin side down on a baking sheet; set aside until later. Cut potatoes in 1-inch cubes and place in a large pot that has a tight-fitting cover. Add leeks, celery and chicken stock, and bring to a brisk boil. Cover tightly, reduce heat and simmer until leeks are tender—approximately 15 to 20 minutes.

3. Puree soup in blender and pour through a fine sieve again into the pot. Bring to a simmer and season to taste with salt, pepper and Tabasco.

4. Prepare the Puffed Potato Skins: Preheat oven to 400°F. and bake skins until puffed and crisp, taking care not to burn. If desired, sprinkle grated cheese of your choice over the skins during the last few minutes of baking. Salt and pepper may also be used.

5. When ready to serve, add cream to soup. Keep over low heat; do not allow to boil. Taste and correct seasonings if necessary. (If egg yolks are used, beat them into the cream before adding slowly to hot soup, careful to prevent curdling.) Serve soup hot or cold, with the hot Puffed Potato Skins and a bowl of roasted peanuts on the side.

LEEK AND WATERCRESS SOUP

SERVES 12

12 medium leeks, cleaned and washed	4 medium potatoes, scrubbed, skins on, cut into 1-inch cubes
3 bunches watercress	2 cups (1 pint) heavy cream
½ cup diced celery	mace, salt, freshly ground black pepper and cayenne
8 tablespoons (1 stick) butter	
12 cups well-seasoned chicken stock	

METHOD:

1. Wash the leeks and watercress. Slice white part of leeks and just 2 inches of the tender green tops into 1-inch pieces. Discard the remaining tops. Cut stems off the watercress and sauté stems with leeks and celery in butter for 2 to 3 minutes, tossing to blend and release flavors.

2. Place 11 cups of chicken stock in a large pot with a tight-fitting cover. Heat, add leek mixture and potato cubes. Bring to boil, cover tightly, reduce heat and simmer until vegetables are tender. Puree mixture in blender and strain through a fine sieve.

3. Bring the remaining cup of chicken stock to boil and blanch the watercress leaves in it until wilted, about 1 minute. Puree watercress

leaves in blender and strain through a fine sieve into leek mixture. Add cream and heat. *Do not boil.*

4. Season to taste with the mace, salt, pepper and cayenne. Serve in hot cups with Southern Corn Sticks (page 271) for dunking.

CREAM OF FRESH MUSHROOM SOUP

SERVES 6

1 *pound fresh mushrooms*
4 *tablespoons butter*
1 *slice onion, chopped*
4 *cups chicken stock*
2 *teaspoons fresh lemon juice,*
 strained
1½ *cups heavy cream*

salt, freshly ground black pepper
 and Tabasco sauce
pinch of sugar
 2 *teaspoons chopped parsley and*
 12 *whole wheat bread fingers*
 (optional) for garnish

METHOD:

1. Wash mushrooms in a sieve or colander under running water. Dry. Remove and chop stems.

2. Slice ¾ pound of the mushroom caps and place in a heavy pan along with chopped stems, 2 tablespoons butter and the chopped onion and stir together over low flame for 2 minutes.

3. Add chicken stock, bring to a boil, cover tightly and simmer 15 minutes. Puree mixture in blender or food processor and pour into a heavy saucepan.

4. Slice remaining ¼ pound of mushroom caps, toss with lemon juice and sauté in the remaining 2 tablespoons butter for 2 minutes. Add to the mushroom puree, cover and bring just to a boil, then lower heat. Mushrooms should remain crisp.

5. Add heavy cream. Do not bring to boil again.

6. Season to taste with salt, pepper, sugar and 1 drop Tabasco. Serve topped with chopped parsley and, if desired, whole wheat bread fingers.

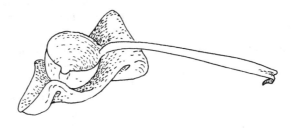

FRESH MUSHROOM CONSOMMÉ

SERVES 6

1 *pound fresh mushrooms*
1 *onion, thinly sliced*
1 *stalk celery*
1 *small garlic clove*
1 *quart cold water*
3 *cups chicken stock*

2 *drops Tabasco sauce*
salt and freshly ground black
pepper
2 *tablespoons dry sherry*
(optional)

METHOD:

1. Wash mushrooms in a sieve or colander under running water. Dry with paper towels and chop coarsely.

2. Combine mushrooms, onion, celery and garlic with the cold water and bring to a rapid boil. Reduce heat and simmer until liquid is reduced by half, stirring occasionally. Strain and discard solids. Measure the strained liquid—there should be about 2 cups. If not, add enough water to make 2 cups and then add the chicken stock. Season to taste with salt and pepper and Tabasco. If desired, add sherry. Serve consommé hot in cups.

Note: ¼ pound dried mushrooms may be substituted for the pound of fresh; they make a stronger-flavored soup.

JELLIED MUSHROOM SOUP

SERVES 6

6 *cups chicken broth*
1 *pound mushrooms, chopped*
1½ *tablespoons (1½ envelopes)*
    unflavored gelatin
2 *tablespoons dry sherry*

¾ *teaspoon salt*
freshly ground black pepper
¾ *cup sour cream and chopped*
    fresh parsley for garnish

METHOD:

1. In a saucepan with a cover, simmer broth and mushrooms together for 30 minutes.

2. Dissolve gelatin in ½ cup cold water and stir into soup.

3. Strain the soup (reserving the mushrooms for another use, if desired) and add sherry, salt and pepper to the mushroom broth.

4. Refrigerate until soup jells. Serve cold garnished with sour cream and chopped parsley.

BAKED SILVER ONION SOUP WITH WHITE WINE AND TOASTED CHEESE FINGERS

SERVES 8

If you can't find silver onions—a special variety of white onions about ¾ inch in diameter—substitute either very small white onions or the smallest yellow onions you can find. In this soup, these small onions are left whole rather than sliced.

1½ pounds small silver onions (or small white or yellow onions), of uniform size if possible
4 tablespoons unsalted butter
¼ cup finely minced celery
7 cups rich chicken broth, preferably homemade
2 tablespoons arrowroot (or 1½ tablespoons cornstarch)
salt and freshly ground white pepper
a small pinch of sugar
¼–½ teaspoon ground mace
1 cup dry white wine

FOR THE TOASTED CHEESE FINGERS (makes 16):
1 stick (8 tablespoons) unsalted butter
4 slices good quality thin white sandwich bread
1 generous cup freshly grated Parmesan cheese
paprika (the medium-hot kind, if available)

2 tablespoons snipped chives for garnish

METHOD:

1. Preheat the oven to 350°F. Peel the onions carefully, leaving them whole. If the onions are larger than bite-size, quarter or halve them partway through the root end.

2. In a bake-and-serve casserole of about 4-quart capacity with a tight-fitting cover, melt the butter over moderate heat. Toss the onions and celery in the butter until coated, then cover the casserole tightly. Place in the center of the oven and bake for 30 minutes, removing the cover and stirring them every 10 minutes or so.

3. Bring 6 cups of the chicken broth to a boil in a saucepan, then lower the heat to a bare simmer. Combine the remaining cup of broth with the arrowroot (or cornstarch), mixing to blend well. Add this mixture to the simmering broth and stir over moderate heat until the broth returns to a boil and is slightly thickened and smooth. Season to taste with salt and pepper, the pinch of sugar and the mace. Reserve.

4. When the vegetables have baked for 30 minutes, add the thickened broth to the casserole in the oven, stirring gently with a wooden spoon. Cover and bake 45 minutes longer, or until the onions are ten-

der but not mushy. Remove the casserole from the oven (leave the oven on for the Toasted Cheese Fingers), place on the stove over moderate heat and stir in the wine. Heat the soup to the simmering point and correct seasoning if necessary.

5. *Meanwhile, prepare the Toasted Cheese Fingers:* Make sure the oven is at 350°F. (It will already be hot if you have just prepared the Silver Onion Soup.) Put the stick of butter into a baking pan (about 7 x 11 inches) and set in the oven, removing the pan when the butter has melted. Meanwhile, cut each slice of bread into four strips. Lay the strips of bread in the butter in the pan and turn them over once so that both sides are lightly coated with butter. Sprinkle the cheese onto the bread fingers, then dust them with paprika. Return the pan to the oven and bake the fingers, without turning them, for 10 to 15 minutes, or until golden. Watch carefully to prevent burning. Keep hot.

6. Sprinkle soup with chives and serve with the hot Toasted Cheese Fingers.

CRUSTED ONION SOUP

SERVES 6

4 *cups thinly sliced onions*	⅓ *cup dry red wine*
3 *tablespoons butter*	*freshly ground black pepper*
1 *tablespoon vegetable oil*	6 *rounds of rye bread*
pinch sugar	1½ *cups mixed grated Swiss and*
1 *teaspoon salt*	*Parmesan cheese*
2 *tablespoons all-purpose flour*	3 *tablespoons melted butter*
1½ *quarts (6 cups) beef stock or*	
bouillon	

METHOD:

1. In a large heavy casserole sauté the onions in the 3 tablespoons butter and the oil, over low heat, covered, about 15 minutes.

2. Remove lid, add sugar and salt, and continue cooking over moderate heat about 30 minutes or until onions turn a deep golden brown.

3. Add flour, stir in thoroughly, add hot stock or bouillon, wine, and pepper to taste, and simmer 30 minutes more.

4. Meanwhile, preheat oven to 325°F.

5. Adjust seasoning if necessary. When ready to serve, bring soup almost to a boil and pour into individual oven-proof crocks.

6. Float rounds of toasted bread atop each, cover with grated cheese, pour melted butter over and bake for 20 to 30 minutes.

PARISIAN ONION SOUP

SERVES 6

4–6 *sweet onions, thinly sliced*
6 *tablespoons butter or vegetable
    oil*
2 *tablespoons all-purpose flour*
*three 10½-ounce cans beef or
    chicken consommé, heated*

*salt and freshly ground black
    pepper*
6 *rounds of French bread, toasted*
6 *tablespoons grated sharp cheese
    (such as Parmesan)*

METHOD:

1. Brown the onions in the butter or oil, blend in flour until smooth and stir constantly while it simmers for 10 minutes.

2. Add the hot consommé, and let mixture simmer slowly until the onions are tender. Season with salt and pepper.

3. Spread the cheese thickly on the toast, and quickly melt it under the broiler. (This is an alternative to putting the toast and cheese on top of the soup and then melting it, since the toast stays crisper.) Pour the soup into a hot tureen, top with the cheese-covered toast and serve at once.

CREAM OF ONION SOUP

SERVES 12

12 *large onions, sliced*
8 *tablespoons (1 stick) butter*
6 *tablespoons flour*
3 *quarts (12 cups) rich veal stock*
2 *cups milk*

*salt and freshly ground black
    pepper*
4 *rolls, cut into croutons and
    lightly toasted*
6 *ounces grated Gruyère cheese*

METHOD:

1. Melt the butter in a large skillet. Add sliced onions and sauté until soft and light golden brown, stirring frequently.

2. Sprinkle flour into onions, stir, then add stock slowly, stirring constantly until blended. Stir in milk and simmer for 20 minutes.

3. Season with salt and pepper to taste. Remove from heat.

4. Pour into individual oven-proof soup bowls and top each with a spoonful or two of croutons and grated Gruyère.

5. Place under broiler (do not turn heat too high), just to let cheese melt on croutons. Serve immediately.

POTATO AND LEEK SOUP

SERVES 6

6 cups chicken broth
12 small potatoes, peeled
6 small onions, peeled
6 leeks (white and tender green part), washed and chopped
½ teaspoon dried chervil

2 tablespoons chopped fresh parsley
1 cup (½ pint) heavy cream
3 tablespoons butter
salt and freshly ground black pepper

METHOD:

1. In a saucepan, simmer chicken broth till heated through.

2. Add the potatoes, onions and leeks. Cover and let simmer an additional 20 to 25 minutes, until the vegetables are tender.

3. Mash the potatoes into the chicken-broth mixture, add the chervil, parsley, cream, butter, salt and pepper to taste and blend well. Reheat but do not let the soup boil. Serve in heated soup bowls.

PUMPKIN SOUP

SERVES 6–8

2 cups whole milk
1 slice onion
4 whole cloves
2 tablespoons chopped fresh parsley or 1 teaspoon dried parsley flakes
1 small garlic clove, left whole
1 bay leaf
2 cups cooked fresh or canned pureed pumpkin (see Note)

1¼ cups or 1 (10½-ounce) can chicken broth
1 cup (½ pint) heavy cream
salt and freshly ground black pepper to taste
1 tablespoon lemon juice
plain whipped cream and toasted, buttered croutons for garnish

METHOD:

1. Scald milk to which onion, cloves, parsley, garlic and bay leaf has been added. Strain the liquid and discard the spices.

2. Place strained milk in top of double boiler, add pureed pumpkin and broth.

3. Heat in double boiler over boiling water until very hot. Just before serving stir in cream, salt, pepper and lemon juice and heat again. Serve soup garnished with a dollop of whipped cream and a sprinkling of croutons.

Note: To make pureed pumpkin from the fresh vegetable, cut pumpkin in half, remove seeds and strings, peel and slice in 2- or 3-inch pieces. Place in saucepan with boiling water 3 or 4 inches above the pumpkin pieces. Cover pan and boil over low heat until tender, about 20 to 30 minutes. Drain well and mash. Let cool.

CREAM OF SORREL SOUP

SERVES 12

Sorrel, or sourgrass, is an acidic, lemony-tasting green which makes a soup of fine flavor and texture because it turns into a puree after cooking. It is grown commercially but may be difficult to find in most supermarkets and vegetable markets—do keep searching, however, because it will be well worth it.

½ pound sorrel	sugar to taste, optional
1½ quarts rich beef bouillon	9 egg yolks, beaten
3 cups heavy cream	cayenne, white pepper and salt

METHOD:

1. Wash, dry and trim the stems and center ribs from the sorrel, then chop the remainder.

2. Bring the bouillon to a boil, drop sorrel into boiling stock and cook for 10 minutes. Add sugar to taste. Let cool.

3. Blend cream into beaten egg yolks, add cayenne and pepper and salt to taste.

4. Stir egg and cream mixture into stock and simmer over very low heat for about 10 minutes. Do not let it boil. Remove from heat and serve hot in cups. This soup may also be served cold.

SPINACH, EGG AND PARMESAN CHEESE SOUP

SERVES 8

2 pounds fresh spinach
4 tablespoons butter
1¼ teaspoons salt
¼ teaspoon freshly ground black
   pepper

⅛ teaspoon grated nutmeg
4 egg yolks
¼ cup grated Parmesan cheese
6 cups boiling chicken stock
bread sticks

METHOD:

1. Pick over, trim tough ends and wash spinach to remove all sand and grit. Place spinach in a skillet or heavy saucepan with only the water that clings to the leaves. Cover and cook for 15 minutes, adding more water if needed. Drain spinach and push through a food mill and into a saucepan.

2. Add butter to spinach puree and season with salt, pepper and nutmeg. Cook gently for two minutes.

3. Beat egg yolks, add to grated cheese and stir into spinach.

4. Add broth and bring to boil. The egg will curdle but that's fine, since this is the desired result. (However, if a smoother soup is preferred, blend mixture in blender and strain.) Serve hot with bread sticks.

FRESH TOMATO BOUILLON

SERVES 6

8–10 large tomatoes, cut in quarters
   (3–3½ pounds)
2 cups chicken broth
1½ teaspoons salt

¼ teaspoon freshly ground black
   pepper
3 drops Tabasco sauce
2 tablespoons chopped chives for
   garnish

METHOD:

1. Place tomatoes and chicken broth in a saucepan and cook over moderate heat until tomatoes are soft.

2. Strain broth through a sieve. Reheat and add seasonings. Serve hot or cold topped with a sprinkling of chives.

PUREE OF TOMATO SOUP

SERVES 12

12 *cups chicken stock*
6 *cups fresh tomatoes, quartered,*
   or two 12-ounce cans
2 *large onions, chopped*
1 *cup finely diced celery*
4 *garlic cloves, sliced*
pinch of sugar

salt and freshly ground black
   pepper
½ *cup Madeira*
1 *cup sour cream*
4 *tablespoons chopped fresh*
   chives for garnish

METHOD:

1. Put chicken stock, tomatoes, onions, celery and garlic in a saucepan and simmer for 30 minutes. Let mixture cool.

2. When cool, puree soup in a blender until smooth. Then strain through a fine sieve and again into saucepan.

3. Season soup with sugar, salt and pepper to taste.

4. Add wine, stirring to blend well and reheat thoroughly. Serve in hot cups, each topped with a heaping tablespoon of sour cream and sprinkled with chives.

ITALIAN TOMATO SOUP

SERVES 6

6 *cups chicken broth*
2 *onions, finely chopped*
2 *scallions, chopped*
2 *garlic cloves, finely chopped*
12 *plum tomatoes, cut in quarters*

1 *tablespoon chopped fresh basil*
   or ½ teaspoon dried
salt and freshly ground black
   pepper
3 *tablespoons butter*
chopped fresh parsley for garnish

METHOD:

1. Place chicken broth in a soup pot and add onions, scallions, garlic and tomatoes. Simmer for 20 minutes.

2. Add basil, salt and pepper to taste. Simmer for an additional 5 minutes.

3. Add butter, stir, and remove from heat. Serve hot, sprinkled with parsley.

WHITE TURNIP SOUP

SERVES 6

6 *white turnips*
6 *medium potatoes*
6 *cups chicken stock or water*
3 *tablespoons butter*

salt
1 *cup milk*
1 *cup (½ pint) heavy cream*

METHOD:

1. Wash, peel and dice the turnips and potatoes.

2. Place them in a soup kettle with stock or water. Bring to a boil, reduce heat and simmer until vegetables are tender—about 15 minutes. Puree in blender until smooth.

3. Return turnip-potato mixture to saucepan, add butter, salt to taste, milk and cream and heat but do not let it boil. Serve hot.

ZUCCHINI SOUP

SERVES 6

6 *cups chicken stock*
1 *large onion, thinly sliced*
2 *stalks celery with leaves, diced*
2 *large garlic cloves, pierced*
3 *medium zucchini, scrubbed to remove sand*

salt, freshly ground black pepper and Tabasco sauce
¾ *cup sour cream*
1 *tablespoon chopped fresh chives and 2 ounces toasted pistachio nuts for garnish*

METHOD:

1. Place stock in a soup pot, add onion, celery and garlic and simmer for 20 minutes. Puree vegetables and liquid in a food mill or food processor and return to pot.

2. When ready to serve, grate zucchini into stock, add seasonings to taste. Heat just to boiling, then lower heat; *do not let soup boil.*

3. Serve in heated cups, each topped with a tablespoon of sour cream and garnished with chives and pistachio nuts.

CHEESE SOUP

SERVES 12

1 cup finely chopped carrots
1 cup finely chopped celery
2 cups boiling water
8 tablespoons (1 stick) butter
¼ cup finely chopped onion
¼ cup all-purpose flour
¾ cup plus 1 tablespoon instant
    nonfat dry milk
4 cups less 2 tablespoons water

4 cups chicken stock or bouillon
1 pound American cheese, diced
½ teaspoon powdered garlic
salt and freshly ground black
    pepper
chopped parsley or watercress or
    sliced pimento-stuffed olives for
    garnish

METHOD:

1. Combine carrots, celery and boiling water and simmer for 15 minutes, or until vegetables are tender. Do not drain.

2. Meanwhile, sauté onion in butter just until tender, but not browned. Add flour and blend well until smooth. Cook 3 to 4 minutes.

3. Combine nonfat dry milk with water, stirring to mix. Gradually add milk and chicken stock to onion mixture. Cook over low heat, stirring constantly, until smooth and thickened.

4. Add cheese, garlic, and salt and pepper to taste; continue cooking and stirring until cheese is melted and blended. Add carrots and celery with their cooking water. Blend and heat through. Keep warm in the top of a double boiler over hot water until ready to serve. Serve hot, topped with parsley, watercress or olives.

GOLDEN CHEDDAR CHEESE
AND BEER SOUP

SERVES 6

2 tablespoons butter
¼ cup all-purpose flour
3 cups hot chicken broth
¼ cup chopped onion
¼ cup chopped celery
¼ cup chopped carrots
¼ cup chopped fresh parsley

¼ cup chopped fresh chives
8 tablespoons (1 stick) butter,
    melted
¼ pound Cheddar cheese, melted
3 cups beer, warmed
popcorn (optional)

METHOD:

1. Melt the 2 tablespoons butter in a saucepan and blend in flour until smooth.

2. Add chicken broth and keep stirring for about 3 to 5 minutes until mixture is smooth and thickened. Then add the onion, celery, carrots, parsley and chives. Simmer the vegetables for 20 minutes or until tender.

3. Add melted cheese and butter, then the warm beer. Bring just to a boil; remove from heat. Serve hot with bowls of popcorn on the side, if desired.

CHICKEN CREOLE SOUP WITH BROWN RICE

SERVES 6

one 5- to-6-pound stewing chicken, disjointed
2 quarts cold water
2 teaspoons salt
2 medium onions, cut in quarters
1 carrot, peeled and cubed
1 cup diced celery
1½ cups brown rice

one 12-ounce can whole tomatoes
1 cup sliced okra, blanched
½ teaspoon turmeric
salt, freshly ground black pepper and cayenne
1 cup cooked peas and 2 tablespoons minced green peppers for garnish

METHOD:

1. Cover chicken with water, add salt and cook for 1 hour or until tender. Remove chicken from stock. Remove skin and bones from entire chicken, reserve one breast and dice remaining meat into cubes.

2. Add onions, carrot, celery, brown rice, tomatoes, okra and turmeric to the stock and cook 20 to 30 minutes or until rice is tender. During the last 5 minutes of cooking time, add the diced chicken.

3. Remove 1 cup of cooked rice, put into blender with the reserved chicken breast and puree until smooth. Add mixture to soup and heat through.

4. Season with salt, pepper and cayenne to taste.

5. Serve soup hot, garnished with peas and green pepper.

CHICKEN CURRY SOUP

SERVES 6–8

6 cups chicken stock
1 cup celery, finely diced
1 cup cooked chicken, cut into
  fine julienne strips
1½ teaspoons curry powder blended
  with 3 tablespoons cold water
  until smooth

1 large, tart apple, peeled and
  grated
1 cup baby green peas, cooked
  for 2 minutes
1½ tablespoons lemon juice
salt and freshly ground black
  pepper
crushed roasted peanuts for garnish

METHOD:

1. Bring chicken stock just to a boil; lower heat, add celery and cook 2 minutes. Add chicken, curry and apple, return to boil, then simmer 5 minutes more.

2. Add cooked peas, lemon juice and season with salt and pepper to taste. Serve garnished with crushed roasted peanuts.

CHICKEN GUMBO SOUP

SERVES 10–12

6 cups chicken stock
1 cup fresh corn, cut from cob, or
  one 8-ounce can corn kernels
  (niblets)
1 onion, minced
2 pounds fresh tomatoes, peeled
  and seeded, or 2 cups canned
  tomatoes
1½ pounds fresh or frozen okra,
  sliced

1 teaspoon sweet paprika
⅛ teaspoon hot pepper sauce
½ cup cooked rice
2 cups cubed cooked chicken
  (dark and white meat)
2 tablespoons butter
salt and freshly ground black
  pepper
chopped fresh parsley for garnish

METHOD:

1. In a soup kettle combine stock with all the vegetables, the paprika and hot pepper sauce.

2. Bring to a boil and simmer, covered, until vegetables are tender.

3. Add 1 cup of vegetable stock to blender along with cooked rice and puree until smooth.

4. Add pureed rice mixture, chicken and butter to vegetables and stock. Season to taste with salt and pepper and heat through. Serve garnished with chopped parsley.

GUMBO

SERVES 6

This is a classic gumbo in the Southern tradition.

8 tablespoons (½ cup) shortening
  (vegetable oil, butter or bacon
  fat—see Note)
3 tablespoons all-purpose flour
3 tablespoons whole wheat flour
1½ cups beef stock
½ pound okra, washed, dried and
  cut across pod (frozen may also
  be used)
1 cup chopped onion
1 medium leek, cut in 1-inch
  pieces, 2 inches of tender green
  top included
¼ cup chopped green pepper
½ cup chopped celery including
  some leaves

2 garlic cloves, chopped
2 cups water
¾ cup tomato sauce
⅓ teaspoon cayenne or to taste
salt and freshly ground black
  pepper
1 cup diced, cooked chicken
  (white and dark meat)
1 pound medium shrimp, shelled
  and deveined
1 pound lump crab meat, bits of
  shell and cartilage removed
1 teaspoon filé powder (optional)
  (see Note)
6 cups hot cooked white rice

METHOD:

1. In a saucepan, make a roux with 6 tablespoons of the shortening and both the flours, cooking and stirring until smooth and a rich golden color. Stir in 1 cup of beef stock and cook 8 to 10 minutes until thickened and smooth. Set aside until later.

2. Sauté okra in the remaining shortening, stirring to prevent sticking. Cook until okra is no longer slippery, then add onion, leek, green pepper, celery and garlic. Add water and cook until vegetables are almost tender.

3. Add tomato sauce, remaining stock, cayenne, salt and pepper. Stir well.

4. Stir in roux and simmer for 20 minutes.

5. Then add chicken, shrimp and crab meat, tossing gently with a

fork. Do not break crab lumps. Bring again to a simmer and cook for 3 minutes. Remove from heat and cover tightly. Let stand at room temperature until cool, then refrigerate overnight.

6. When ready to serve, heat slowly over low heat—*do not boil*. Add filé powder, stirring gently until the gumbo thickens. Serve in large bowls with a ball of hot fluffy rice in the center of each.

Note: Bacon fat adds greatly to the flavor—just be sure it has not been scorched. Filé powder, which can be purchased in gourmet shops or supermarkets with a good selection of spices, is made from drying the young leaves of *Sassafras varifolium*, which are then ground to powder in a mortar. Dried okra, allspice, coriander and sage are sometimes added. It should never be allowed to boil and should be added only to a hot dish, otherwise it will sting the tongue. Filé powder is a truly American ingredient. It was originally produced by the Choctaw Indians and then later obtained by the French colonists. In Creole cooking it is used to thicken gumbo.

BOSTON CLAM CHOWDER

SERVES 6

3 *slices salt pork or bacon, diced*
2 *onions, diced*
1½ *pints fresh shucked clams or a*
    17-ounce can minced or
    whole clams
1½ *cups water*
3½ *cups diced potatoes*
1½ *teaspoons salt*

½ *teaspoon ground pepper*
3 *teaspoons Worcestershire sauce*
3 *cups milk*
3 *tablespoons unsalted butter*
3 *tablespoons all-purpose flour*
    (optional)
soda crackers

METHOD:

1. Sauté pork or bacon in saucepan or kettle until light brown; skim out pieces. Cook onions in fat until golden brown.

2. Drain clams, then strain the liquor and reserve. If the clams are large, chop them coarsely. Add clam liquor to fat with water and potatoes. Cook until potatoes are tender; add seasonings, then add clams. Scald milk and add. If no further thickening is desired add the butter at this point. If you are thickening soup, blend butter and flour together until creamy, add and cook 10 minutes longer, being careful not to let mixture boil.

3. Pour chowder over crackers in tureen or separate bowls and serve.

CREAM OF CLAM SOUP MANHATTAN

SERVES 6

1 quart (approximately 2 dozen)
  clams in shells
4–5 cups cold water
4 tablespoons butter
4 tablespoons all-purpose flour
4 egg yolks

1 cup light cream or half-and-half
a few grains of cayenne pepper
pinch of nutmeg
salt and freshly ground black
  pepper

METHOD:

1. Scrub clams and let them soak in cold water for 1 hour. Place clams in a pot with the 4 or 5 cups cold water and cook gently until shells open. Discard any clams that remain closed. Remove clams from cooking water, and from shells, and either leave whole or chop; set aside. Strain liquid through a double thickness of cheesecloth and reserve. Measure liquid and, if necessary, add enough water to make 5 cups.

2. In a saucepan, melt butter, and add flour. Blend well. Let mixture brown, stirring constantly. Gradually pour in the clam liquid and cook over moderate heat, stirring, until it begins to thicken. Remove from heat.

3. Whip egg yolks, stir in cream or half-and-half, then blend with the thickened clam mixture, return to low heat, add clams, and cook for about 5 minutes, stirring to a nice smooth cream. Do not allow to boil.

4. Add cayenne, nutmeg, and salt and pepper to taste. Serve in heated bowls.

LOBSTER BISQUE

SERVES 12

3 two-pound live lobsters (or any
  number equal to 6 pounds
  lobster)
2 carrots, peeled
2 onions
2 celery stalks
3/4 pound (3 sticks) unsalted butter
2/3 quart (about 2 1/2 cups) dry
  white wine
3 quarts (12 cups) fish stock
  (see Note)

salt and freshly ground black
  pepper
3 bay leaves
2/3 teaspoon dried thyme
3/4 cup rice
3 or 4 peppercorns
1 1/2 cups tomato puree
2 cups (1 pint) heavy cream
1/4 cup brandy

METHOD:

1. Kill the lobster by inserting a sharp knife where the head meets the shell. Separate heads and tails of lobster (reserve the claws and body for another dish). Cook tails in boiling water for 10 minutes, then set aside.

2. Finely chop carrots, onions, celery. Pound lobster heads until the pieces are as small as possible.

3. Melt 1/4 pound (1 stick) butter over high heat.

4. Sauté together in the butter the crushed lobster heads until they are deep red, and the carrots, onions and celery until somewhat limp—about 4 or 5 minutes total. Add wine, fish stock, salt, pepper, bay leaves, thyme, rice, peppercorns and tomato puree. Simmer for 45 minutes. Strain bisque through a fine sieve, then bring again to a simmer and check seasoning.

5. Add remaining butter and cream and brandy.

6. Dice lobster-tail meat into 1/8-inch pieces, add to the bisque and serve.

Note: When you buy the lobster, ask your fish man for bones and heads of white-meated fish that he has fileted that day. Simmer these in 3 quarts of water with bay leaves, parsley, onion, celery and peppercorns. Strain and use as fish stock. (Or use 1 1/2 quarts of water to 1 1/2 quarts of bottled clam juice.)

MUSSEL STEW

SERVES 6

4 *pounds mussels*
1 *small onion, chopped*
2 *garlic cloves, chopped*
1 *cup dry white wine*
7 *tablespoons butter*
1 *tablespoon rice flour*
2½ *teaspoons milk*

1¼ *cup heavy cream*
2 *leeks, white part only, trimmed, washed and finely chopped*
salt and freshly ground black pepper
pinch of sweet paprika

METHOD:

1. Wash mussels well in a colander under running water to remove the sand. Scrub with a stiff brush and cut off their fibrous beards. Let them soak further in cold water for 30 minutes or so to get rid of any remaining sand. Then place them in a saucepan.

2. Add onion, garlic and wine. Steam slowly, covered, until mussels are open, discarding any that remain closed. Remove from heat. Strain liquid through a double thickness of cheesecloth. Take the mussels out of their shells. Set mussels and broth aside.

3. Melt butter in saucepan and add the rice flour, which has been dissolved in milk. Blend until smooth, then slowly add the cream and chopped leeks.

4. Simmer for a few minutes, just long enough for the leeks to cook (do not boil), then stir in the mussels and broth. Season with salt and pepper to taste.

5. Serve stew piping hot (over hot, freshly cooked rice, if desired) with a dash of paprika for color.

OYSTER STEW

SERVES 6

1 *quart oysters (about 24), shucked, with their liquor*
1 *tablespoon finely grated onion*
½ *cup milk*
½ *cup celery, minced*

1 *cup heavy cream*
1 *tablespoon dry sherry*
salt and white pepper to taste
4 *tablespoons (½ stick) softened butter*

METHOD:

1. Strain liquor from oysters into a saucepan, bring to a boil, and skim off the foam from the surface. Set the boiled oyster liquor aside.

2. In another saucepan combine oysters with onion, simmer over very low heat until oysters curl (do not overcook) and remove from heat.

3. In another saucepan cook milk and celery over moderate heat for 5 minutes, stir in heavy cream and bring almost to a boil. Remove pan from heat and add oyster liquor, oysters, sherry and salt and pepper to taste.

4. Ladle stew into wide soup bowls and top each with 2 teaspoons of softened butter.

FRESH CORN AND SHRIMP CHOWDER

SERVES 6

6 *cups well-flavored chicken stock, preferably homemade*
1½ *pounds shrimp, shelled and deveined*
1 *cup minced celery, including some leaves*
2 *tablespoons minced green pepper*
½ *cup minced onions*
4 *tablespoons bacon fat (can be obtained from frying bacon for garnish)*
2 *medium carrots, peeled and sliced*

2 *cups fresh corn, cut from cob (frozen corn on the cob may be used; do not use canned)*
1½ *cups heavy cream*
salt
freshly ground black pepper
cayenne pepper
2 *tablespoons butter*
unsweetened whipped cream
6 *slices bacon, fried crisp, drained on paper towel and crumbled, for garnish*

METHOD:

1. Bring 3 cups of the stock to boil, lower heat and add shrimp, cover and steam for 3 minutes only; do not boil. Remove shrimp from stock and set both aside.

2. Sauté celery, onion and pepper in bacon fat for 2 minutes, stirring once or twice. Add carrots and stir again to blend with other vegetables. Add mixture to the chicken stock that was used to cook shrimp, reheat and let simmer 5 minutes. Add corn and return to simmer for 2 minutes only.

3. Combine half the shrimp in blender with the remaining 3 cups of chicken stock and, when well blended, add to the vegetable-chicken stock mixture.

4. Over low heat, add heavy cream, salt, pepper and cayenne. When ready to serve, cut remaining shrimp in half, add to soup and swirl in butter. Do not let soup boil. Serve in hot cups topped with whipped cream and crushed, crisp bacon.

LIVER SOUP

SERVES 6

1½ pounds calf's liver
6–7 cups beef stock
  2 medium onions, sliced
  2 tomatoes, peeled, seeded,
    chopped
  4 teaspoons chopped fresh parsley

2 tablespoons raw rice
salt and freshly ground black
  pepper
  2 eggs, well beaten
juice of 2 lemons

METHOD:

1. Bring the beef stock to a boil in a soup pot or saucepan with a cover. Wash liver, slice into small pieces and simmer in stock until tender. Cool, remove gristle and grind the liver fine in meat grinder, blender or food processor. Reserve the stock.

2. Add the ground liver, onions, tomatoes, rice, salt and pepper to the stock and simmer, covered, until onions and rice are cooked. Remove from heat.

3. Before serving make an egg sauce: Add the lemon juice to well-beaten eggs and continue beating until well blended. Gradually add egg mixture to the soup, heat gently (do not boil) and serve.

OXTAIL-BARLEY SOUP

SERVES 6

2½ pounds oxtails, cut up
3 tablespoons butter
1 large onion, chopped
2 stalks celery, chopped
1 garlic clove, minced
2 sprigs parsley
¼ teaspoon dried thyme
¼ teaspoon dried rosemary

¼ teaspoon dried marjoram
1 teaspoon salt
freshly ground black pepper
2 cups water
4 cups beef broth
1 cup dry red wine
½ cup barley
¼ cup Madeira

METHOD:

1. In a large skillet brown oxtails in butter over moderate heat. Add vegetables, herbs and seasoning, mix thoroughly and continue cooking for 15 minutes.

2. Transfer mixture to a large casserole, deglaze skillet with the 2 cups water, and add this liquid plus beef broth and red wine to casserole. Bring to boil, reduce heat, cover and simmer 3 hours.

3. Strain soup into large saucepan, discarding vegetables. Bone and dice meat and add to broth along with barley. Skim fat, bring soup to a boil, reduce heat and simmer 30 minutes or until barley is tender. Add Madeira, stir thoroughly, taste for seasoning, and serve hot.

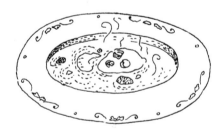

CHAPTER THREE
MEATS, SPECIALTY CUTS AND GAME

BEEF

BEEF WELLINGTON (BEEF IN PASTRY)

2¾- to 3-*pound filet of prime beef,*
trimmed and all fat removed
½ *cup vegetable oil or shortening*
8 *tablespoons (1 stick) butter*

FOR THE PUFF PASTRY:
1 *cup (2 sticks) sweet butter*
8 *ounces pastry flour, sifted*
4–6 *tablespoons ice-cold water*
1 *small egg, beaten (to brush on*
pastry before baking)

FOR THE DUXELLES STUFFING:
(makes about 3 cups—any leftover
Duxelles may be refrigerated
for future use)
2 *pounds fresh mushrooms*

1 *large onion, peeled*
8 *tablespoons (1 stick) butter*
2 *tablespoons chopped fresh*
parsley
salt, freshly ground black pepper
and ground thyme

FOR THE MADEIRA SAUCE:
4 *cups strong beef stock*
1½ *cups Madeira*
½ *cup Duxelles*
salt and freshly ground black
pepper
2 *tablespoons arrowroot (optional,*
for a thicker sauce)

watercress for garnish

METHOD:

1. *Prepare the Puff Pastry:* Knead the butter with your fingers or spoon in ice water or cold running water until soft but still chilled, folding it over and over until it is supple. Cut 2 tablespoons of the butter into the sifted pastry flour, add the ice-cold water and knead the dough for 5 minutes on a lightly floured board. Roll the dough to a scant ¼ inch in thickness, keeping the pastry in a rectangular shape and the corners square. Place remaining butter in center and spread evenly on lower half of dough. Cover with upper half of dough and fold right side under and the left side over. Roll to a scant ¼ inch thickness once again. Repeat this process of folding and rolling 4 more times. Wrap the pastry tightly with waxed paper and refrigerate 1 hour, until dough is firm.

2. For the filet of beef: Heat oil and butter in a large sauté pan.

Sauté filet, turning it with tongs (a fork should not be used as it punctures the meat, allowing some of its precious flavor, to escape) until golden brown over entire surface. Remove and cool at room temperature on paper towels—the towels will absorb the excess fat.

3. *Meanwhile, prepare the Duxelles Stuffing:* Wash mushrooms in a sieve or colander. Shake dry or blot with paper towels. Chop the mushrooms and onion by hand (do not use a food processor or blender) until medium fine. Melt butter in a large sauté pan, add mushroom-and-onion mixture and parsley. Sauté, stirring frequently, until all the liquid has evaporated, about 35 to 40 minutes. Season with salt, pepper and ground thyme to taste. (Thyme has a "powerful" flavor so it is wise to add only a little and then taste—too much will detract from the flavor of the beef.) Cool. Place in a jar with a cover and refrigerate until ready to use. Duxelles will keep a week or longer in refrigerator, so this step may be done well in advance.

4. Preheat oven to 400°F.

5. Unwrap pastry and roll out to a rectangle 18 by 9 inches and ¼ inch thick. Spread about ¾ cup of the Duxelles in a 3-inch-wide line in the center of pastry. Lay cooled filet, rounded side down, on top of Duxelles. Spread another ¾ cup Duxelles over the filet. (Another ½ cup will be used for the Madeira Sauce.) Fold the 2 long sides of the pastry over the filet, overlapping them. Seal them together and cut off and reserve any excess pastry. Next, fold the ends in an envelope fashion and seal, cutting away excess pastry and reserving it.

6. Turn filet over so that the rounded top is up (and the folded ends of the pastry are underneath) and place on a large, lightly greased baking pan.

7. Roll pastry trimmings and cut small squares or rounds and lay over top of pastry in a design. Brush entire surface with the beaten egg.

8. To bake the filet, place it on the center of lower rack in oven for 40 to 45 minutes or until pastry is a light golden color. Filet should be quite rare.

9. *Meanwhile, prepare the Madeira Sauce:* Reduce the beef stock in a saucepan until it yields 3 cups and reduce the Madeira in another saucepan to 1 cup. Add it to the reduced beef stock and boil together for 5 minutes. Add the Duxelles and heat. Season with salt and pepper to taste. If a thicker sauce is desired, stir in arrowroot until dissolved.

10. Remove filet from oven and let stand at room temperature 6 to 8 minutes before slicing. Set 6 very hot plates out, slice filet and serve 4 slices on each plate. Do this as fast as possible so that meat will not get cold.

11. Spoon ¼ cup Madeira Sauce around (*not on*) each serving of

beef. Garnish each plate with a large sprig of watercress and serve immediately.

Note: If you'd like, substitute rich pie pastry (your favorite recipe) for the puff pastry.

FILET OF BEEF BURGUNDY

SERVES 12

1 *whole filet of beef, about 6 pounds*
1½ *teaspoons salt*
¼ *teaspoon freshly ground black pepper*
1 *teaspoon dried rosemary leaves*
10 *bacon slices*
1 *cup Burgundy*
½ *cup (1 stick) butter*
2 *pounds large mushrooms*

FOR THE BORDELAISE SAUCE:
¼ *cup (½ stick) butter*
2 *shallots, finely chopped*
2 *garlic cloves, finely chopped*
2 *onion slices*
2 *carrot slices*

2 *sprigs parsley*
10 *whole black peppercorns*
2 *whole cloves*
2 *bay leaves*
3 *tablespoons all-purpose flour*
one *10½-ounce can condensed beef broth, undiluted*
1 *cup Burgundy*
¼ *teaspoon salt*
freshly ground black pepper to taste
2 *tablespoons chopped fresh parsley*
½ *teaspoon meat extract (optional)*

chopped fresh parsley and watercress sprigs for garnish

METHOD:

1. Trim excess fat from beef. Sprinkle filet all over with salt, pepper and rosemary.

2. Tuck narrow end of filet under to make uniformly thick; fasten with skewer.

3. Arrange bacon slices over top of beef and wrap string around beef to secure them.

4. Place beef on rack in shallow roasting pan and then under broiler so that meat is 4 inches from heat. Broil 45 minutes, turning meat every 10 minutes.

5. Remove meat from roasting pan to discard string and bacon and pour off excess fat from bacon. Reduce oven temperature to 300°F. Put meat back in roasting pan.

6. Pour Burgundy over beef. Roast filet in oven, basting occasionally with pan juices, until done (it will take 30 minutes for rare).

7. Meanwhile, in hot butter in large skillet, sauté mushrooms, stirring occasionally, until tender. Remove from heat and keep warm.

8. Remove filet to serving platter. Cover and keep warm while making sauce.

9. *Prepare the Bordelaise Sauce:* In hot butter in medium-size skillet, sauté shallots, garlic, onion, carrot, parsley, peppercorns, cloves and bay leaves until onion is golden, about 3 minutes. Remove from heat, stir in flour, blending until smooth. Cook, stirring constantly, over low heat, until flour is lightly browned—about 5 minutes. Remove from heat. Stir broth and ¾ cup of Burgundy into flour mixture. Cook over low heat, and bring just to boiling, stirring constantly. Reduce heat, and simmer, uncovered, for 10 minutes, stirring occasionally. Strain sauce, discarding vegetables and spices. Return sauce to skillet. Add salt, pepper, the 2 tablespoons parsley and remaining Burgundy. Reheat gently—do not boil. (If you are using meat extract, add it to sauce now.)

10. To serve, cut meat into slices ¾ inch thick. Surround slices with mushrooms. Garnish with chopped parsley and watercress. Serve the Bordelaise Sauce on the side.

BEEF STROGANOFF

SERVES 6

3 *pounds filet of beef, cut against grain into narrow strips*
4 *tablespoons lemon juice*
6 *tablespoons butter*
2 *cups finely chopped onion*
2 *cups sliced mushrooms*
4 *tablespoons flour*

salt and freshly ground black
    pepper
2 cups sour cream
small black or small green ripe
    olives for garnish
cooked rice or noodles

METHOD:

1. Sprinkle beef with lemon juice.

2. Melt 2 tablespoons butter in a frying pan. Add onions and cook gently until golden brown. Remove onions from pan.

3. Add sliced mushrooms, cook for 5 minutes and remove.

4. Dust beef lightly with flour. Reheat the pan, add remaining butter and heat until sizzling, then add beef. Shake pan occasionally while cooking beef over brisk fire for 5 minutes.

5. Return onions and mushrooms to pan and cook for 3 or 4 minutes. Season with salt and pepper.

6. Pour on the sour cream. Heat but do not boil.

7. Garnish with small ripe olives, and serve with noodles or rice.

SIRLOIN STEAK WITH SHERRY SAUCE

SERVES 3–4

2-inch-thick porterhouse or sirloin
    steak
freshly ground black pepper
juice of 2 lemons
    2 garlic cloves, halved
salt to taste

FOR THE SHERRY SAUCE:
1 cup beef consommé
1 cup dry sherry
1 tablespoon all-purpose flour
    mixed with 2 tablespoons cold
    water (optional)
2 tablespoons chopped fresh
    parsley

METHOD:

1. Rub the steaks with pepper and half the lemon juice. Rub garlic over the steak.

2. Broil steak just 4 inches from the flame under a hot broiler. Cook for 4 minutes, salt well, turn the meat over and broil 6 to 8 minutes on other side, or until steak is done to your preference. Remove steak from the pan to a platter and keep warm. Discard garlic.

3. Pour the pan drippings into a saucepan and add the consommé, sherry, remaining lemon juice and more salt if desired. Bring to a boil. Skim off the excess fat and serve the sauce plain or thicken it with flour-and-water paste, letting it come to a boil before serving. Add chopped parsley to the sauce and serve with the steak.

SKILLET MUSHROOM-PEPPER STEAK

SERVES 4

16 large mushrooms, washed
1½ cups chicken broth
    2 pounds steak (sirloin, top round
    or flank)
⅓ teaspoon salt
⅛ teaspoon freshly ground black
    pepper

1 garlic clove
4 tablespoons butter
1 small onion, sliced
1 green pepper, sliced
toasted crusty bread

METHOD:

1. Cover mushrooms with chicken broth and let stand 30 minutes. Drain broth; remove stems and discard (save for another dish if desired).

2. Cut steak in thin strips (crosswise to the grain if round or flank steak is used). Sprinkle meat with salt and pepper.

3. Melt butter in saucepan, add garlic and meat. Sauté quickly until nicely browned. Remove meat from pan and keep warm.

4. Add onion, green pepper and mushrooms to pan.

5. Sauté, stirring, until vegetables are tender, about 5 minutes. Return steak to pan along with any juices they have given up. Heat, stirring, a few minutes longer. Serve with toasted crusty bread.

STEAK DIANE FLAMBÉ

SERVES 6

six 10-ounce strip sirloin steaks
salt and freshly ground black
    pepper
vegetable oil
2¼ sticks (1 cup plus 2 tablespoons)
    butter
12 medium mushrooms, thinly
    sliced
24 shallots or 12 small onions,
    thinly sliced

¾ cup brandy
6 tablespoons A-1 sauce
2 tablespoons Worcestershire
    sauce
1½ cups sherry
1 tablespoon chopped fresh chives
2 tablespoons chopped fresh
    parsley

METHOD:

1. Lay steaks between sheets of wax paper and pound to ¼-inch thickness. Season with salt and pepper and rub lightly with oil.

2. In a hot skillet, brown steaks quickly on both sides (it is essential to maintain a rare center) and remove.

3. Melt 1½ sticks butter in skillet and when moderately hot add mushrooms and shallots or onions. Sauté until golden. Return steaks to skillet and place on top of sautéed mushrooms and shallots.

4. Pour brandy into skillet. Heat well and ignite with a match (stand back and be careful). When flame has died down, add A-1 sauce, Worcestershire sauce, remaining butter, sherry, chives and parsley. Stir to mix. Turn steaks over in sauce and serve.

Note: This will undoubtedly have to be done in 2 skillets, if you want to prepare the steaks all at one time. Or cook them 2 or 3 at a time, keeping the cooked steaks warm as you prepare the rest. In that case, divide the rest of the ingredients accordingly.

MINUTE STEAKS WITH WHITE WINE

SERVES 6

1¼ cups (2½ sticks) butter
6 thin sirloin steaks
1 tablespoon chopped fresh
   parsley
3 green onions, finely chopped

6 fresh mushrooms, sliced
1 tablespoon all-purpose flour
9 ounces dry white wine
salt and freshly ground black pepper

METHOD:

1. Melt butter in frying pan and sauté steaks quickly on both sides; they should cook in less than 10 minutes.

2. Remove steaks to hot platter and keep warm. Into the same pan put the parsley, onions and mushrooms. Sauté and remove.

3. Blend the flour into the juices in the pan and continue to mix while adding the wine. Stir until sauce thickens and is cooked, about 4 minutes. Then add the sautéed onion and mushroom mixture and stir again.

4. Pour sauce over the steaks and serve hot.

FLANK STEAK IN WINE

SERVES 6

2 pounds flank steak
4 tablespoons butter
2 garlic cloves, crushed
¼ cup chopped fresh parsley
½ teaspoon salt
¼ teaspoon dried rosemary
¼ teaspoon dried basil
¼ teaspoon dried oregano
one 8-ounce can tomato sauce

1 cup dry red wine
½ pound fresh mushrooms, thinly
   sliced
2 tablespoons water
1 tablespoon flour
one 8-ounce package noodles
2 tablespoons chopped parsley
   for garnish

METHOD:

1. Wipe steak with paper towels. Trim excess fat.

2. Cut steak crosswise into diagonal slices ¼ inch thick.

3. Melt butter in large Dutch oven and sauté slices quickly a few at a time until browned on both sides. As slices brown, remove them from the pot. Continue until all slices are browned. Remove from heat. Pour the drippings off.

4. Add garlic, parsley, salt, rosemary, basil, oregano, tomato sauce, wine and meat to pan.

5. Simmer, covered, stirring occasionally, about 1 hour, or until meat is tender.

6. Add mushrooms and simmer, covered, 5 minutes longer.

7. In a small bowl, combine water and flour and mix well. Stir into beef mixture; bring to a boil, stirring constantly. Reduce heat; simmer 1 minute or until mixture is thickened.

8. Meanwhile, cook noodles and drain.

9. To serve, spoon beef and sauce into center of deep serving dish and surround with noodles. Sprinkle with chopped parsley.

ROAST HIP OF BEEF

SERVES 12

1 *hip (sirloin) of beef (approximately 15 pounds, bone in; 11 pounds, boned)*	3 *cups Burgundy*
salt and freshly ground black pepper	2 *cups beef stock*
about 1 tablespoon grated horse-radish	16 *tiny carrots, peeled*
2 *tablespoons prepared mustard*	24 *small onions, peeled*
	18 *crab apples, sautéed in melted butter and cinnamon, and sprigs of fresh parsley for garnish*

METHOD:

1. Wipe beef with damp cloth.

2. Rub all over with salt and pepper. Mix mustard with horseradish and rub mixture into both sides of the beef.

3. Place in a large bowl or pan and pour Burgundy over meat. Cover and let stand 6 to 8 hours, turning the meat over every 2 hours.

4. Preheat oven to 450°F.

5. Remove meat from marinade and place in a roasting pan; pour beef stock over meat. Reserve the marinade. Put in oven and roast for 45 minutes. Reduce heat to 350°F. and continue to roast for 1 to 1½

hours, basting frequently with marinade. Reduce heat to 200°F. and continue to roast approximately 20 minutes per pound for medium, or, if using meat thermometer, remove meat from oven when it registers the degree of doneness you prefer.

6. When roast is almost done, steam carrots and onions separately until just tender. Toss with butter and keep warm until ready to serve.

7. Remove meat from roasting pan and set in a large hot platter. Arrange vegetables around and garnish with crab apples and sprigs of parsley.

MARINATED RUMP OF BEEF

5–6 *pounds rump of beef*
 2 *cups sliced onions*
 ½ *cup chopped shallots or green*
  onions
 2 *garlic cloves, chopped*
 1 *bay leaf*
 ½ *teaspoon dried thyme, crumbled*
4 *or 5 sprigs of parsley*

1 *teaspoon black peppercorns*
1 *teaspoon salt*
2 *cups dry red wine*
5 *tablespoons melted butter*
two 10½-*ounce cans condensed beef*
  broth
1 *tablespoon all-purpose flour*

METHOD:

1. Put meat in stainless steel or enamel pan just large enough to hold it. Combine onions, herbs, peppercorns, salt and wine; pour over meat. Cover. Refrigerate 8 to 12 hours, turning meat occasionally.

2. Heat oven to 475°F. Remove meat from marinade; pat dry. Reserve marinade. Place meat on rack in shallow roasting pan.

3. Roast 30 minutes, basting once or twice with 4 tablespoons of butter. Reduce heat to 400°F. Roast 40 to 45 minutes. Estimate total roasting time at about 12 minutes per pound for rare. Baste occasionally with pan drippings, adding a little of the marinade if there is not enough liquid. Remove meat to warm platter. Let stand 15 to 20 minutes before carving.

4. Strain the drippings into a saucepan, discarding vegetables and herbs. Heat to boiling; cook 1 minute. Remove as much fat as possible. Add reserved marinade. Bring to a boil and cook until reduced to just a few tablespoons. Add broth. Blend together remaining 1 tablespoon butter and flour. Add to pan. Cook, stirring constantly, until sauce is thick and smooth. Correct seasoning and strain sauce before serving.

5. Slice beef and serve with sauce.

SPICY ROAST OF BEEF WITH
GINGERSNAP GRAVY

SERVES 6–8

5 *pounds rump or round of beef*
2 *cups wine vinegar*
1 *ripe tomato, chopped*
2 *bay leaves*
½ *teaspoon whole cloves*
½ *teaspoon whole black pepper-*
  corns
¼ *cup all-purpose flour*

½ *teaspoon freshly ground black*
  pepper
1 *teaspoon salt*
½ *teaspoon allspice*
4 *tablespoons butter*
½ *cup sliced onions*
12 *gingersnaps, crumbled*
boiled potatoes

METHOD:

1. Place the meat, vinegar, tomato, bay leaves, cloves, peppercorns and enough water to cover meat in a bowl. Refrigerate overnight or even another day if you like a spicier meat. Turn meat in marinade 2 or 3 times to coat evenly.

2. Remove meat, reserving marinade, and rub with a mixture of flour, pepper, salt and allspice.

3. Melt butter in a large deep skillet or kettle, then add onions and meat; brown meat on all sides.

4. Add 3 cups of the rserved marinade and cook, covered, over low heat for 2 to 3 hours, or until the meat is tender.

5. Add the crumbled gingersnaps and continue to cook, stirring, until gravy has thickened. Remove meat to a hot serving dish and strain the gravy into a sauceboat. Serve with boiled potatoes.

APPLEJACK BEEF STEW

SERVES 6

1½ cups applejack (apple brandy)
    4 tablespoons vegetable oil
    4 shallots, chopped
juice of 1 lemon
    2 garlic cloves, pierced
    ⅛ teaspoon ground thyme
salt and freshly ground black pepper
Tabasco sauce
    1 bay leaf

3 pounds beef chuck, cut into
    1½-inch pieces
2 cups beef stock
2 medium carrots, peeled and cut
    in 1-inch rounds
2 small turnips, peeled and cubed
½ pound parsnips, peeled and cut
    in 1-inch rounds

METHOD:

1. Mix 1 cup of the applejack, the oil, shallots, lemon juice and garlic in a large bowl. Season with thyme, salt, pepper and Tabasco and add bay leaf.

2. Add the meat, turning to coat it well. Refrigerate for 3 hours, turning the meat over occasionally.

3. Preheat oven to 325°F. Place meat and marinade in 3-quart bake-and-serve casserole with a tightly fitting cover.

4. Add the beef stock, cover and bake in oven until meat is tender, about 3 hours. Add the vegetables during the last hour of cooking time. When done, remove cover and cook long enough to reduce sauce to a thick gravy. Correct seasoning. Warm the remaining applejack, pour over the stew and flame. Serve in the baking casserole.

BOURBON BEEF AND OYSTER POT

SERVES 8

4 pounds beef chuck, top or bottom
    round, cut into 1½-inch pieces
2 tablespoons lemon juice
salt and freshly ground black pepper
4 tablespoons vegetable oil
2 tablespoons butter
5 ounces Bourbon
4 cups boiling beef stock or beef
    broth
4 cups boiling water
1 large carrot, cut in 1-inch pieces
2 stalks celery, cut in 1-inch pieces
1 large potato, peeled and cut in
    half

1 medium onion, studded with
    2 whole cloves
2 tablespoons tomato sauce
1 small bay leaf
1 garlic clove, pierced
¼ teaspoon ground thyme
Tabasco and Worcestershire sauces
    to taste
3 dozen fresh shucked oysters,
    plus their liquor, picked over to
    remove bits of shell
crisp toast points and watercress
    or parsley for garnish
grated horseradish

METHOD:

1. Dry meat thoroughly with paper towels, sprinkle on lemon juice, and let stand 10 minutes. Dust with salt and pepper.

2. Sauté meat in a skillet in oil and butter on all sides until golden brown. Pour 4 ounces (½ cup) Bourbon over meat and flame. When flame dies out, place meat in a large stew pot attractive enough to bring to the table. Pour boiling beef stock and water over beef. Discard fat from skillet the meat was browned in, scrape brown bits with a little water and pour over the meat. Add the vegetables, tomato sauce and all spices except Tabasco and Worcestershire. Bring to a brisk boil, reduce heat, then cover and simmer until meat is tender (approximately 3 hours).

3. Remove meat, pour sauce into blender jar, add the vegetables, and blend until pureed and smooth. (If too thick, add extra beef stock.) Season with Tabasco and Worcestershire to taste. Return meat and sauce to stock pot.

4. When ready to serve, reheat beef until bubbly hot, add oysters with their liquor, and heat just until oyster edges curl. Heat the remaining ounce (2 tablespoons) of Bourbon, pour over beef, and flame. Spoon into serving bowls; garnish with toast points and watercress. Pass the grated horseradish.

PICADILLO-STUFFED ONIONS

SERVES 6

6 large onions, about ¾ pound
   each, peeled
boiling water
salt
3 tablespoons olive oil
¾ pound lean ground beef
¾ pound lean ground pork
one 16-ounce can plum tomatoes,
   drained
6-ounce can mild chili peppers,
   drained, chopped
¾ cup raisins

3 tablespoons tomato paste
2 garlic cloves, minced
1 tablespoon cider vinegar
½ teaspoon cinnamon
¼ teaspoon ground cloves
1 cup pimento-stuffed green olives,
   drained, coarsely chopped
½ cup chopped pimento
salt and freshly ground black pepper
two 10¾-ounce cans beef broth
minced fresh parsley for garnish

METHOD:

1. Preheat oven to 350°F.

2. With a melon-ball cutter, scoop out the centers of the onions, leaving a firm shell.

3. Chop enough of the centers to measure 1½ cups.

4. In a large saucepan of salted boiling water, cook the onion shells over moderate heat for 5 minutes. Drain shells and invert on a rack and/or paper towels to dry.

5. In a stainless steel or enameled skillet cook the chopped onions in olive oil over moderate heat, stirring, until softened. Add meat and cook until it is no longer pink. Add the tomatoes, chili peppers, raisins, tomato paste, garlic, vinegar, cinnamon, clove, salt and pepper to taste. Stir in the chopped olives and pimento.

6. Stuff the onion shells with this mixture. Arrange the onions in a flameproof casserole just large enough to hold them. Heat broth on top of stove, then pour around the onions, making sure there is enough to reach ½ inch up the sides of the onions. Bring to a boil over moderate heat, and then bake in oven for 45 minutes or until tender. Transfer the onions with a slotted spoon to a heated serving dish, sprinkle with minced fresh parsley and serve.

VEAL

BAKED STUFFED VEAL CHOPS WITH MARSALA AND MUSHROOM CAPS

Excellent accompaniments for this dish are artichokes, buttered broccoli, and Potatoes Anna (page 216).

6 *double-rib veal chops (about 8 ounces each)*
3 *tablespoons grated Swiss cheese*
3 *thin slices baked ham*
salt and freshly ground black pepper
flour to coat chops
1½ *sticks (12 tablespoons) butter*

18 *whole mushroom caps*
½ *cup chicken stock*
1½ *cups dry Marsala*
¾ *cup dry sherry*
3 *tablespoons flour to thicken sauce*
parsley or watercress for garnish

METHOD:

1. Preheat oven to 475°F.

2. Cut a slit in the side of each chop to form a pocket. Place ½ tablespoon cheese in each pocket, then a half slice of ham. Fasten each chop closed with a skewer or toothpicks.

3. Dust chops with salt and pepper, then with flour.

4. Add 2 tablespoons butter to flameproof casserole and melt over burner. Add mushroom caps, sauté 2 to 3 minutes and remove. Then melt remaining butter, add chops and sauté until a light golden brown on both sides.

5. Place mushroom caps on top of chops. Add chicken stock, cover and bake in oven for 25 minutes. Then add the Marsala and sherry and bake uncovered for 10 minutes or until chops are brown and tender. Remove chops and mushroom caps to a hot serving platter. Scrape all the bits from the sides and bottom of the casserole so they are incorporated into the pan drippings. Pour drippings into a bowl and strain off the fat, reserving ¼ cup of it. Place fat in the casserole, heat over burner and add flour, stirring until smooth and thickened. Stir in slowly 2 cups of the pan drippings (if more liquid is needed to make 2 cups, then add additional wine and broth). Correct seasoning. Pour sauce over the chops and the mushroom caps. Garnish with parsley or watercress.

VEAL CHOPS ORLOFF

SERVES 8

8 *rib veal chops, each ¾ to 1 inch thick*
salt and freshly ground black pepper
flour for dredging
8 *tablespoons (1 stick) butter*
1 *cup minced onion*
1 *pound mushrooms, finely chopped*
¾ *teaspoon salt*

2 *dashes freshly ground black pepper*
1 *tablespoon lemon juice*
4 *tablespoons all-purpose flour*
2 *cups light cream*
¾ *cup grated Swiss or Parmesan cheese*
parsley or watercress sprigs for garnish

METHOD:

1. Sprinkle chops with salt and pepper.

2. Dredge in flour; shake off excess. Melt half the butter in large skillet over medium heat. Cook chops 10 to 12 minutes on each side. Remove from skillet. Keep warm.

3. Add onions to fat left in skillet. Cook 1 minute, scraping bottom of skillet with wooden spoon. Add mushrooms; sprinkle with ½ teaspoon salt, dash of pepper and lemon juice. Cook 5 to 6 minutes, stirring occasionally.

4. Melt remaining butter in a small saucepan. Stir in flour. Cook 1 minute, stirring constantly. Stir in slowly the cream, the ¼ teaspoon salt and a dash of pepper. Cook over medium heat, stirring rapidly with wooden spoon or wire whisk, until sauce bubbles. Remove from heat. Stir sauce into mushroom mixture; mix well. Correct seasoning to taste.

5. Place chops on cookie sheet or in shallow roasting pan. Top each with mushroom mixture, dividing evenly among chops. Sprinkle with cheese. Place under broiler for a few minutes until cheese melts and is lightly browned. Arrange chops with their sauce on heated serving platter. Garnish with parsley or watercress.

VEAL CORDON BLEU

SERVES 8

8 double-rib veal chops, each
   weighing 8 or 9 ounces
salt and freshly ground black pepper
8 thin slices prosciutto or baked
   ham
8 thin slices Swiss cheese

8 tablespoons (1 stick) butter,
   melted
flour for dusting
¾ cup beef stock
½ cup dry Marsala

METHOD:

1. Preheat oven to 350°F.

2. Cut a deep pocket in the side of each chop (unless your butcher has already done this for you).

3. Dust chops with salt and pepper.

4. Place 1 slice each of ham and cheese in each pocket. Fasten with skewers or toothpicks.

5. Brush chops generously with melted butter and then dust with flour.

6. Place chops in well-greased baking casserole, add ½ cup of stock and bake about 20 minutes. Turn to brown other sides of chops and bake until done, 20 to 30 minutes.

7. Remove chops to hot serving platter. Pour off fat and deglaze casserole on top of stove by adding the remaining (hot) stock, stirring and scraping the solidified pieces from the bottom and sides. Add the Marsala and boil the liquid rapidly until syrupy. Season sauce to taste and serve poured over the chops.

ROAST VEAL WITH ORANGE SAUCE

SERVES 8

4–5 pounds veal from the leg,
   boned and tied
2 tablespoons butter, softened
½ teaspoon mace
salt and freshly ground black pepper
½ cup beef consommé

½ cup dry red wine
1 teaspoon grated orange rind
1 teaspoon grated lemon rind
1 peeled orange, sliced and cut in
   sections

METHOD:

1. Preheat oven to 325°F.

2. Put the meat on a rack in a roasting pan and spread with the softened butter.

3. Sprinkle with mace, salt and pepper.

4. Roast in oven for about 2 hours, basting frequently with a mixture of consommé and red wine.

5. Transfer roast to heated platter.

6. Skim off the fat from the juice of the roast and stir grated orange and lemon rinds into remaining juice. Cook sauce until reduced slightly and stir in the orange sections. Serve the sauce separately.

HERBED MIXED GRILL

SERVES 12

FOR THE CREOLE SAUCE:
2 tablespoons vegetable oil
2 tablespoons chopped onion
½ green pepper, chopped
½ cup sliced mushrooms
1 garlic clove, crushed
1 cup dry white wine
¼ cup tomato puree
1 fresh tomato, peeled and seeded
½ bay leaf
1 cup tomato sauce
½ bay leaf
salt and freshly ground black pepper
2 tablespoons chopped parsley

12 ribs of lamb, each weighing
    about 6 ounces
3 pounds filet of beef, trimmed,
    cut into 12 slices
1 pound small sausages (12 to a
    pound), parboiled

salt and freshly ground black pepper
smoke-flavored seasoning
2¼ pounds calf's liver cut in
    36 one-ounce portions
12 slices bacon, partially cooked,
    each slice cut in thirds
36 sage leaves or 1 teaspoon ground
    sage
seasoned pan juices (reserved from
    broiling meats)
melted butter
12 firm, ripe tomatoes, cored,
    blossom end removed
12 baked potatoes

FOR THE SOUR CREAM TOPPING:
2 cups (1 pint) sour cream
2 tablespoons bacon crumbs made
    from crisply fried bacon
2 tablespoons chopped chives

watercress for garnish

METHOD:

1. *Prepare the Creole Sauce:* Heat oil in a saucepan until hot, then add onion, green pepper and mushrooms and sauté a few minutes; add garlic. Cover pan and let simmer gently until tender, about 10 minutes.

Then add the wine and reduce volume by half. Add tomato puree and fresh tomato. Cook slowly over low heat for another 10 minutes and add tomato sauce, bay leaf, salt and pepper. Continue cooking slowly for another 20 minutes. Correct seasoning and add parsley.

2. While the sauce is cooking, prepare the meats: Dust lamb and beef lightly with salt, pepper and smoke-flavored seasoning and broil, with the sausage, to desired doneness; keep warm.

3. Meanwhile, wrap a bacon slice around each piece of liver, enclosing a sage leaf in between, and fasten it with a skewer. If ground sage is used, dust liver lightly before skewering. Broil on both sides until brown and keep warm.

4. Save the pan juices from the broiled meats and skim off the fat. Keep warm and reserve to serve with meats.

5. Brush tomatoes generously with melted butter and broil 6 minutes.

6. *Prepare the Sour Cream Topping:* Mix bacon crumbs and chives with sour cream.

7. To serve, arrange broiled meats, potatoes and tomatoes on hot serving platter. Top each tomato with a spoon of hot Creole Sauce. Slit potatoes open and fill openings with Sour Cream Topping. Garnish with watercress and serve the seasoned meat-juice gravy on the side.

LAMB

LAMB AND VEGETABLE POT PIE

SERVES 6

1 *lamb shoulder, boned (about*
2½ pounds), excess fat removed,
cut into 1½-inch pieces
flour
salt and freshly ground black pepper
½ cup bacon fat
boiling water to cover (about
8 cups)

2 *cups diced celery, leaves*
included
3 *cups sliced onions*
6 *cups diced potatoes*
2 *cups carrots sliced ½ inch thick*
2 *cups green peas, fresh or frozen*
(if frozen, thaw slightly)
biscuit dough (page 278) for 6 large
biscuits

METHOD:

1. Dredge lamb in flour and dust with salt and pepper. In a large saucepan or stew pot, heat half the bacon fat and brown the meat. Cover with boiling water, bring to a boil and simmer until meat is tender—approximately 1 hour.

2. Sauté celery and onions in remaining bacon fat in another pan and add to meat. Simmer until vegetables are tender, approximately 20 minutes. Remove meat-vegetable mixture from heat, cool, and skim off excess fat.

3. Preheat oven to 350°F.

4. Drain 2 cups of the liquid from the lamb and discard (or save for another dish). Add potatoes and carrots to the lamb and cook on top of stove for 10 to 15 minutes. Then add peas and stir well. Correct seasoning. Place lamb-vegetable mixture in casserole, top with biscuit dough and bake until biscuits are done—approximately 15 minutes—and serve immediately.

LAMB STEW

SERVES 6

3½ *pounds shoulder of lamb, boned,*
  cut in 1½-inch cubes
flour for dredging
salt and freshly ground black pepper
  3 *tablespoons vegetable oil or*
    shortening
 12 *small white pearl onions*

 3 *carrots, peeled and cut in*
   quarters
 2 *stalks celery, chopped*
 2 *sprigs fresh thyme*
 2 *garlic cloves, chopped*
2½ *cups dry white wine*
 1 *cup (½ pint) heavy cream*

METHOD:

1. Trim the meat of fat and gristle.

2. Mix flour with salt and pepper and rub all over meat. Heat the oil in a large stew pot or Dutch oven, add lamb and brown well.

3. Skim off any excess fat. Add onions, carrots, celery, garlic and thyme and then pour in enough wine to just barely cover the meat.

4. Cover and cook very slowly, stirring occasionally, for 1½ hours or until meat is tender.

5. Add cream and blend well. For a thicker sauce, reduce the cream by boiling it down rapidly over high heat. Season to your taste with salt and pepper and serve hot.

BAKED LAMB HASH AU GRATIN

SERVES 12

3 *cups diced potatoes*
1 *cup chopped onion*
1 *cup diced green pepper*
¾ *cup diced pimento*
12 *cups cooked, diced lamb*
2 *cups lamb gravy (see Note)*

1 *cup tomato puree*
salt and freshly ground black pepper
3 *tablespoons butter (or more)*
6 *ounces American or Parmesan*
   cheese, grated
sweet paprika

METHOD:

1. Preheat oven to 350°F.

2. Plunge potatoes, onions and green peppers into boiling water to blanch. Remove immediately. Add pimento and lamb to vegetables.

3. Combine gravy and tomato puree in a large pot, adding a little hot water to thin it if necessary.

4. Add vegetable-meat mixture to sauce; heat. Season with salt and pepper.

5. Butter 12 individual flat gratin dishes with half the butter and add hash mixture. Dot tops with remaining butter, sprinkle cheese over and dust with paprika. Bake for 15 to 20 minutes.

Note: A very tasty lamb gravy can be made from the drippings of roast lamb. Just deglaze the roasting pan (after you have strained off the fat) with about 2 cups of lamb, veal or beef stock and blend in 2 tablespoons of flour to thicken it.

ROAST CROWN OF MUTTON STUFFED WITH PRUNES AND RICE

SERVES 8

2 racks mutton (about 8 pounds),
  trimmed for roasting
¼ cup lemon juice
½ teaspoon grated lemon rind
½ cup olive or vegetable oil
½ teaspoon salt
½ teaspoon freshly ground black
  pepper
⅛ teaspoon sweet paprika

FOR THE STUFFING:
1 cup minced celery

1 cup chopped apple
2 tablespoons minced onion
2 tablespoons butter
1 tablespoon lemon juice
½ teaspoon grated lemon rind
¾ pound cooked prunes, chopped
  (about 1¾ cups pitted,
  uncooked)
2 cups cooked rice or 3 cups soft
  bread crumbs
salt and freshly ground black pepper

METHOD:

1. Mix the lemon juice, rind, oil and seasonings together well and spoon over the mutton racks; marinate 2 hours, turning from time to time.

2. Preheat oven to 400°F.

3. *Prepare the stuffing:* Sauté the celery, apple and onion in the butter for 2 minutes. Remove from heat. Add the lemon juice, rind and chopped prunes, and toss in the rice or bread crumbs and season.

4. Shape the 2 racks in the form of a crown and fasten them together with skewers. Roast for 10 minutes per pound.

5. Remove from oven and fill the crown with the stuffing. Return to oven, lower the heat to 350°F. and roast for 25 minutes more or until ribs are crisp and golden. Do not overcook—the meat should be pink inside.

PORK

STUFFED CROWN ROAST OF PORK

SERVES 10–12

juice of 2 lemons
 7-pound crown roast of pork
 8 tablespoons (1 stick) butter
 3 tablespoons grated onion
 3 apples, peeled and cubed
 2 garlic cloves, minced
 3 cups bread cubes
 ⅓ cup dry white wine

½ cup sugar or to taste
½ teaspoon dried marjoram
¼ teaspoon dried thyme
 2 tablespoons chopped fresh
 parsley
salt and freshly ground black pepper
parsley sprigs for garnish

METHOD:
1. Preheat oven to 325°F.
2. Sprinkle the pork with lemon juice.
3. In a large skillet, melt butter and sauté onions, apples, garlic and bread cubes.
4. Add wine, sugar and herbs and mix well. Season with salt and pepper to taste.
5. Make certain the pork is tied securely into a crown roast with a bit of twine. Stand in roasting pan and stuff the center of crown firmly with all the stuffing.
6. Roast for 3 to 4 hours, or until well done as registered on a meat thermometer.
7. Remove from oven, set roast on a hot platter and garnish with parsley sprigs.

FENNEL PORK ROAST

SERVES 8

5-pound boneless pork roast
4 tablespoons olive oil
flour for dusting
1½ cups chicken broth
1½ cups dry white wine
1 teaspoon fennel seeds

3 garlic cloves, finely chopped
1 tablespoon fresh rosemary or
   1 teaspoon dried
1 tablespoon fresh sage or
   1 teaspoon dried
salt and freshly ground black pepper

METHOD:

1. Preheat oven to 350°F.

2. Rub the pork on all surfaces with about 1 tablespoon of the olive oil and then dust with flour. Place a heavy roasting pan with remaining oil on high heat, add pork and brown on all sides (use more oil if necessary).

3. Next, in a saucepan, combine chicken broth, wine, fennel seeds, garlic, rosemary, sage, salt and pepper. Bring mixture to a boil, then simmer for 10 minutes to blend flavors.

4. Pour half this marinade over the pork in the roasting pan, and roast uncovered in the oven for 3 hours or until done. Baste every 15 to 20 minutes, adding more marinade after each basting and as liquid evaporates. When pork is done, remove to plate to cool 10 minutes before carving. Skim off the fat from the marinade-pan juice mixture in roasting pan and pour into a saucepan.

5. On top of the stove, reduce the marinade and pan juices by half. Pour into a gravy boat. Serve with sliced pork and hot steamed rice on the side.

SOY-HONEY GLAZED BARBECUED SPARERIBS

SERVES 8

This dish should be started a day in advance as the spareribs need to marinate overnight.

6 *pounds lean spareribs*

FOR THE MARINADE:
½ *cup soy sauce*
½ *cup honey*
⅔ *cup lemon juice*
1 *teaspoon crushed anise seed*

1 *teaspoon ground ginger*
1 *teaspoon dry mustard*
½ *teaspoon mace*
½ *teaspoon ground cloves*
½ *teaspoon salt*
2 *tablespoons dry sherry*

METHOD:

1. Place spareribs in a shallow baking dish (not metal).

2. *Prepare the marinade:* Combine all marinade ingredients and mix well. Pour over ribs and toss to coat. Refrigerate overnight, covered.

3. When ready to cook the ribs, prepare a charcoal fire. Adjust grill 4 inches from coals.

4. Cut a piece of heavy-duty foil, 30 by 18 inches, place spareribs in center of foil and carefully pour marinade over them. Bring long sides of foil together and fold over twice to seal securely. Then fold in ends to completely seal package.

5. Place foil package, seam side down, in center of another 30-by-18-inch rectangle of heavy-duty foil. Wrap again as directed above.

6. Place foil package on hot grill: grill 30 minutes. Turn and grill 30 minutes longer on other side.

7. Raise grill 2 inches, remove spareribs from foil, pour off the marinade and place ribs directly on grill. Cook ribs 5 minutes on each side or until well done and browned, basting with marinade if you wish. Cut into serving-size pieces.

PRAGUE HAM EN CROÛTE WITH CHAMPAGNE

SERVES 12

The Prague ham from central Europe is perhaps the most prized of all hams. It can be purchased here in good butcher shops, particularly European ones. It has a mild sweet taste derived from first being salted, then mildly brined and lightly smoked over beechwood embers.

7-pound Prague ham, uncooked	salt and freshly ground black pepper
2 bottles champagne (approximately 3 cups each)	beef or chicken stock
½ teaspoon dried or 1 tablespoon chopped fresh thyme	1 recipe for Puff Pastry (see Beef Wellington, page 84)
1 tablespoon chopped fresh parsley	3 egg yolks, beaten
1½ bay leaves	1 pound mushrooms, stems removed
2 medium carrots, chopped	7 tablespoons butter
2 medium onions, chopped	1 cup (½ pint) heavy cream
	1 cup Madeira

METHOD:

1. Soak the ham for 24 hours in water to cover (about 7 quarts), changing the water 2 or 3 times to free it of salt. When ready to cook the ham, rinse it thoroughly.

2. Pour the champagne into a braising pan and add the thyme, parsley, bay leaves, carrots, onions, salt and pepper. Place the ham in the pan; it should be covered with the champagne. If necessary add some stock. Bring to a boil and simmer for 2½ hours. Leave the ham to cool in the liquid. Remove the rind and bone the ham, keeping the meat intact.

3. Preheat oven to 450°F.

4. Roll out the pastry to a rectangle large enough to wrap around the ham. Cover the ham entirely with the pastry, tucking the ends underneath. For an attractive decorative effect, cut any remaining pastry scraps with a sharp knife into flower petals and leaves or a design of your choice. Moisten one side of the shapes to attach them to the pastry. Brush the entire surface of the pastry with one of the beaten egg yolks for a lovely golden glaze.

5. Bake the ham at 450° for 5 minutes, then reduce the temperature

to 350° and cook for 25 to 30 minutes more, or until the crust is light golden brown.

6. Finely dice the mushroom caps and cook them in 2 tablespoons of the butter. Reduce the liquid from the ham to ⅕ of the original volume, then strain through a fine sieve. Add the cream, mushrooms, remaining egg yolks and Madeira. Heat this sauce gently on a low flame, but do not allow it to come to a boil. Remove the pan from the fire and stir in the remaining butter, divided into small pieces. Taste for seasoning. Serve the ham on a hot platter with the sauce on the side.

HAM AND SWEET POTATOES

SERVES 6

3 *pounds ham steak*	½ *cup whole cranberry sauce*
3 *pounds sweet potatoes*	½ *cup chili sauce*
2 *tablespoons butter*	⅓ *cup vinegar*
	pineapple chunks and/or watercress
FOR THE PINEAPPLE CRANBERRY	*sprigs for garnish* (*optional*)
SAUCE:	
one 12-ounce jar pineapple preserves	

METHOD:

1. Preheat oven to 350°F.

2. Boil sweet potatoes until tender, 25 to 30 minutes, peel and arrange in a buttered dish. Set aside.

3. *Prepare the Pineapple Cranberry Sauce:* In a small bowl combine pineapple preserves, whole cranberry sauce, chili sauce and vinegar. Mix well to blend. (Use to brush over ham and sweet potatoes.)

4. Place ham steak in baking dish or pan and brush some sauce over it. Bake in oven for 40 minutes.

5. Glaze the potatoes with some of the sauce and bake in oven during the last 15 or 20 minutes that the ham is cooking. Keep glazing the potatoes until they turn light brown. Glaze the ham with the remaining sauce.

6. Remove ham and potatoes from oven. Place ham steak in center of a hot platter, arrange potatoes around and serve with any remaining sauce. Garnish with pineapple chunks and watercress sprigs if you like.

HAM PATTIES WITH ORANGE-CELERY SAUCE

SERVES 12

4 ounces dark seedless raisins
¼ can (10½-ounce size) cream
  of celery soup
6 ounces (1⅔ cups) pancake mix
½ ounce instant minced onion
¼ teaspoon freshly ground black
  pepper
1½ pounds smoked cooked ham,
  ground

1½ pounds fresh pork, ground

FOR THE ORANGE-CELERY SAUCE:
¼ can (10½-ounce size) cream
  of celery soup
¼ cup orange juice
¼ teaspoon grated orange rind
½ teaspoon whole cloves tied in
  a small piece of cheesecloth

METHOD:

1. Soak raisins in tepid water for several hours to plump them; drain.

2. When ready to prepare patties, preheat oven to 350°F.

3. Mix soup, pancake mix, onion and raisins in mixing bowl of electric mixer (or in blender or food processor). Add ground meat and mix on low speed until just blended, using a spatula to scrape mixture from sides of bowl. Do not overmix.

4. Divide mixture into 12 patties, place on greased baking sheet and flatten. Bake 30 to 45 minutes or until done.

5. *Meanwhile, prepare the Orange Celery Sauce:* Combine sauce ingredients in a saucepan, bring to a boil, stirring, lower heat at once and simmer for 10 minutes. Serve on the side with the ham patties.

BAKED HAM HASH AND TOMATOES

SERVES 6

6 *medium tomatoes*
1 *teaspoon powdered mustard*
3 *cups cooked chopped ham*
3 *tablespoons finely chopped*
  sweet red pepper

9 *eggs*
3¾ *cups milk*
salt and freshly ground black pepper
  2 *tablespoons chopped fresh*
  parsley

METHOD:
1. Preheat oven to 350°F.
2. Grease 6 individual casserole dishes and set aside.
3. Scald tomatoes in hot water for a few minutes to remove skin easily.
4. Slice tomatoes ¼ inch thick and place a sliced tomato in each dish.
5. Dissolve the mustard in a little water and mix with the ham. Add chopped sweet pepper and mix well.
6. Spread ½ cup of ham mixture over tomato slices in each dish.
7. Whip eggs well (but not to a froth) and add milk.
8. Pour equal portions over the tomato slices and ham in each dish.
9. Season with salt and pepper and sprinkle a teaspoon of chopped parsley over each dish. Bake in oven until eggs are set and a light golden brown. Serve immediately.

SPECIALTY CUTS AND GAME MEATS

VEAL KIDNEY AND MUSHROOMS FLAMBÉ

SERVES 6

6 veal kidneys, membrane removed, washed, trimmed, sliced
flour for dusting
6 tablespoons melted butter
1 cup sliced mushrooms

4 tablespoons chopped shallots
⅔ cup brandy
salt and freshly ground black pepper
1½ cups heavy cream
1 tablespoon dry mustard

METHOD:

1. Dust veal kidneys with flour and sauté briefly in melted butter in sauté pan.

2. Add sliced mushrooms and shallots and continue to sauté 4 to 5 minutes or until kidneys are brown.

3. Heat the brandy in a separate pan. Add the warm brandy to kidney-mushroom mixture and ignite—stand back and be careful. (Never flambé for more than 1 minute or kidneys will toughen.) When flame dies out, sprinkle with salt and pepper.

4. Pour heavy cream into a small saucepan and stir in dry mustard; cook until cream is hot. Serve as sauce for kidneys.

SWEETBREADS WITH PEARS

SERVES 6

2 pounds veal sweetbreads
6 cups boiling water
3 cups chicken stock
2 small onions, peeled, halved
2 small carrots, peeled, halved
2 small leeks (white part only),
trimmed and well washed, cut
into small pieces

2 cups (1 pint) heavy cream
3 tablespoons butter
3 firm pears, pared, cored and
sliced
2 tablespoons all-purpose flour
2 tablespoons pear brandy
2 teaspoons fresh lemon juice
salt and freshly ground black pepper

METHOD:

1. Rinse sweetbreads well under cold running water. Put in bowl with enough cold water to cover. Refrigerate 4 to 6 hours, changing the water 2 or 3 times; drain well. Place sweetbreads in single layer in shallow baking pan; cover with plastic wrap. Place smaller baking pan inside larger on top of sweetbreads; weight down with 5-pound weight, such as 5 one-pound cans. Refrigerate overnight.

2. Next day rinse sweetbreads well and drain. Blanch in 6 cups rapidly boiling water in large saucepan for 1 minute; drain immediately. Carefully peel off membrane. With tip of small sharp knife, cut out fat and connective tubes and discard these.

3. Combine stock, onions, carrots and leeks in medium saucepan; heat to simmering. Add sweetbreads and simmer, covered, until tender—about 40 minutes. Transfer sweetbreads and broth to bowl. Let sweetbreads cool in broth. Discard vegetables; skim off fat. Strain broth through sieve lined with double thickness of damp cheesecloth and reserve. Cut the sweetbreads into 1-inch pieces. Cover with plastic wrap; reserve.

4. Heat cream in medium saucepan over low heat to boiling. Boil slowly, stirring often, until reduced to ¾ cup, about 25 minutes. While cream is reducing, heat reserved broth in separate saucepan to boiling point; boil over medium heat until reduced to ¾ cup, about 15 minutes. When both liquids are reduced, pour broth into cream; cook over medium-low heat until reduced to 1 cup, about 10 minutes. Reserve.

5. Melt butter in skillet. Add pear slices and sauté over medium heat until lightly browned on both sides, about 5 minutes. With a slotted spatula, transfer the pears to warm serving platter, cover and keep warm.

6. Toss sweetbreads with flour; add to skillet. Sauté over medium heat until heated through, about 3 minutes. Arrange sweetbreads in mound on serving platter with pears.

7. Reheat sauce over medium heat. Add brandy and lemon juice; season with salt and pepper to taste. Pour over sweetbreads and serve immediately.

FRIED PIG'S TROTTERS

SERVES 6–8

Trotters, also known as pig's petitoes, are simply pig's feet. These fried trotters are delicious served Southern style with butter, mustard and gingerbread.

8 *pig's trotters (feet)*
2 *quarts beef stock*
1 *tablespoon vinegar*
salt

¼ *cup all-purpose flour, seasoned with salt and freshly ground black pepper*
vegetable oil

METHOD:

1. Clean the trotters and soak for 3 hours in cold water, then drain.

2. Place in a large pot with stock, vinegar and a little salt; bring to a boil. Skim off the fat that surfaces to the top, cover and simmer 2½ to 3 hours or until tender.

3. Remove the trotters, drain, cut in half. Coat with seasoned flour. Heat oil in a shallow frying pan and fry trotters in hot oil for 10 to 15 minutes or until brown. Drain on paper towels and serve immediately.

TARRAGON RABBIT

SERVES 6–8

3 *rabbits, each weighing 2 to 3 pounds, cleaned, cut in serving portions*
flour for dusting
1 *tablespoon dried tarragon leaves*

salt and freshly ground black pepper
12 *ounces (3 sticks) butter*
3 *cups dry white wine*
2–4 *tablespoons all-purpose flour*

METHOD:

1. Blend the flour, half the tarragon, salt and pepper together well.

2. Toss the pieces of rabbit in flour mixture to coat thoroughly.

3. Melt butter in a sauté pan and brown rabbit pieces on all sides. Lower heat, add wine and simmer, covered, until tender—about 45 minutes. Add remaining tarragon and cook 5 minutes more.

4. Remove the rabbit to a warm platter.

5. Strain the fat off the pan drippings, reserving 4 tablespoons of it,

and place in a saucepan. While fat is heating, blend in 2 to 4 tablespoons of the flour and stir with a wire whisk until mixture has thickened and is well combined. Then add the pan drippings, and cook slowly, stirring constantly, until smooth. Season to taste, pour sauce over rabbit and serve very hot.

CAJUN TURTLE STEW

SERVES 6

Turtle meat may not always be available in the markets of your area, but if you can obtain it, particularly the meat of small, tender turtles, you'll experience a delicious new taste. Wild rice is a fine accompaniment for this dish.

3 pounds turtle meat cut into 1½-inch cubes
juice of 1 lemon, strained
1½ tablespoons minced shallots
1 garlic clove, crushed
salt and freshly ground black pepper
1 bay leaf
2 or 3 black peppercorns
1½ stalks celery cut into 2 or 3 pieces
3 tablespoons vinegar

FOR THE CREOLE SAUCE:
3 tablespoons vegetable oil

3 tablespoons sliced onions
1 green pepper, sliced
3 ounces mushrooms, sliced
1 garlic clove, crushed
1½ quarts dry white wine
¾ cup tomato puree
1 medium-size fresh tomato, peeled, seeded and chopped
2 cups tomato sauce
½ bay leaf
salt and freshly ground black pepper
1 tablespoon chopped fresh parsley

METHOD:

1. Marinate turtle meat in lemon juice, shallots, garlic, salt and pepper for several hours.

2. Drain. Place in a large pot, cover with water and add bay leaf, black peppercorns, celery and vinegar. Boil gently for 3 hours.

3. *Meanwhile, prepare the Creole Sauce:* Heat oil in a sauté pan and sauté onions, green pepper and mushrooms for a few minutes; add garlic. Then cook slowly for 10 minutes until vegetables are tender. Add the white wine and reduce by rapid boiling to half its volume. Add tomato puree and fresh tomato. Cook very slowly for another 10 minutes, then add tomato sauce, bay leaf, salt and pepper. Cook slowly for another 20 to 30 minutes. Correct seasoning and add chopped parsley.

4. Drain turtle meat, simmer briefly in the Creole Sauce, then serve.

VENISON RUMP ROAST

SERVES 6

4 *pounds boneless venison rump roast*

2½ *cups dry red wine*

1 *teaspoon dried rosemary, crushed*

salt and freshly ground black pepper

fat salt pork for browning

METHOD:

1. Preheat oven to 450°F.

2. Place venison in a glass bowl, cover with wine, sprinkle rosemary over and let stand for 4 hours, turning it often.

3. Remove meat, reserving the wine. Dry the meat with paper towels and season with salt and pepper.

4. Place salt pork in a roasting pan and heat in the oven. When the fat gets very hot, add the meat and let it sear, browning it evenly on all sides.

5. Heat the reserved wine-and-rosemary mixture. Lower the oven to 325°F., cover roast with the warmed liquid and roast for 45 minutes or until done to taste.

6. Transfer roast to a platter and keep warm. Serve with the sauce on the side.

VENISON POT ROAST

SERVES 6

The venison must be marinated 2 to 3 days at room temperature before cooking, so plan ahead when preparing this dish.

3–4 *pounds venison* (*boned shoulder, rump or round*)

FOR THE MARINADE:
2 *cups dry red wine*
1 *cup vinegar* (*wine or cider*)
1 *medium onion, sliced*
1 *garlic clove, crushed*
2 *cups water*
2 *medium carrots, sliced*
6 *whole black peppercorns*
1 *teaspoon salt*
4 *sprigs parsley*
2 *celery tops*
½ *teaspoon dried rosemary* (*optional*)

½ *teaspoon dried thyme*
¼ *teaspoon dried marjoram*

salt and freshly ground black pepper
flour for dusting
4 *tablespoons peanut oil*
3 *cups beef stock or bouillon*
4 *large carrots, peeled, whole*
6 *medium potatoes, peeled, whole*
6 *medium onions, peeled, whole*
6 *small turnips, peeled, whole*
3 *stalks celery, cut in 2-inch pieces, tops included*
2–3 *tablespoons all-purpose flour*

METHOD:

1. *Prepare the marinade:* Mix all ingredients together very well. Place meat in a glass or ceramic bowl and pour marinade over meat.

2. Marinate at room temperature for 2 to 3 days, turning often. Drain, reserving marinade, and pat dry.

3. Add salt and pepper to the flour for dusting and dredge the meat very well.

4. Heat oil in heavy iron kettle and sear meat on all sides, browning it evenly. Add the stock. Cover and simmer over low heat for 2 to 3 hours or until meat is tender. If more liquid is needed, use some of the reserved marinade. Add the vegetables during the last 30 minutes of cooking time and cook until tender. Remove meat to a heated platter, arrange vegetables around it and keep warm.

5. Skim the fat off the pan drippings, reserving 4 tablespoons of it. Place reserved fat in a saucepan over medium heat. Blend in 2 to 4 tablespoons flour as it heats and stir with a wire whisk until mixture is well combined and has thickened. Then add the pan drippings and cook slowly, stirring constantly, until smooth. Season to taste, pour gravy around meat and serve.

CHAPTER FOUR
POULTRY AND GAME BIRDS

CHICKEN

ROAST BONELESS GOLDEN CHICKEN WITH CURRIED CHUTNEY GLAZE AND SEEDLESS GREEN GRAPES

2 roasting chickens, 3 or 3½
  pounds each, oven ready
2 tablespoons lemon juice, strained
4 tablespoons butter
3 cups diced celery (¼-inch
  dice), some leaves included
24 garlic cloves, peeled, cut into
  thirds
2 eggs, lightly beaten
2 tablespoons chopped fresh
  parsley
2–3 cups soft bread crumbs

salt, freshly ground black pepper
  and Tabasco sauce
1 cup chicken stock (made with
  bones and giblets of the
  chickens)

FOR THE CURRIED CHUTNEY GLAZE:
½ teaspoon curry powder
1 cup chutney, chopped
4 ounces butter, melted
¾ pound seedless green grapes

METHOD:

1. Bone and split chickens according to your favorite method. Brush with lemon juice and lay open on large sheets of aluminum foil.

2. Melt butter and sauté celery and garlic for 2 minutes. Celery should remain crunchy. Remove. Cool and then stir in eggs, tossing to prevent a sticky mess.

3. Mix parsley with crumbs and blend into celery-garlic-egg mixture. Season with salt, pepper and Tabasco to taste. Do not overmix; the stuffing should remain in a loose state.

4. Place half of stuffing on breast area of each chicken. Fold skin from the wingside part of the chicken over the stuffing; fold skin from tail end neatly over this. Then pull the skin from neck over all, folding under lightly and creating a pillow effect.

5. Wrap the chickens in the aluminum foil, crushing the ends in tightly, and refrigerate several hours or overnight. This to set the shape and to prevent them from falling apart while roasting.

6. *Prepare the Curried Chutney Glaze:* In a saucepan, stir curry into chutney, then add butter, stirring to mix well. Add grapes, toss to coat

well, and heat. (Most of this will be spooned over chicken as it roasts, but leave a little to add to the sauce made from pan juices.)

7. Preheat oven to 500°F.

8. When ready to roast, lay foil-covered chickens on rack in a shallow roasting pan. Add the chicken stock and roast 30 minutes at 500°F. Reduce heat to 350°F. and roast another 30 minutes, pricking the foil with a fork from time to time to release juices into pan and to test for tenderness. Transfer the chickens to another pan, remove foil and roast until they begin to brown, then spoon glaze over chickens. Turn oven again up to 500°F. and continue to roast until the glazed skin is brown (about 5 minutes more), basting with the pan juices. Remove from oven and keep warm. Pour pan juices through a strainer and into a bowl. Skim off the fat from the surface with a large ladle or spoon, blotting any remaining fat from juices with paper towel. Pour into a saucepan and reduce by rapid boiling until sauce is thick. Season with salt to taste.

9. Serve the chickens sliced into serving portions, on hot platters, with the extra glaze spooned over. Rice is a good accompaniment.

CHUTNEY-GLAZED ROAST CHICKEN WITH PECAN STUFFING

SERVES 8–10

2 roasting chickens, about 4½
  pounds each
1 lemon, cut in half
salt and freshly ground black pepper
8 tablespoons (1 stick) unsalted
  butter

FOR THE PECAN STUFFING:
1¼ cups (2½ sticks) unsalted butter
the reserved livers of the chickens,
  diced
1½ cups (about ½ pound) shallots
  or onions, peeled and minced
2 cups diced celery, with leaves
2 garlic cloves, peeled and minced
1 tablespoon salt
1 teaspoon freshly ground black
  pepper
pinch of cayenne

1 teaspoon crumbled dried rosemary, or to taste
1 tablespoon chopped fresh parsley
2 cups (about 7 ounces) large
  pecan halves
1 loaf (about 1 pound) home
  style white bread, crusts
  removed, cut into ¼-inch cubes

FOR ROASTING AND GLAZING:
2 cups or more strong chicken
  stock (preferably homemade)
two 9-ounce jars Major Grey's
  Chutney (or any other mango
  chutney)

FOR THE GRAVY:
¼ cup all-purpose flour
2–3 tablespoons chopped parsley
  (no stems)

METHOD:

1. Preheat the oven to 450°F.

2. Remove and reserve the giblets, necks, and all excess fat that can be pulled from the cavities of the chickens. Chop the livers coarsely and reserve for the stuffing. Rinse and dry the chickens, then rub them inside and outside with the lemon halves. Sprinkle inside and out with salt and pepper. Cut the stick of butter into about 16 thin pats and reserve, refrigerated, on a plate.

3. *Prepare the Pecan Stuffing:* In a small pan melt 1 stick of the butter, then set it aside. In a large skillet or flameproof casserole, melt the remaining 1½ sticks of butter. Sauté the diced chicken livers for about 2 minutes over moderate heat, then remove them with a slotted spoon and reserve, leaving the butter in the skillet. Add the shallots or onions to the butter in the skillet and sauté, stirring, until slightly softened, about 5 minutes. Add the celery and garlic; toss to coat with the butter. Sauté for 3 or 4 minutes longer, until the vegetables are slightly translucent (they should retain some crispness). Remove the vegetables from the heat and season with salt, pepper, cayenne, rosemary, and parsley. Stir in the pecans, then add the cubed bread and the reserved livers and toss everything together. Add just enough of the reserved melted butter to bind the mixture lightly. Correct all seasonings; the flavoring should be assertive but not overpowering.

4. Stuff the chickens: Spoon the stuffing into the cavities of the chickens, packing it loosely (don't stuff the neck cavities). If there is leftover stuffing, place it in a shallow baking dish and bake it separately later (see step 11).

5. Beginning with the loose flap of skin at the neck end gently lift the skin over the breast of each chicken by working your fingers between the skin and the flesh. Lay 8 of the reserved chilled butter pats under the skin of each chicken's breast. Lay the reserved chicken fat over each breast. Carefully remove the skin from each reserved chicken neck, slitting it open lengthwise. Lay the neck skin over the fat on the breast; this will help baste the chicken as it roasts. Skewer closed, or sew up, the large cavity and neck cavity of each chicken; then truss the birds. To truss: For each chicken cut a length of kitchen string about 30 inches long, center the chicken on top of it, breast up, with the string lying under the tail. Crisscrossing the string, make a loop around the tip of each leg and pull the legs together firmly. Run the string along the underside of the legs, toward the wings. Turn the bird breast down, fold the wings against the back, make a loop around each wing, and tie the ends of the string between the wings. Place the chickens breast up

in a large roasting pan (preferably one with a cover) and scatter the necks, gizzards and hearts around them.

6. Pour the chicken stock into the roaster and cover the pan tightly with heavy aluminum foil. Set the cover, if there is one, in place. Set covered pan in the lower third of the preheated oven and roast the chickens for 20 minutes.

7. After 20 minutes, reduce the heat to 325°F. and roast the birds 45 minutes longer. Remove the cover and foil, and check the chickens. They should be tender and almost done (an instant-reading thermometer inserted in a thigh will record a temperature of 165° to 170°F.; or, when the thigh is pricked, the juices will still run somewhat pink). Raise the heat to 450°F. and roast the birds uncovered for another 10 minutes, browning the chickens slightly. If no chicken stock remains in the pan, add enough to cover the bottom.

8. While the chickens are roasting puree the chutney in a food processor or blender until smooth.

9. When the chickens have browned, remove them to an ovenproof platter (lined with foil if you like), setting aside the roasting pan. Brush the chutney glaze over the chickens, covering them well. Return the birds to 450°F. oven and roast until the glazed skin is golden brown, 5 minutes or more. Remove the chickens from the oven and lower the oven to 375°F. Allow the chickens to rest for at least 10 minutes before carving.

10. *Prepare the Gravy:* Pour the juices from the roasting pan through a strainer into a bowl. Use a ladle or large spoon to remove the fat from the surface, reserving it all in a bowl. Blot any remaining fat from the pan juices with paper towels. Pour about ¼ cup reserved fat into saucepan and stir in the flour. Stir over moderate heat for 2 or 3 minutes, until the roux is smooth, pale and slightly foamy. Pour the degreased pan juices back into the roaster, and with a wooden spoon, scrape up and stir in the browned bits clinging to the bottom and sides. Whisk the juices into the roux in the saucepan and continue to whisk until well blended; simmer for 8 or 10 minutes. If the gravy is too thick, whisk in more chicken stock. Correct seasoning and swirl in the parsley.

11. If you have leftover stuffing or if you have made extra stuffing, moisten it with a little gravy and heat through in the 375° oven for 15 or 20 minutes. Serve the chickens hot, with the stuffing and gravy passed separately.

ROAST CHICKEN WITH CHAMPAGNE STUFFED WITH VEGETABLES

SERVES 6

1 *large roasting chicken, about 5 pounds*
1/4 *teaspoon each of dried thyme, dill, and rosemary (or 1 1/2 teaspoons chopped fresh herbs)*
salt *and freshly ground black pepper*
4 *or 5 garlic cloves, crushed*
3/4 *cup (1 1/2 sticks) butter, chilled*
1/2 *pound mushrooms, sliced*

3 *shallots, chopped coarsely*
6 *small carrots, diced*
10 *pearl onions, left whole*
2 *leeks, white part only, washed and cut up*
3–3 1/2 *tablespoons all-purpose flour*
3/4 *cup heavy cream*
2 *cups dry champagne*
fresh parsley sprigs for garnish

METHOD:

1. Preheat oven to 400°F.

2. Wash chicken well under running water. Pat dry.

3. Using your fingers, loosen the skin from the chicken carefully, from the cavity toward the neck.

4. Mix thyme, dill, rosemary, salt and pepper together and rub the cavity and outside of the chicken very well with the mixture.

5. Place the crushed garlic cloves and 4 tablespoons of the chilled butter, cut in little bits, under the skin.

6. Mix together in a bowl the mushrooms, shallots, carrots, onions, leeks and 4 tablespoons of butter, cut in little bits. Stuff the chicken and the neck cavity with the mixture. Stitch up the cavities with a strong string and large needle or use skewers. Tie the legs together.

7. Put stuffed chicken in large roasting pan. Baste with the remaining butter, melted, and half the champagne. Place in the oven and bake for 15 minutes. Lower the heat to 375°F. and baste again. Continue basting every 15 or 20 minutes, turning the chicken over and from side to side, until it is a golden brown—about 1 to 1 1/4 hours. Insert a meat thermometer into the thickest part of the thigh or breast. When the thermometer registers 165° the chicken should be cooked; or pierce a fork into thigh; the juice should run out clear when chicken is done.

8. Remove chicken from the pan onto a hot platter. Pour drippings from the pan through a strainer into a bowl. Using a ladle or large spoon, skim off any fat from the surface. Return to pan and cook on top of stove over moderate heat, adding the remaining champagne. De-

glaze roasting pan by stirring and scraping solidified juices from bottom and sides and add to the rest. Thicken sauce with the flour that has been dissolved in a little cream, and continue to cook until smooth and thick. Remove from heat and strain through a fine sieve. Add the remaining cream. Taste for seasoning. Heat sauce again and pour over the chicken, or serve separately in a gravy boat. Garnish with sprigs of parsley.

CHICKEN IN COCOTTE

SERVES 6

3 chickens, 2½ pounds each, trussed
salt and freshly ground black pepper
½ cup olive oil
½ teaspoon dried rosemary
½ teaspoon sweet paprika

1 pound mushrooms
¾ cup heavy cream
salt and cayenne pepper
4 tablespoons butter
6 shallots, finely chopped
½ cup dry white wine
4½–6 ounces brandy

FOR THE VELOUTÉ SAUCE:
5⅓ cups chicken stock

watercress for garnish

METHOD:

1. Preheat oven to 450°F.

2. Dust chicken well with salt and pepper. Rub with olive oil and then sprinkle with rosemary and paprika.

3. Roast in tightly covered casserole for 35 to 40 minutes, turning twice.

4. *Meanwhile, prepare the Velouté Sauce:* Rapidly boil stock with ¾ pound of the mushrooms until reduced to about 4 cups. Add cream, stirring constantly, and cook gently a few minutes longer. Season with salt and cayenne pepper to taste. Strain through a sieve; reserve the mushrooms for another use. If sauce is not used immediately, put a little butter on top to prevent a crust from forming. Slice remaining mushrooms and sauté in half the butter; add to sauce.

5. Sauté shallots in remaining butter until golden and place on the bottom of three individual casseroles. Remove chicken from oven and place in casseroles. Pour wine over chickens and cover with some of the Velouté Sauce. Return to the oven and bake 10 to 12 minutes.

6. To serve, warm the brandy, pour over the chickens and flame each chicken (stand back and be careful as you ignite it), adding extra sauce as the flame dies down. Cut chickens in half, garnish with watercress

and serve with the remaining Velouté Sauce. Fresh green vegetables such as asparagus, broccoli or whole green beans make excellent accompaniments.

BAKED CHICKEN MARSALA

SERVES 6

3 chickens, each weighing
   2½ pounds
¾ cup dry Marsala
¼ cup vegetable oil for brushing
1½ medium onions, sliced
3 cups diced celery
½ cup all-purpose flour
1 tablespoon salt

¾ teaspoon dried oregano
salt and freshly ground black pepper
¾ cup (1½ sticks) butter
1¼ cups water
2 pounds whole button mushrooms
1 pound egg noodles, cooked
2¼ cups fresh or frozen cooked
   green peas

METHOD:

1. Split chickens and soak in Marsala for 1 hour.

2. Preheat oven to 500°F.

3. Remove chickens, drain, reserving wine, and dry chickens on paper towels. Brush chickens well all over with the oil.

4. Place sliced onions and diced celery in bottom of baking pan or dish.

5. Blend together flour, salt, oregano and pepper to taste. Dust over chickens.

6. Lay chickens in pan on top of the onions and celery, and pour the water over them. Bake for 20 minutes, basting with reserved wine marinade. When chickens begin to brown, turn down the temperature to 350°F. and continue to bake until tender (total cooking time is about 1 hour).

7. Melt butter and sauté button mushrooms for 3 to 5 minutes and set aside. Pour the juices from the pan used to roast the chickens through a strainer into a bowl. Use a ladle or large spoon to remove the fat from the surface. Blot any remaining fat with a paper towel. Add strained drippings to mushrooms and reheat. Slice chickens in half and serve each half in a nest of egg noodles, garnished with green peas. Serve the pan juices on the side.

CHICKEN SAUTERNE

SERVES 6–8

2 chickens, 3 or 3½ pounds each,
    disjointed
½ cup olive oil
2 garlic cloves, chopped
2 tablespoons chopped shallots
1 medium onion, diced
1 cup sauterne
2 medium eggplants, diced

6 medium zucchini, diced
6 medium-size ripe tomatoes,
    diced
salt and freshly ground black pepper
12 black olives, sliced, 12 anchovy
    filets and 2 tablespoons chopped
    chives for garnish

METHOD:

1. Heat olive oil in a skillet and sauté chicken pieces until golden brown, 15 to 20 minutes.

2. Add garlic, shallots, onion and sauterne. Simmer for 20 minutes.

3. Add eggplant, zucchini and tomatoes and simmer until chicken and vegetables are done, about 10 minutes. Season with salt and pepper.

4. Serve chicken with the vegetables, garnished with olives, anchovy filets and chopped chives.

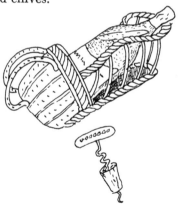

BRUNSWICK STEW

SERVES 6

One of the original American dishes.

½ cup vegetable oil
one 3-pound chicken, quartered
  1 pound boneless chuck, trimmed
    and cut into chunks
  1 cup chopped celery with leaves
  1 cup chopped onions
  1 medium ham hock, trimmed
  3 tomatoes, chopped
  2 sprigs parsley, chopped

1 small hot red pepper, seeded
  and minced
1 teaspoon salt
½ teaspoon dried basil
½ teaspoon dried thyme
2½ quarts water
1½ cups corn kernels
1½ cups sliced okra
1½ cups lima beans
1½ cups cooked mashed potatoes

METHOD:

1. Heat half the vegetable oil in a heavy skillet and brown chicken; transfer to a dish. Then brown chuck in same skillet, and transfer to the dish with the chicken.

2. In a large pot heat the remaining oil, add celery and onions and sauté lightly. Add chicken, beef, ham hock, tomatoes, parsley, red pepper, seasonings and water to pot.

3. Bring to a boil, reduce heat and simmer, covered, for 45 minutes. Remove chicken with slotted spoon to a platter and continue to simmer the rest 1½ hours.

4. When chicken has cooled, remove and discard skin and bones and shred the meat. Set aside the shredded meat.

5. Add corn, okra and lima beans to simmering liquid mixture and cook over medium heat 30 minutes. Remove ham hock with slotted spoon; bone and shred the meat. Return it to casserole along with reserved chicken.

6. Add mashed potatoes, stir well, and continue cooking 15 minutes more. Serve hot.

GINGER CHICKEN

SERVES 8

2 chickens, 3½ pounds each,
  disjointed
⅔ cup all-purpose flour
salt and freshly ground black pepper
4 teaspoons ground ginger

8 tablespoons (1 stick) butter
6 tablespoons peanut oil
3 cups chicken stock
1 cup (½ pint) heavy cream
preserved ginger, sliced, for garnish

METHOD:

1. Mix flour with salt, pepper and ground ginger and dredge the chicken pieces in this mixture. Reserve the seasoned flour that's left. Heat the butter and oil in a large skillet and sauté chicken until golden brown.

2. Remove chicken from skillet. Add reserved seasoned flour to the skillet, blending well with butter and oil until smooth, and then gradually add chicken stock. Bring to a boil, stirring until thickened and smooth.

3. Replace chicken in skillet, cover and simmer in sauce about 45 minutes.

4. Transfer chicken to serving platter, stir cream into sauce and pour over chicken. Garnish with slices of preserved ginger. To serve cold, chill for at least 2 hours in advance.

VELVET SLICED CHICKEN

SERVES 6

6 whole chicken breasts, boned
  and skinned
8 egg whites
3 tablespoons cornstarch
1 teaspoon salt
¾ cup chicken broth

2 cups peanut oil
2 teaspoons dry sherry
½ teaspoon sugar
2 tablespoons minced cooked
  Smithfield ham for garnish

METHOD:

1. Slice each raw chicken breast with the grain into $\frac{1}{16}$-by-2-inch pieces. Beat the egg whites until slightly foamy. Add sliced chicken to egg whites, toss to coat, and set aside.

2. Mix the cornstarch, salt and chicken broth to a smooth paste.

3. Have a strainer with a pot underneath ready. Heat oil in a wok to 250°–280°F. Then lower heat to medium high.

4. Stir the egg white and chicken mixture again and pour into the oil. When the egg whites start to set—it takes only 5 seconds—gently turn over with spatula. If they start to turn fluffy and yellow, the heat is too high, and if the heat is too low they will soak up the oil—so be careful to adjust the heat. As soon as the egg whites are smooth and set and chicken turns white, pour the contents of the wok (including the oil) into a strainer to drain. Place drained chicken on platter.

5. Heat the same wok with one tablespoon of the strained oil on high heat. Blend in the cornstarch and chicken broth mixture until smooth. Then return the egg white-and-chicken mixture to the wok and add sherry and sugar. Stir and turn a few times to heat through. Transfer to a serving dish and garnish with minced ham. Serve hot.

BAKED CHICKEN HASH

SERVES 6

Leftover roast chicken is excellent for this dish. The flavor is better if both dark and white meat are used.

2 *large baking potatoes (approximately 1 pound)*
6 *tablespoons butter, melted*
2 *cups diced, cooked chicken, skin and gristle removed*
1 *cup minced celery*
½ *cup minced onion*
3 *cups chicken stock, heated*
3 *tablespoons all-purpose flour*
1 *cup milk, scalded*

salt, freshly ground black pepper and cayenne
3 *large fresh mushrooms, sliced*
½ *cup cooked sweet peas*
sweet paprika
2 *roasted sweet red peppers, each cut in 6 strips and 1 tablespoon chopped fresh parsley for garnish*

METHOD:

1. Preheat oven to 500°F.

2. Scrub potatoes but do not peel; slice across paper thin and toss in 2 tablespoons melted butter to coat.

3. Place celery and onion in a saucepan, add ½ cup of the chicken stock, cover, and steam for 3 minutes. Strain vegetables and add the stock in which they were cooked to the remaining chicken stock. Toss the celery and onion with the diced chicken.

4. Heat the remaining butter in a saucepan. Stir in the flour, blending until smooth and thick; then add the stock and scalded milk. Cook to thicken and season with salt, pepper and cayenne to taste.

5. Line the bottom and sides of a heavy 2-quart casserole (about 7 by 7 by 2 inches) with half of the potato slices overlapping to form a crust.

6. Place the sliced mushrooms over the potato slices.

7. Spoon half the sauce over the mushrooms.

8. Add the chicken mixture, sprinkle the peas on top, and pour the remaining sauce over chicken, pushing it well against the sides of casserole.

9. Lay the remaining potato slices over the top and dust lightly with paprika.

10. Bake at 500°F. for 10 minutes, reduce heat to 350°F., cover top with foil to prevent overbrowning and bake 10 to 15 minutes longer until golden. Serve piping hot, each portion garnished with 2 roasted red pepper strips, and sprinkled with parsley.

ROCK CORNISH GAME HEN AMANDINE, SOUTHERN STYLE

SERVES 8

This dish can be prepared either in an electric frying pan or in the oven.

4 *Rock Cornish game hens, each weighing about 1¼ pounds*
2 *tablespoons all-purpose flour*
1 *teaspoon salt*
3 *teaspoons sugar, or to taste*
pinch curry powder
pinch paprika
¾ *cup (1½ sticks) butter*

4 *sprigs parsley*
3½ *tablespoons brandy*
1 *cup canned cherries, pitted, juice reserved*
¾ *cup cherry juice from canned cherries*
⅔ *cup slivered almonds*

METHOD:

1. Defrost hens (if frozen); split and dry the hens. Blend together flour, salt, 1 teaspoon sugar, curry and paprika. Lay hens on wax paper and dust well with flour mixture.

2. Set electric skillet or oven at 275°F. Melt butter in skillet or roasting pan, bruise parsley with wooden spoon and add. Heat until butter bubbles (do not overheat).

3. Place hens in skillet (or in uncovered pan if using oven), cover, close vent (or oven), increase temperature to 400°F. and cook for 5 minutes. Reduce temperature to 300°F. and cook 10 minutes more. Turn hens and cook another 10 minutes or until tender and golden brown.

4. Remove hens. Skim off whatever fat you can from the pot. Scrape up all bits from browning with a spoon and add brandy, 2 teaspoons sugar (or to taste), cherries and cherry juice, stirring after each addition. Cook gently until cherries are hot. Push cherries to one side; replace hens, baste with cherry sauce until they are hot and well glazed. Mix almonds with the cherries, spoon over the hens, with any remaining glaze, and serve.

ROASTED GUINEA HEN

SERVES 6

3 guinea hens
3 tablespoons butter
salt and freshly ground black pepper

1 onion, chopped
1 pound salt pork, sliced
3 cups chicken stock

METHOD:

1. Preheat oven to 350°F.

2. Clean, wash and truss the guinea hens, and rub all over with butter.

3. Place in roasting pan, sprinkle with salt and pepper and chopped onion.

4. Place the slices of salt pork in layers on the breast of the hens, and pour chicken stock into the pan.

5. Bake the hens until tender, about 50 or 60 minutes; baste every 15 minutes with the stock and juices. Turn the heat up to 500°F. and continue to bake for 5 to 8 minutes, or until the guinea hens are a golden brown. Keep checking; don't let the hens overbake.

BRAISED PIGEON

SERVES 6

6 pigeons, approximately ¾ pound each

juice of 3 lemons

fresh parsley sprigs

salt and freshly ground black pepper

¾ cup bacon fat or ¾ cup (1½ sticks) butter

2 cups dry red wine (or cider, beer or orange juice)

water

METHOD:

1. Pluck and clean the birds thoroughly, then rub them well inside and outside with lemon juice.

2. Place sprigs of parsley into the cavity of each bird and season with salt and pepper.

3. Melt the bacon fat or butter in a sauté pan. Add the pigeons and sauté until browned on all sides.

4. Add about 1½ cups of the wine (or the liquid of your choice). Cook slowly, covered, for 20 to 30 minutes, basting frequently and adding more liquid if necessary.

5. When the birds are cooked, remove from heat, serve immediately, or place in a warmed covered dish until ready to use.

STUFFED ROAST SQUAB

SERVES 2

Squabs are very young pigeons that never weigh more than 14 ounces, and are prized for their delicate, sweet meat. They need plenty of butter or fat to keep them moist.

2 squabs, cleaned, washed and dried
3 tablespoons butter, melted
2 cups bread crumbs
½ cup chopped onions

a small sprig of fresh thyme, chopped
salt and freshly ground black pepper
chicken broth or roast pork or beef drippings
parsley and pimentos for garnish

METHOD:

1. Preheat oven to 350°F.

2. Mix bread crumbs into melted butter and add onions, herbs and seasonings; blend well.

3. Stuff into cavities of squabs. Place in a roasting pan, and roast in a slow oven for 50 to 60 minutes, basting frequently with broth.

4. When squabs are almost done, increase heat to 450°F. to brown.

5. Serve each squab on an individual platter, garnished with parsley and pimentoes.

TURKEY

BONELESS STUFFED TURKEY

SERVES 12 OR MORE

one 10-pound turkey
1–2 garlic cloves, crushed
½ cup finely chopped celery
salt and freshly ground black pepper
  5 pounds ground veal, lightly
    seasoned with salt and pepper
  3 pounds ham, cut into ¼-inch
    strips
  ¼ pound sliced bacon
  3 cups sliced mushrooms

2 small cans truffles, boiled,
  sliced (optional)
1 quart chestnuts, blanched,
  peeled and chopped
sweet paprika
¾ cup (1½ sticks) butter, softened
12 cooked carrots and/or beets,
  6 hardboiled eggs, parsley and
  cranberry jelly (chilled and
  sliced) for garnish

METHOD:

1. Bone the turkey as neatly as possible using method described for boning duck on page 139. Spread out the turkey, skin side down, on a chopping board, pat it flat and shape it into a rectangle for rolling (as you would a jelly roll).

2. Preheat the oven to 350°F.

3. Sprinkle the turkey flesh with garlic, celery, salt and pepper. Spread half the veal evenly on the turkey. Lay down half the strips of ham in a row, then a row of mushrooms, a row of truffles, if using them, a row of chestnuts and half the bacon. Repeat the layers, beginning with the veal, until everything is used up.

4. Tuck in the boned wings and legs as neatly as possible. Roll up turkey tightly and tie with kitchen twine in a secure manner. Sprinkle with salt, pepper and paprika and rub all over with butter. Wrap tightly in foil and place in the oven.

5. Bake at 15 minutes per pound (about 2½ hours), removing foil from the turkey for the last 45 minutes. Baste with the melted butter and juices. The turkey should then be nicely browned. When the turkey is done remove from oven, place on platter and allow to cool before slicing.

6. Decorate with the carrots, beets, eggs (stuffed, if desired), parsley and any other fancy decoration. Serve with cranberry jelly slices on the side.

SMOKED BREAST OF TURKEY
WITH BROCCOLI

SERVES 6

5 tablespoons butter	dash of ground mace
5 tablespoons whole wheat flour	12 small spears broccoli, cooked
3–4 cups seasoned turkey or chicken broth	1½ pounds smoked breast of turkey, thinly sliced
1½ cups (¾ pint) light cream	⅓ cup grated Cheddar cheese

METHOD:

1. Melt butter in a skillet. Add flour and stir until smooth; then add broth. Stir until sauce is thick and smooth. Stir in the cream and season with ground mace.

2. Add the broccoli stalks to the sauce and mix lightly. Cover with the sliced turkey.

3. Blanket the turkey with the cheese.

4. Simmer gently until sauce bubbles up through the turkey and cheese begins to melt. With a sharp knife cut into wedge-shaped pieces. Serve hot.

DUCK

ROAST GOLDEN DUCK WITH WILD RICE STUFFING, TOPPED WITH APPLE RINGS AND PRUNES AND RED WINE SAUCE AND FLAMBÉED WITH APPLE BRANDY

SERVES 6

3 ducks weighing 5 pounds each,
boned (see steps 1–3 below),
excess fat removed

2 tablespoons melted butter
12 large prunes, cooked and pitted
2 tablespoons chutney

FOR THE WILD RICE STUFFING:
1½ cups wild rice
2 cups water
3 tablespoons butter
salt

FOR THE RED WINE SAUCE:
3 cups duck stock
2 cups Burgundy
salt and freshly ground black pepper
lemon juice

FOR THE APPLE RINGS AND PRUNES:
3 large apples, cored and seeded,
each sliced in 4 rings

¾ cup apple brandy

METHOD:

1. How to Bone Ducks: Lay oven-dressed birds breast side down on cutting board. Using a boning knife, cut off wing tips. Run knife around next joint of wing, cutting through skin and flesh. Then cut the skin and flesh around the bottom joint of leg. Make an incision down the length of back along the spine, cutting through skin and flesh down center back. Remove tail bone.

2. Starting at neck, cut skin and flesh away from back, carefully pulling the flesh away from the bones, with the skin attached, and any tissue holding flesh to bones, all the way down to the tail area. Pull the leg bone up, cutting flesh away from bone, but leaving flesh attached to the skin. Work up to the wing area, pulling and cutting flesh and skin from rib cage to the breastbone. Do not cut through skin. Pull wing bone up through skin, carefully cutting flesh attached to skin, pulling bone out. Turn and repeat on the other side.

3. When all flesh and skin have been removed from both sides of

breast (remove carefully to avoid breaking the skin), using a very sharp knife cut away all excess fat. Fold together and refrigerate the ducks until ready for stuffing. Reserve all bones for preparing the stuffing and the stock for the sauce.

4. *Prepare the Wild Rice Stuffing:* Wash wild rice and cook in water until tender and fluffy, about 40 minutes. Sauté whatever bits of duck meat you can cut away from the leg and backbones in 3 tablespoons butter until tender. Season lightly with salt and stir into cooked rice. Correct seasonings.

5. *Prepare the Apple Rings and Prunes (to top ducks):* Lay apple slices on a baking sheet. Brush liberally with melted butter and place a pitted cooked prune in the center of each. Spoon ½ teaspoon chutney over each. Bake 10 minutes in 350°F. oven.

6. Spread chilled ducks open on a large sheet of heavy-duty aluminum foil. Spoon ½ cup stuffing over breast area of each duck and, beginning at the tail end, fold skin up and over stuffing. Then fold the other end over so that it overlaps the stuffed end. Fold in the sides to form a pillow shape.

7. Fold foil ends up and wrap duck completely in foil. Refrigerate 1 hour to let ducks set to hold their shape.

8. Preheat oven to 500°F. for 10 minutes.

9. Lay foil-covered ducks and reserved bones on a rack over a pan of hot water to depth of ½ inch. Do not let the ducks touch the water. Roast the ducks and reserved bones 30 minutes. Remove the bones and save for the Red Wine Sauce (step 13).

10. Lower oven to 350°F., and remove foil from ducks. Replace ducks in oven and roast 1½ hours, checking to be sure water doesn't evaporate from pan.

11. Then lower oven to 300°F. and roast until ducks are tender when pierced with a fork and skin is crispy brown.

12. Remove ducks to a tray and hold in a warm oven until serving time. Save the pan drippings.

13. *Meanwhile, prepare the Red Wine Sauce:* In a partially covered saucepan, simmer stock, roasted bones and the pan drippings, with all fat removed, for 30 minutes or until the flavor is concentrated. Meanwhile, reduce the Burgundy to 1 cup by rapid boiling and add to the stock. Season with salt and pepper and a little lemon juice. No thickening is needed for this fine sauce. Keep warm.

14. Place ducks on a hot serving platter. Cut them with a sharp, thin-bladed knife in 3 slices each and cut each slice in half, making 6 squares for each duck.

15. Place a preheated apple ring on each duck square. Heat ¼ cup

apple brandy, pour over each duck, ignite (stand back and be careful) and serve flaming. Serve the Red Wine Sauce on the side.

HAPPY DUCKLING IN BURGUNDY

SERVES 6

3 ducklings weighing about 4½
   pounds each
4 tablespoons all-purpose flour
2 teaspoons salt
freshly ground black pepper
8 tablespoons (1 stick) butter
4 sprigs fresh parsley
8 celery tops
8 strips of orange peel

1½ teaspoons Kitchen Bouquet
1½ cups Burgundy
4 cups hot chicken stock
2 duck livers, scalded in boiling
   water and sieved
1½ cups canned apricot juice
16 apricots, cooked and sieved
4 tablespoons sugar

METHOD:

1. If ducks are frozen, defrost. With a small, sharp knife remove the skin and all the fat from the ducks by cutting skin down center of breast and pulling skin and fat away, being careful not to cut flesh. Fat may be rendered for future use.

2. Cut ducklings in quarters. Lay on wax paper and dust with flour, salt and pepper.

3. Set a large skillet over low heat and melt butter.

4. Tie parsley, celery and orange peel with string, bruise with wooden spoon and add to the butter. Cover skillet and heat this bouquet for about 3 minutes; then push it to one side and place the ducks in skillet cut side up. (This will probably have to be done in 2 skillets or at least 2 batches—in that case divide all other ingredients equally.)

5. Increase temperature to high, cover and cook until all pieces are *well browned*. Tilt skillet(s) occasionally to spread butter evenly.

6. Add Kitchen Bouquet, ½ cup Burgundy, 2 cups stock and baste until all pieces are well covered. Replace cover and heat for 5 full minutes; then reduce temperature to medium and braise until tender, about 1¼ hours. Baste frequently, adding the remaining stock as needed. Remove duckling quarters to a hot platter.

7. Discard bouquet; add sieved livers and simmer a few minutes. Add remaining Burgundy, apricot juice, sieved apricots and sugar.

8. Season with pepper and salt to taste; pour sauce through a fine strainer and return duckling juices (from the platter) to skillet. Lay duckling pieces in, heat and baste until well glazed. Serve hot.

GOOSE

EAST HAMPTON ROAST GOLDEN GOOSE WITH FRUIT STUFFING

SERVES 6–8

If you can buy a fresh goose, choose one with a soft, pliable bill. This indicates that the bird is young.

FOR THE FRUIT STUFFING:
- ½ *pound (1½ cups, approximately) extra-large dried apricots and/or prunes, washed and drained in a sieve*
- ½ *cup seedless dark raisins, washed and drained*
- 1 *cup port wine*
- 1 *lemon, thinly sliced, seeds removed*
- 4 *tablespoons butter*

the liver from the goose
- 1 *medium onion, peeled and chopped*
- 1 *large sour apple, peeled, cored and coarsely chopped*
- 1 *cup walnuts, coarsely chopped*
- ½ *teaspoon mace*

salt and freshly ground black pepper
- 2 *tablespoons fresh lemon juice, strained*
- ½ *cup minced celery, leaves included*
- 2 *cups soft white or whole wheat bread, cut into ½-inch cubes*

FOR THE GOOSE:
one 12- to 14-pound fresh young goose (or a frozen goose, defrosted)
- 1 *lemon cut in half, seeds removed*

salt and freshly ground black pepper

FOR THE PORT WINE GRAVY:
the juices from the roasting pan
the port wine reserved from the stuffing
- 2 *tablespoons arrowroot or corn-starch mixed with 2 tablespoons cold water or chicken stock*
- ¾ *cup chicken stock*

salt and freshly ground black pepper

METHOD:

1. *Prepare the Fruit Stuffing:* Soak the apricots and raisins in the port wine and refrigerate overnight. When ready to cook, add the lemon slices and simmer until almost tender in a large saucepan, about 5 or 6 minutes. Drain well, reserving the wine for the gravy.

2. Chop the cooked apricots, lemon, and raisins coarsely.

3. Melt 1 tablespoon of the butter and sauté the goose liver until firm but not browned. Chop liver and add it to the fruit.

4. Sauté the onion in another tablespoon of the butter just until translucent (do not brown). Add to the stuffing.

5. Add the apple, walnuts and mace. Season with salt and pepper to taste and add the remaining 2 tablespoons of butter, melted, lemon juice, celery and bread cubes. Toss all together.

6. *Prepare the Goose:* Preheat oven to 500°F., or to its highest possible setting (if lower than 550°).

7. Remove all excess fat from the goose and save for another use if desired. Rub cavity and skin with the cut lemon; dust the bird inside and out with salt and pepper. Pierce the skin around the legs and wings with a fork.

8. Stuff the bird loosely and sew or skewer the cavity; truss the wings and legs.

9. Place the bird, breast down, on a rack in a shallow roasting pan. Roast at 550°F. for 30 minutes. Reduce the heat to 300° and continue to roast, basting frequently with pan juices and pricking the skin often with a fork to release the fat.

10. After 2 hours, turn the goose breast up. Cover the breast with foil. Continue to roast until the joints move readily and the meat feels soft. The juices will run clear from a small cut in the thigh when the bird is done; approximate roasting time in all, 3 hours.

11. Remove the foil from the breast, turn the heat up to 450°F., and brown the breast skin to a crisp gold. Remove the bird to a hot serving platter.

12. *Prepare the Port Wine Gravy:* Skim off and discard all but 3 tablespoons of fat from the juices in the roasting pan.

13. Add the reserved port wine and stock. Set over heat and scrape the browned bits from the bottom and sides of the pan.

14. Stir in the arrowroot or cornstarch and simmer until thickened. Season with salt and pepper and serve in a sauceboat.

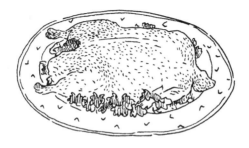

ROAST GOOSE WITH SAVORY FRUIT STUFFING

Ideal accompaniments to goose are turnips or Brussels sprouts and applesauce.

a 12- to 14-pound goose (fresh or frozen and thawed), ready to cook
juice of 2 lemons
salt and freshly ground black pepper

3 cups chopped apples
3 cups uncooked pitted prunes, chopped
⅓ cup plus 1 tablespoon lemon juice

FOR THE SAVORY FRUIT STUFFING:
¼ cup finely chopped onion
6 tablespoons butter, melted
1 teaspoon salt
½ teaspoon marjoram
3 cups celery in ¼-inch dice
8 cups bread cut in ¼-inch cubes

FOR THE SAUCE:
2 cups goose broth (made from goose giblets, neck and heart) or chicken broth
2 or 3 tablespoons all-purpose flour
2 or 3 tablespoons water
salt and freshly ground black pepper

METHOD:
1. Preheat oven to 325°F.
2. Rub goose well with lemon juice, salt and pepper.
3. *Prepare the Savory Fruit Stuffing:* In a skillet, brown onion in butter and then add other ingredients. Taste and correct seasoning if necessary.
4. Stuff the bird loosely with fruit stuffing and sew or skewer the cavity; truss the wings and legs.
5. Roast immediately (do not leave stuffed bird uncooked for any length of time). Place breast side down on the rack of a large, shallow roasting pan.
6. Roast slowly for 3¾ to 4 hours, basting frequently. Drain off fat as it accumulates. Prick the fatty skin around the legs to release extra fat. When done, joints will yield readily, the meat will feel very soft, and skin will be brown and crisp.
7. *Prepare the Sauce:* When the meat is done remove it from the roasting pan and pour off fat. Deglaze pan on top of stove with goose broth, stirring and scraping the solidified juices and bits from bottom and sides. Bring to boil and reduce heat, then add the flour, which has

been mixed with 2 or 3 tablespoons of water. Keep stirring until sauce thickens and is smooth. Correct seasoning with salt and pepper to taste.

8. To serve, remove stuffing and place portions on hot serving plates. Carve birds and serve a piece of breast, a piece of drumstick and some crisp brown skin on each plate. Pass the goose sauce separately.

SMOTHERED QUAIL

SERVES 6

These tiny birds need to be covered with fat to keep the very tasty meat from drying out. Sometimes referred to as partridge, the quail is both a sportsman's and a gourmand's delight.

12 *quail, oven-ready*	¼ *cup vegetable oil*
½ *cup gin*	*freshly ground black pepper*
½ *teaspoon salt*	8 *tablespoons (1 stick) butter*
2 *drops Tabasco sauce*	6 *small onions, peeled*
6 *juniper berries, crushed*	12 *thin slices fatback (pork fat)*
1 *large onion, sliced*	2 *teaspoons arrowroot*
2 *stalks celery, chopped, leaves*	2 *cups chicken broth*
included	

METHOD:

1. Mix gin, salt, Tabasco, juniper berries, onion, celery, oil and pepper together and pour over the quail. Marinate in refrigerator overnight, turning twice.

2. Preheat oven to 400°F.

3. Remove quail from marinade and wipe dry. Melt butter in skillet and sauté quail until golden on all sides.

4. Lay quail on bottom of a large shallow heatproof casserole with a tight-fitting cover and place one of the small onions inside each quail. Strain the marinade over the birds. Place a slice of fatback over each breast. Cover casserole. Set on the bottom rack of oven and roast 45 minutes, basting with pan juices 2 or 3 times, until quail are fork tender. Remove birds to hot serving platter and keep warm.

5. Ladle excess fat from casserole. Place casserole on top of stove and mix in arrowroot, stirring and scraping the brown bits from sides and bottom. Then add about 1½ cups chicken broth and cook the sauce (do not boil) until smooth and thick. Season to taste with salt and pepper and add remaining broth if sauce is too thick. Serve quail immediately with the sauce on the side.

QUAIL WITH CHAMPAGNE

SERVES 6

12 *quail, oven-ready*
12 *strips larding pork (approximately 1/4 inch thick, 1 inch wide, 3/4 inch long)*

3/4 *cup (1 1/2 sticks) butter*
2 *cups champagne*
6 *truffles, thinly sliced (optional)*
salt and freshly ground black pepper

METHOD:

1. Cover the breasts of the birds with the strips of larding pork.

2. Melt the butter in a heatproof casserole with a cover and put in the quail. Sauté until delicately brown all over, about 15 minutes.

3. Add the champagne and slices of truffle, if you are using them. Season with salt and pepper.

4. Place the lid on the casserole and simmer gently for 12 to 15 minutes.

5. Serve hot in a deep serving dish with the sauce in which they were cooked, and surrounded with the slices of truffle, if you have used them.

PHEASANT WITH MARSALA

SERVES 6

Select an old bird for this delicious recipe.

1 *pheasant, oven-ready, liver reserved and diced (if the bird was freshly killed, it should have been aged for 4 or 5 days)*
2 *small oranges*
4 *tablespoons lard*
12 *small fresh mushrooms*
3 *small shallots, chopped*
4 *tablespoons butter*

1 *tablespoon all-purpose flour*
1 *cup Marsala*
salt and freshly ground black pepper
8 *juniper berries*
a sprig of fennel
fried hominy (optional)
red currant jelly (optional)
parsley (optional) for garnish

METHOD:

1. Preheat oven to 400°F.

2. Peel and section the oranges and mix with the diced liver. Place

in the cavity of the bird. Sew skin of cavity together with thread or fasten with skewers.

3. Rub the bird all over with lard and brown in a skillet for 15 minutes, turning often from side to side to brown all over. Remove from pot.

4. In the hot fat remaining in the skillet, sauté mushrooms lightly.

5. Melt the butter in a saucepan, add the minced shallots and brown. Stir in the flour and blend well. Slowly pour in the Marsala while gradually stirring the sauce. Season to taste with salt and pepper.

6. Place the bird in an earthenware casserole, add the juniper berries and fennel and pour the wine sauce on top.

7. Cover and do not disturb while it roasts for 25 minutes. Serve with the sauce and, if desired, with fried hominy and red currant jelly, and garnish with parsley.

CHAPTER FIVE

FISH AND SHELLFISH

STRIPED BASS STEWED IN CHAMPAGNE

a whole striped bass, 7 or 7½ pounds
   3 tablespoons butter, for oiling
      baking dish
   5 shallots, peeled and minced
 10 whole mushrooms, chopped,
      stems removed
a sprig of thyme
   1 bay leaf
   1 garlic clove, crushed

salt and freshly ground black pepper
   2 bottles (6 cups) champagne
   1 pint (2 cups) heavy cream
 1⅓ cups butter
juice of ½ lemon
puff pastry crescents (can be store-
      bought) and 10 thin slices
      truffle for garnish

METHOD:

1. Preheat oven to 350°F.

2. Make sure the bass is fresh—gills should be red and clear, eyes full and bright. If fish has been caught by you or a friend, remove entrails and wash well under cool running water; otherwise, the fish store will have done this for you.

3. Butter a long, deep baking dish with the 3 tablespoons of butter and add the shallots, mushrooms, thyme, bay leaf, garlic, salt and pepper. Lay the fish on this bed, pour the champagne over and cover with buttered, greaseproof paper. Bake for 35 to 40 minutes, basting frequently with liquid in which the fish is cooking. When done it should flake easily when tested with a fork.

4. When cooked, remove the fish at once, keep warm, and strain the liquid into a shallow pan. Reduce by rapid boiling to half, add the cream and again reduce by half. Lower the heat. Add the butter cut into small bits, stirring with a wooden spoon, but do not bring to boil again. Adjust seasoning, add the lemon juice and strain through a fine sieve.

5. To serve: Remove the skin with a knife, place the fish on a long serving dish and spoon half the sauce over it; pour the rest of the sauce into a sauceboat and serve on the side. Garnish with puff pastry crescents and thin slices of truffle.

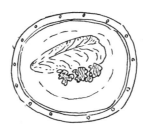

BAKED FLOUNDER AMANDINE

SERVES 6

There are many ways of preparing flounder. This dish offers a change from the routine amandine preparation. The addition of onions as a base and a variety of herbs place it in a gourmet category with just a little extra work.

3 pounds flounder filet, in 6–8-
  ounce portions
2 bay leaves, finely crushed
fresh thyme
2 medium onions, thinly sliced
2 tablespoons lemon juice
1¾ tablespoons grated lemon peel

1½ teaspoons sweet paprika
½ teaspoon salt
⅓ teaspoon freshly ground black
  pepper
1 cup chopped blanched almonds
1 cup (2 sticks) butter, softened

METHOD:

1. Preheat oven to 350°F.

2. Sprinkle crushed bay leaves and thyme over onion slices. Toss to mix well, then sprinkle with lemon juice.

3. Combine remaining seasonings with almonds and butter and blend well. Divide onion mixture among 6 individual buttered casseroles. Arrange filets over the onions. Spoon almond mixture over filets.

4. Bake for 20 to 25 minutes or until fish flakes easily when tested with a fork.

CHAMPAGNE HALIBUT STEAK WITH HOLLANDAISE SAUCE

SERVES 6

six 8-ounce halibut steaks
1½ cups hot water
1½ cups champagne
8 shallots, peeled and chopped

FOR THE HOLLANDAISE SAUCE:
3 tablespoons lemon juice

6 egg yolks
3 tablespoons melted butter
1 cup fish stock (reserved from
  cooking fish)
salt and cayenne pepper to taste

METHOD:

1. Place halibut steaks in a skillet, cover with hot water and bring to slow boil. Cover, lower heat and simmer 5 minutes.

2. Add champagne and shallots and simmer another 5 minutes.

3. Place steaks on flameproof serving platters.

4. Reduce fish-cooking liquid to 1 cup by rapid boiling and set aside to add to Hollandaise Sauce.

5. *Prepare the Hollandaise Sauce:* Cook lemon juice and egg yolks in top of double boiler over hot water, stirring continuously. Do not boil. Using a wire whisk beat melted butter gradually into mixture. Continue beating until sauce thickens, then slowly blend in the reserved fish stock. Add salt and cayenne to taste.

6. Spread sauce over fish on the flameproof platters. Broil just long enough to brown lightly and serve immediately.

FILETS OF SALMON WITH CHAMPAGNE

SERVES 6

1 *whole salmon, 4 or 5 pounds*
  (*or 2 pounds, fileted*)
salt and freshly ground black pepper
1 *large onion stuck with 5–6*
  cloves
bouquet garni: bay leaf, thyme,
  basil, parsley

½ *cup bread crumbs*
8 *tablespoons (1 stick) butter,*
  melted
½ *bottle (1½ cups) champagne*
1½ *cups sliced mushrooms*

METHOD:

1. Remove the bone from the salmon (if the fish market has not done this for you), wash and pat dry.

2. Cut 2 filets from each half. Place the filets in a pot and season with salt and pepper.

3. Add onion, bouquet garni, bread crumbs and melted butter. Pour the champagne over the salmon.

4. Sprinkle the sliced mushrooms over the top.

5. Simmer the salmon until the liquid is reduced and the fish starts to flake when tested with a fork (10 to 15 minutes). Serve hot with sauce.

BAKED SALMON IN RHINE WINE

SERVES 12

6-*pound piece of salmon (prefer-*
ably from the middle section
of the fish)
salt and freshly ground black pepper
2 *tablespoons chopped fresh*
parsley
2 *tablespoons finely chopped*
onions
½ *teaspoon thyme*

2 *bay leaves*
1 *cup (2 sticks) plus 7 table-*
spoons butter, softened
¾ *cup dry white Rhine wine*
1¾ *cups fish stock made with fish*
trimmings and strained
lemon slices and parsley sprigs for
garnish

METHOD:

1. Preheat oven to 375°F.

2. Wash the salmon and dry it on paper towels. Place in a baking pan and season with salt and pepper.

3. Mix parsley, onions, thyme and bay leaves together with 1 cup (2 sticks) of butter, and spread mixture on the inside and outside of the salmon.

4. Mix the wine with 1 cup of fish stock, pour over and around the salmon. Cover with aluminum foil, place in oven, and bake 40 to 45 minutes, basting with pan juices.

5. When done, remove salmon from pan and set aside to keep warm. Add the remaining fish stock to the baking pan, set on top of the stove and reduce by rapid boiling to about 1½ cups. Then add the 7 table-spoons of butter. Pour over the salmon and keep hot until ready to serve. The sauce may also be presented in a separate bowl. Garnish with lemon slices and parsley sprigs.

BAKED HERBED SALMON

SERVES 8

This tasty salmon recipe can also be served for a special breakfast.

8 *salmon filets, each weighing*
  about 6 ounces
2 *teaspoons salt*
¼ *teaspoon white pepper*
¼ *teaspoon dried thyme or 1½*
  teaspoons chopped fresh thyme
12 *tablespoons unsalted butter*

FOR ONION RINGS AND GREEN PEPPER
  RINGS:
3 *large onions, peeled, sliced ¼*
  inch thick
5 *tablespoons all-purpose flour*
salt and freshly ground black pepper
½ *cup milk*
¾ *cup vegetable oil*
4 *medium-size green peppers, cut*
  in ¼-inch rings

½ *cup dry white wine*

METHOD:

1. Preheat oven to 375°F.

2. Combine salt, pepper and thyme and rub filets with this mixture.

3. Melt 8 tablespoons of the butter and dip the filets into it to coat them. Place filets in a pan with a cover, pour the remaining melted butter over, cover and bake, basting frequently, until flesh flakes easily when tested with a fork—about 10 minutes.

4. Meanwhile, separate onions into rings. Blend flour, salt and pepper together. Dip the onion rings into the milk and then into flour mixture. Pour ¼ cup oil in a warm skillet and let it get very hot. Drop in the onion rings and sauté until light golden brown.

5. Pour the remaining oil in another skillet and let it get very hot. Add pepper rings and keep turning in oil for 6 minutes or until tender. Remove and drain on paper towels. Season with salt and pepper to taste.

6. Remove filets to a hot serving platter. Deglaze the pan in which they baked on the top of stove by adding the wine while scraping the browned bits from the sides. Then add the remaining 2 tablespoons butter, stir, and heat until melted. Pour this sauce over the salmon, garnish with onion rings and green pepper rings and serve.

SALMON SEVICHE WITH ARTICHOKES AND RED PEPPER MAYONNAISE

SERVES 6

2 pounds fresh salmon filets,
  skinned
1 cup olive oil
6 tablespoons fresh lemon juice
2 medium-size red bell peppers
juice of 2 lemons
6 large artichokes
4 egg yolks, at room temperature

2 tablespoons chopped fresh basil
  leaves or 1 teaspoon dried basil,
  crumbled
1 teaspoon salt
¼ teaspoon freshly ground black
  pepper
2 tablespoons minced fresh chives
3 large fresh ripe tomatoes
fresh basil sprigs for garnish

METHOD:

1. Cut salmon diagonally and across the grain into the thinnest possible slices. Arrange in a single layer on large platter. Whisk oil and 6 tablespoons lemon juice together in a small bowl; brush evenly over the salmon. Refrigerate, covered, 30 minutes to 1 hour.

2. Meanwhile, heat broiler. Roast red peppers on broiler pan, 4 inches from heat, turning frequently, until skin is charred and blistered on all sides, about 10 minutes. Peel or rub skin away from peppers. Cut peppers open and remove stems, seeds and white parts. Dice into ¼-inch pieces.

3. Stir lemon juice into a large bowl of cold water. Trim artichokes by first cutting off the stem flush with the base. Then remove the outer leaves by pulling each leaf outward so that it snaps off the base, until you reach the tender, yellow-green inner leaves. Cut off the tops of the artichokes about ⅔ of the way down and discard them. Drop each artichoke into the lemon water immediately after you cut off the top (this will prevent discoloration). Starting at the base of the choke, pare away the dark bases of the leaves, then drop into the acidulated water again. Pare away the dark green parts of the leaves at the top in the same manner. Remove artichokes from the water one by one and pull out the leaves in the center so that the choke is visible. Scoop out the hairy chokes with a teaspoon and drop the artichokes into the lemon water once again.

4. Again removing them one by one, cut hearts vertically into slices ⅛ inch thick. Immediately drop slices into the lemon water. Cook slices

in a large saucepan of boiling water until crisp-tender, about 3 minutes. Drain and pat dry.

5. Drain marinade from salmon and reserve. Process egg yolks, basil leaves, salt and pepper in blender or food processor until frothy. With motor running, add reserved marinade in a slow steady stream to make a mayonnaise. Blend until thickened. Add diced peppers and puree. Transfer mayonnaise to small bowl and stir in chives.

6. Blanch tomatoes in boiling water for 30 seconds. Rinse under cold water; peel off and discard skins. Cut tomatoes lengthwise in half, then cut crosswise into thin slices.

7. For dramatic presentation arrange the elements of this as follows: Arrange salmon in semicircle near edge of each plate; follow with a row of artichoke slices. Next place semicircles of tomato slices, with cut sides of slices facing the center of the plate. Spoon mayonnaise onto plate so that it touches the cut sides of the tomatoes. Place basil sprigs in center for garnish.

FILETS OF SOLE WITH CHAMPAGNE

SERVES 8

⅓ *bottle (1 cup) champagne*	4 *egg yolks*
salt and freshly ground black pepper	6 *tablespoons heavy cream*
1 *small onion, finely chopped*	8 *thin slices truffle*
1 *cup (2 sticks) butter*	*parsley sprigs for garnish*
8 *thick sole filets (about ½ pound each)*	

METHOD:

1. Preheat oven to 300°F.

2. Put champagne in a saucepan. Add salt, pepper, onion and half the butter and bring to a slow boil, then reduce the heat. Simmer very gently for 6 to 8 minutes.

3. Place filets in a serving dish that has been well buttered with the remaining butter.

4. Pour the champagne mixture over the filets and place in oven to bake for 5 minutes. Remove from oven and turn temperature up to 350°F.

5. Beat egg yolks and cream briskly with a whisk until well mixed. Pour over filets, then add sliced truffles on top, return to oven and bake 20 to 25 minutes, or until fish flakes when tested with a fork.

6. Remove from oven. Garnish with sprigs of parsley and serve hot.

SOLE STUFFED WITH LOBSTER

SERVES 6

two 11-ounce lobster tails, cooked
    and shelled
8 tablespoons (1 stick) butter
2 teaspoons finely chopped green
    onion
2 teaspoons finely chopped celery
2 teaspoons finely chopped green
    pepper

salt and freshly ground black pepper
    to taste
6 medium-size sole filets (about
    2 pounds)
1 teaspoon chopped fresh parsley
1 cup chicken consommé or stock
2 tablespoons lemon juice
2 tablespoons minced onion

METHOD:

1. Remove meat from lobster tails and dice.

2. Melt half the butter in a skillet, preferably nonstick, and sauté green onion, celery and green pepper. Season with salt and pepper to taste. Cook until vegetables are somewhat soft (approximately 5 minutes). Remove from heat and mix with the diced lobster meat.

3. Spread mixture on sole filets and sprinkle with parsley. Roll up and fasten with toothpicks.

4. In same skillet, combine remaining ingredients and cook for a few minutes to blend flavors. Place stuffed sole in liquid, simmer, and poach for 10 minutes, or until sole flakes easily when tested with a fork.

BRAISED TROUT WRAPPED IN LETTUCE

SERVES 6

6 whole trout, 8 ounces each,
    cleaned
1/3 cup finely chopped carrots
1/2 cup finely chopped onions
1 cup finely chopped celery
1/2 cup finely chopped shallots
10 tablespoons (1 1/4 sticks) butter

salt and freshly ground black pepper
6 large lettuce leaves
2 tablespoons butter, melted
4 tablespoons heavy cream
2/3 cup champagne or other dry
    white wine

METHOD:

1. Preheat oven to 400°F.

2. Butterfly the trout to remove the backbone (see Trout Barnee, below).

3. Cook the carrots, onions, celery and shallots slowly in butter until soft. Season with salt and pepper to taste.

4. Blanch the lettuce leaves: Dip them into a bowl of hot water for 2 minutes, then quickly into cold water; pat dry. With a sharp knife remove hard center of lettuce leaf. Then brush leaves with the 2 tablespoons melted butter.

5. Stuff the trout with the vegetable mixture and wrap each fish in a blanched lettuce leaf.

6. Lay wrapped fish in deep, well-buttered fireproof dish.

7. Add the champagne. Poach in the oven, basting frequently until done, 15 to 20 minutes. When done, add cream, and reduce by rapidly boiling on top of stove, while basting all the time, until the sauce is of a thick enough consistency to coat the trout.

8. Serve the trout in the dish in which it has cooked.

TROUT BARNEE STUFFED WITH WILD RICE AND TOPPED WITH MACADAMIA NUT BUTTER SAUCE

SERVES 6

6 *rainbow trout, 6 ounces each, boned and butterflied (see Note)*

3 *tablespoons butter*

salt *and freshly ground black pepper to taste*

4 *ounces wild rice, cooked according to package directions*

6 *half-inch slices from large tomatoes*

6 *large mushroom caps*

12 *small strips king crab meat, cooked*

sweet *paprika*

FOR THE MACADAMIA NUT BUTTER SAUCE:

8 *tablespoons (1 stick) butter*

1 *cup macadamia nuts*

paprika *and chopped fresh parsley*

6 *large lettuce leaves or shredded lettuce*

fresh *parsley sprigs and Spiced Crab Apples (recipe below) or lingonberry jam for garnish*

METHOD:

1. Preheat oven to 350°F. Butter the bottom and sides of a baking pan with the 3 tablespoons of butter.

2. Lightly salt and pepper boned and butterflied trout on inside. Place cooked rice on opened trout, then a slice of tomato and a mushroom cap on top. Sprinkle with paprika.

3. Bake for about 15 minutes or until meat of trout is white but still juicy.

4. Lay a strip of king crab meat on each side of mushroom cap and return to oven for 5 or 10 minutes.

5. While fish is baking, *prepare Sauce:* Melt the stick of butter in saucepan, add chopped nuts, parsley and paprika. Cook just long enough to heat thoroughly.

6. Serve trout on a lettuce leaf or a bed of shredded lettuce, garnished with parsley and Spiced Crab Apples or lingonberry jam. Pour the Macadamia Nut Butter Sauce over the trout or serve separately.

Note: To butterfly fish, use a very sharp knife and cut from just below the head straight through the belly; open fish slightly and then cut the backbone away from the flesh on both sides. Sever the backbone, leaving the head and tail intact. Spread fish out flat.

SPICED CRAB APPLES

6 *crab apples*
¼ *cup brown sugar*
¼ *cup granulated sugar*
¼ *cup water*

3 *cloves or a small piece of*
   cinnamon stick
1 *teaspoon fresh lemon juice*

METHOD:

1. Wash the apples and remove the stems. Prick each apple a few times with the point of a sharp knife.

2. Add the sugar to the water in a saucepan and bring to a rapid boil. Add apples, cloves or cinnamon stick and lemon juice. Cook about 15 minutes, or until apples are just tender.

3. Remove from heat and let cool in syrup before using. (Apples in syrup will keep for a few weeks in a jar in the refrigerator.)

FISH STEW AMERICAINE

SERVES 8

4 *leeks, white part only, trimmed,*
   well washed and cut into 2-inch
   pieces
2 *garlic cloves*
1 *cup onion slices*
4 *carrots, cut into 2-inch pieces*
2 *tomatoes, skinned, seeded and*
   quartered
2 *bay leaves*
2 *tablespoons chopped fresh*
   parsley
2 *teaspoons salt*
¼ *teaspoon saffron*
1 *teaspoon dried thyme*
1 *teaspoon dried basil*

¼ *teaspoon freshly ground black*
   pepper
3 *cups water*
2 *South African lobster tails, 6*
   to 8 ounces each, slightly
   thawed and cut into 2-inch
   segments
12 *medium clams, scrubbed*
12 *mussels, scrubbed and beards*
   removed
1 *pound shrimp, shells on*
1 *pound halibut filet*
½ *cup olive oil*
½ *cup dry white wine*
buttered French bread
8 *cherry tomatoes for garnish*

METHOD:

1. Put leeks, garlic, onion, carrots, tomatoes, herbs and spices in deep kettle, add water and bring to boil. Let simmer about 10 minutes.

2. Add lobster tails, clams, mussels, shrimp and halibut. Pour in olive oil and wine. Simmer, covered, until fish, lobster meat and shrimp are cooked but still firm, and shells of clams and mussels are open, 15 to 20 minutes. Discard any clams or mussels which do not open.

3. Serve in large soup bowls. Place slice of buttered French bread in each bowl, add portion of each fish and shellfish, then add broth. Garnish with a cherry tomato.

MUSSELS WITH RICE AND CHAMPAGNE

SERVES 6

36 *mussels*
1½ *cups rice*
1¾ *cups water*
2 *cups champagne*
6 *tablespoons butter*

herb bouquet: 2 or 3 sprigs of
parsley and ¼ teaspoon dried
thyme, tied together in small
square of cheesecloth
salt and freshly ground black pepper

METHOD:

1. Scrub mussels well and remove the hairy beards with a sharp knife. Soak them in cold water until needed.

2. In a saucepan, bring the rice to a boil in the water for 2 or 3 minutes.

3. Add the champagne, butter, herbs, salt and pepper. Let simmer very slowly, covered, until rice is cooked—about 20 minutes. Remove the cheesecloth with the herbs.

4. While the rice is cooking, place the mussels in a large pot with ½ inch of boiling water, cover tightly, and let them cook until they open—no longer then 10 minutes. Discard any mussels that do not open. Remove mussels with a slotted spoon, and remove meat from shells.

5. Add the mussels to the rice and toss lightly to blend. Serve hot.

Note: If you prefer a more intense mussel flavor in your rice, then strain the liquid from cooking the mussels and add some to the finished rice.

MARYLAND CRAB TARTAR ROLLED IN VIRGINIA HAM

SERVES 8

1½ pounds lump (backfin)
   Maryland crab meat
8 large thin slices baked Virginia
   ham
sweet butter for greasing casseroles

FOR THE TARTAR SAUCE:
(makes approximately 2½ cups)
  ½ cup finely chopped onion
  ¼ cup chopped fresh parsley
  ½ cup finely chopped sweet pickle
  2 tablespoons chopped capers

¼ cup apple cider vinegar
2 tablespoons lemon juice
salt, freshly ground black pepper
   and hot sauce to taste
1½ cups mayonnaise, preferably
   homemade

4 tablespoons bread crumbs
sprigs of watercress or parsley for
   garnish

METHOD:

1. Preheat oven to 350°F.

2. Remove all bits of shell from the crab meat.

3. Place a ham slice in each of 8 well-buttered casseroles, half the slice covering the bottom, and spoon the crab meat carefully over the ham.

4. *Prepare the Tartar Sauce:* Blend onion, parsley, pickle and capers together. Add vinegar and lemon juice. Stir. Season with salt, pepper and hot sauce. Fold in mayonnaise. (If you wish to make sauce ahead of time, refrigerate until ready to use.)

5. Spoon 2 tablespoons of Tartar Sauce over the crab in each casserole. Fold the other half of the ham slice over crab meat, enclosing carefully so filling does not ooze out. Spoon 1 tablespoon of Tartar Sauce over the ham.

6. When ready to serve, sprinkle the crumbs over the top and place in the oven for 6 to 8 minutes. Garnish with watercress or parsley.

SOUTHERN CRAB CAKES

SERVES 6

3 *cups cooked crab meat,*
cartilage and bits of shell
removed
2 *teaspoons salt*
1½ *teaspoons dry mustard*
2 *egg yolks*
2 *tablespoons mayonnaise*
3 *teaspoons minced fresh parsley*

flour for dredging
2 *eggs, slightly beaten with 2*
tablespoons water
1 *cup finely sifted dry bread*
crumbs
4 *tablespoons butter*
parsley sprigs, 6 tomato wedges,
and 6 lime slices for garnish

METHOD:

1. Mix crab meat, salt, mustard, egg yolks, mayonnaise and parsley together. Press mixture into 6 firm cakes and refrigerate until well chilled. Just before serving, dip each crab cake in flour, then egg beaten with water, and then in bread crumbs.

2. Melt butter in frying pan, sauté cakes quickly, a few at a time, over high heat until golden brown, turning once. Garnish with parsley sprigs, a wedge of tomato and a slice of lime and serve immediately.

LOBSTER STEW

SERVES 6

4 *live Maine lobsters, 2½–3*
pounds each
4 *quarts water*
8 *tablespoons (1 stick) butter*

2 *quarts light cream*
pilot crackers (a large round soda
cracker that can be bought in a
supermarket)

METHOD:

1. To cook lobsters, heat water in a large kettle with a tight-fitting cover until boiling. Drop live lobsters in, cover tightly, bring to a boil again and simmer until done, approximately 20 minutes. Remove lobsters, drain and allow to cool enough to be handled.

2. Place each lobster on its back and split in half lengthwise in the soft underside. Remove and discard the stomach, intestinal vein and

spongy lungs. Remove coral and the tomally (green liver). In a soup pot, melt butter and sauté coral and tomally for 3 or 4 minutes.

3. Remove meat from the shells of the lobsters. Cut meat in 1½-inch pieces, add to the tomally mixture and sauté over a low flame for 5 minutes.

4. Remove from heat and add the cream *very slowly*, stirring constantly. Return pot to fire and heat to boiling point, *but do not boil*.

5. Set pot on back of stove and let stand 5 or 6 hours, or place in refrigerator and let age 1 or 2 full days. Stew will be a rich salmon color.

6. To serve, reheat but do not boil. Spoon into large individual tureens. As accompaniment, place a large bowl of pilot crackers in center of table.

OYSTERS MORNAY

SERVES 6

FOR THE SAUCE:
2 *tablespoons butter*
2 *tablespoons all-purpose flour*
1¼ *cups milk*
1 *egg, slightly beaten*
1 *cup sour cream*
¼ *teaspoon sweet paprika*
¼ *teaspoon finely chopped garlic* (*optional*)

18 *oysters, shucked, dried on paper towels, shells washed and reserved*
1 *cup cheese-cracker crumbs*
1 or 2 *tablespoons butter, melted*
freshly ground black pepper
1 *cup grated Cheddar cheese*

METHOD:

1. *Prepare the sauce:* Melt butter in saucepan, blend in flour to make a smooth paste, then add milk and slightly beaten egg, stirring constantly. Continue to cook for 5 to 8 minutes until it is a smooth cream. Blend in the sour cream, paprika and garlic, if you are using it.

2. Add the oysters.

3. Spoon the oyster-cream sauce mixture into oyster shells (or other suitable containers).

4. Sauté the cheese-cracker crumbs in the melted butter. Sprinkle grated cheese over the top of each shell or dish, and top with sautéed crumbs. Dust lightly with pepper.

5. Place under broiler just long enough for cheese to melt. Serve immediately.

MUSHROOM SHRIMP HOT POT WITH LEMON-BUTTERED RICE

SERVES 12

20 *medium mushrooms*
warm water
  3 *tablespoons cooking oil*
  1 *cup chopped onion*
  2 *tablespoons chicken stock base*
  1 *tablespoon curry powder*
  4 *dashes Tabasco sauce*
  2 *sixteen-ounce cans tomatoes*

  3 *pounds large shrimp, shelled*
    and deveined

FOR THE LEMON-BUTTERED RICE:
  6 *cups hot cooked rice*
  4 *tablespoons butter*
1½ *teaspoons grated lemon peel*

salt to taste

METHOD:

1. Cover mushrooms with warm water. Let soak for a few minutes and drain; remove and discard stems, or save for another use.

2. Heat oil in a skillet and cook onion until soft. Add chicken-stock base, curry, Tabasco and tomatoes.

3. Cover and simmer 15 to 20 minutes. Add mushroom caps and shrimp. Simmer uncovered for 5 minutes or until shrimps turn pink and are done.

4. Taste and add salt if necessary.

5. *Prepare the Lemon-Buttered Rice:* Combine hot rice, butter and grated lemon peel and mix well. Serve the shrimp and mushrooms over the hot rice.

SHRIMP KEBABS

SERVES 12

3 *pounds medium shrimp, shelled
and deveined*
3 *medium avocados, peeled and
cut into 1-inch chunks*
2 *cans (14½ ounces each) whole
artichoke hearts, drained*

FOR THE MARINADE:
¾ *cup lemon juice, strained*

¼ *cup red wine vinegar*
¾ *cup vegetable or olive oil*
½ *teaspoon salt or to taste*
1 *tablespoon Worcestershire sauce*
½ *teaspoon garlic powder*
few drops of hot pepper sauce
freshly ground black pepper to taste
1 *teaspoon dried oregano*

METHOD:

1. Place shrimp, avocado chunks and artichoke hearts in a shallow baking dish (not metal).

2. *Prepare the marinade:* In a jar with tight-fitting cover, combine all the rest of the ingredients. Shake vigorously to blend. Pour over shrimp mixture.

3. Refrigerate shrimp, covered, at least 2 hours, turning the mixture occasionally.

4. Prepare a charcoal grill, adjusting grill 5 inches from prepared coals—or use a hibachi.

5. Thread the shrimp, avocado and artichoke hearts alternately on small skewers or hibachi sticks; brush with marinade.

6. Place wire rack over grill. Grill kebabs on rack, turning occasionally and basting with the marinade, until the shrimp is done, about 10 minutes.

7. Brush with marinade again just before serving, if desired.

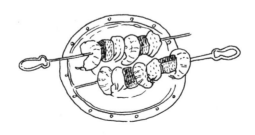

CHINESE VEGETABLE SCAMPI

SERVES 8

3 *pounds jumbo raw shrimp,*
shelled and deveined
¼ *cup soy sauce*
salt and freshly ground black pepper
pinch of garlic powder
8 *tablespoons (1 stick) butter*
1½ *tablespoons lemon juice*
2 *tablespoons chopped parsley*
2 *tablespoons chopped chives*

1¼ *cups beef bouillon*
1 *tablespoon minced onion or*
1½ *teaspoons dehydrated onion*
flakes
1½ *teaspoons soy sauce*
3 *cups sliced mushrooms*
1½ *cups fresh bean sprouts*
1½ *cups chopped green pepper*

METHOD:

1. Preheat oven to 350°F.

2. Place shrimp in a shallow baking dish and marinate in the soy sauce, salt, pepper and garlic powder for 5 to 10 minutes, turning occasionally.

3. Bake shrimp with marinade for about 9 minutes.

4. In the meantime, melt butter in a skillet, add remaining ingredients and cook, stirring, until vegetables are tender but still crisp. Serve shrimp over the vegetables.

CHAPTER SIX

EGGS, CHEESE, VEGETARIAN DISHES, RICE AND OTHER GRAINS

OMELET WITH KIDNEYS

1½ pounds beef kidneys (see below)
4 cups water
2 tablespoons lemon juice
7 ounces (2 cups) mushrooms, washed, sliced
7 tablespoons butter

2 or 3 tablespoons all-purpose flour
¾ cup champagne
salt and freshly ground black pepper
12 eggs
1½ tablespoons chopped fresh parsley for garnish

METHOD:

1. How to clean kidneys: Cut in half lengthwise, remove all fat. Place in a bowl with water and lemon juice. Let kidneys soak for 1 hour, rinse and pat dry. Cut in thin slices.

2. Melt half the butter in a skillet and sauté mushrooms. Then add the remaining butter and sauté the sliced kidneys for a couple of minutes.

3. Strain off the pan drippings from the mushroom-kidney mixture and place in another sauté pan, stir in the flour and mix until smooth. Add the champagne, stirring until sauce thickens, and simmer for a couple of minutes. Add the kidneys and mushrooms. Season with salt and pepper and cook over low heat until heated through.

4. Make the omelet as usual. Put the kidney and mushroom mixture into it before folding over. Garnish with parsley and serve immediately.

CHEESE AND EGGS

8 slices white bread, trimmed and cut into small pieces
2½ cups milk
4 tablespoons (½ stick) butter
1 pound sharp Cheddar cheese, coarsely grated
8–10 eggs, depending on size

salt and freshly ground black pepper
1 tablespoon chopped fresh parsley
sweet paprika
2 or 3 red apples, unpeeled, cut in wedges and fried in 6 table- spoons butter until tender
sprigs of parsley for garnish

METHOD:

1. Soak the bread in the milk for a few minutes.

2. Melt butter in heavy frying pan over medium heat, add bread

mixture and mash thoroughly with a fork, blending until it is a consistency of a soft roux.

3. Add cheese and mix thoroughly with bread mixture until well blended.

4. Beat eggs and add to cheese mixture, stirring constantly until eggs are set.

5. Add salt and pepper to taste. Transfer to a warm chafing dish or platter. Sprinkle with parsley and paprika, arrange the apple wedges and parsley sprigs around the edge, and serve.

CHEESE FONDUE ON TOAST

SERVES 6

1 *pound sharp Cheddar cheese,*
  grated
2 *cups beer*
2 *eggs*
½ *teaspoon dry mustard*

⅛ *teaspoon Tabasco sauce*
salt to taste
12 *slices hot buttered toast*
sweet paprika

METHOD:

1. Preheat broiler.

2. Melt cheese in top of double boiler over boiling water; add beer slowly, stirring constantly.

3. Beat eggs and blend in. Add mustard, salt and Tabasco. Cook until fondue thickens.

4. Remove from heat. Spread over hot buttered toast, sprinkle with paprika and place under broiler to brown lightly. Serve immediately.

BAKED TOMATOES AND CHEESE

SERVES 6

butter for greasing individual dishes
6 medium Italian plum tomatoes
   (regular tomatoes may also be
   used)
3 cups grated Cheddar cheese

9 eggs
3¾ cups milk
6 tablespoons wheat germ
salt and freshly ground black pepper
sweet paprika

METHOD:

1. Preheat oven to 350°F.
2. Butter 6 individual cook-and-serve dishes and set aside.
3. Dip tomatoes in hot water for easy removal of skin.
4. Slice the tomatoes. Divide sliced tomatoes among the dishes.
5. Sprinkle ½ cup grated cheese on top of tomato slices.
6. Whip eggs for a few minutes (not too frothy), add milk, salt and pepper to taste.
7. Divide the egg mixture among the 6 dishes.
8. Sprinkle 1 tablespoon wheat germ and a little paprika on top.
9. Place dishes in a large, shallow pan with a little water. Bake for 30 to 35 minutes or until done (when tested with a knife, the knife should come out clean) and a nice golden brown and puffed up. Serve immediately with rolls or muffins of your choice.

QUICHE LORRAINE
(Swiss Cheese Pie)

SERVES 6–8

FOR THE PASTRY SHELL:
2 cups all-purpose flour
⅔ cup butter
½ teaspoon salt
1 egg yolk, slightly beaten
3 or 4 tablespoons ice-cold water

12 ounces Switzerland Swiss
   cheese, grated

1½ tablespoons all-purpose flour
1¾ cups light cream
¼ teaspoon salt
pinch each of dehydrated onion,
   cayenne and grated nutmeg
4 eggs, slightly beaten
8 slices broiled bacon, crumbled

METHOD:

1. *Prepare the Pastry Shell:* Preheat oven to 350°F. Mix flour and salt and sift together. Cut in butter with pastry blender. Add whipped egg yolk and just enough water to combine the mixture so that it will hold together in a ball. Chill for 1 hour, then roll out lightly on floured pastry board, about ¼ inch thick. Line a greased 9-inch pie or quiche pan with the pastry, making it about 2 inches wider than pan. Flute the edges high or crimp with a fork, and prick the bottom and sides well. Bake for 10 minutes, remove from oven and let cool slightly, then refrigerate a short while before filling with quiche mixture.

2. Turn oven up to 425°F.

3. Place cheese in pastry shell. Add the flour, toss together, using fingers, and distribute cheese mixture evenly in the shell.

4. Add seasonings to cream, stir well, and add to eggs. Beat to blend well.

5. Ladle the egg mixture slowly over cheese.

6. Bake at 425°F. for 15 minutes. Reduce heat to 325° and bake about 35 minutes or until quiche is set. The quiche will puff up, the center will remain soft and the top may crack (this is OK). Remove from oven and let set 10 minutes before cutting. Quiche may be baked early in the day and reheated as needed. When reheating, just let it sit in a hot oven with the heat turned off. Cut into wedges to serve and place strips of crisp bacon over wedges.

ONION PIE

SERVES 10–12

5 *cups thinly sliced onions*	2 *cups (1 pint) half-and-half*
8 *tablespoons (1 stick) butter*	¼ *cup grated Parmesan cheese*
two 9-inch prebaked pastry shells	¼ *cup grated Cheddar cheese*
(*see Quiche Lorraine, above*)	*salt and freshly ground black pepper*
8 *eggs*	*sweet paprika*
2 *cups (1 pint) heavy cream*	*parsley sprigs for garnish*

METHOD:

1. Preheat oven to 350°F.

2. Melt butter in a skillet and cook onions until limp. Drain off any extra liquid.

3. Spread onions over bottoms of pastry shells.

4. Whip eggs, add cream, half-and-half, Parmesan and Cheddar cheese. Season with salt and pepper to taste.

5. Pour mixture over onions, sprinkle with a little paprika.

6. Bake for 45 minutes or until done—test for doneness by inserting a knife in center. It should come out clean.

7. Remove pies from oven and let stand for 15 to 20 minutes before cutting into wedges. Garnish with parsley.

TOMATO CHEESE PIE

SERVES 6–8

4 tablespoons butter
2 large onions, thinly sliced
2 large firm ripe tomatoes, thinly
   sliced
one 9-inch prebaked pastry shell
   (see Quiche Lorraine, page 172)
   brushed with egg white
2 tablespoons chopped celery

1 cup grated Gruyère cheese
4 eggs, beaten
2 teaspoons celery powder
¼ teaspoon grated nutmeg
¼ teaspoon cayenne
salt and freshly ground black pepper
1 cup (½ pint) heavy cream

METHOD:

1. Preheat oven to 350°F.

2. Melt the butter in a skillet. Sauté half the onion slices in butter, then mix with raw onion.

3. Place sliced tomatoes in the pastry shell and scatter the onion and celery between the slices; then sprinkle on half of the grated cheese.

4. Whip the eggs, add celery powder, cayenne, nutmeg, salt and pepper. Add cream and blend well.

5. Pour over the tomato, onions and celery in shell. Sprinkle the remaining half of grated cheese over the top of the pie. Bake about 45 minutes or until a sharp knife, inserted in the center, comes out clean. Let cool slightly and serve in wedges.

MOCK CHEESE SOUFFLÉ

SERVES 8

16 *slices white bread*
butter
  8 *slices sharp Cheddar cheese,*
    ⅜ inch thick

3 *cups milk*
6 *eggs, slightly beaten*
crisp bacon strips (optional) for
  garnish

METHOD:

1. Preheat oven to 350°F.
2. Butter the slices of bread on one side.
3. Place 8 slices of buttered bread, buttered side down, in a baking dish or pan to fit. Cover each slice with a slice of cheese, top with remaining bread slices, buttered side facing cheese.
4. Combine milk and eggs and pour mixture over bread.
5. Bake in the oven for about 45 minutes, or until a sharp knife when inserted in center comes out clean. If desired, garnish with crisp bacon strips.

MACARONI AND CHEESE SOUFFLÉ

SERVES 6

⅓ *cup uncooked elbow macaroni*
2 *tablespoons butter*
3 *tablespoons all-purpose flour*
½ *teaspoon salt*
½ *teaspoon dry mustard*

⅛ *teaspoon freshly ground black*
  pepper
1 *cup milk*
1½ *cups grated Cheddar cheese*
  4 *eggs, separated*
flour or grated cheese for dusting

METHOD:

1. Cook macaroni until just done—not too soft. Drain and chop into small pieces and reserve.
2. Preheat oven to 350°F.
3. Melt butter in saucepan. Remove from heat. Combine flour, salt, mustard and pepper. Blend into melted butter until smooth. Stir milk in slowly and cook over medium heat, stirring constantly, until mixture thickens.

4. Gradually add cheese; continue to cook and stir until cheese is melted. Stir in the macaroni. Remove from heat and cool for 1 minute.

5. Beat egg yolks until thick. Fold egg yolks into cheese-macaroni mixture.

6. Beat egg whites until stiff. Slowly pour mixture onto beaten egg whites, folding lightly.

7. Butter a 1½-quart casserole and dust with flour or sprinkle with additional grated cheese. Spoon mixture into the casserole, set it in a baking pan filled with hot water to depth of 1 inch, and place in oven. Bake until top is lightly browned and feels somewhat dry when touched lightly with finger—about 1 hour. Serve immediately.

HOMINY GRITS SOUFFLÉ

SERVES 8

Hominy grits are a coarse meal made from the broken grains of hominy—corn with the hull and germ removed. It is the mainstay of Southern cooking, particularly at breakfast, when it is prepared as a hot cereal.

flour for dusting soufflé dish	*4 egg yolks, well beaten*
1 *cup boiling water*	*salt*
¾ *cup uncooked hominy grits*	*white pepper*
2 *cups milk*	6 *egg whites*
3 *tablespoons melted butter*	

METHOD:

1. Preheat oven to 350°F. Grease a 2½-quart soufflé dish and dust with flour.

2. Pour rapidly boiling water into the top of a 1½-quart double boiler and add the grits. Cook directly over medium heat for 2 minutes, stirring constantly.

3. Stir in 1 cup of milk and set the pot over the bottom of the double boiler, which has been filled with a few inches of boiling water.

4. Cook for 30 minutes, stirring constantly. Remove from heat and stir in the remaining cup of milk and the melted butter.

5. Place this again over boiling water and stir until mixture is smooth and heated through.

6. Remove saucepan from heat and stir the beaten yolks into the grits. Cool to lukewarm.

7. Meanwhile, in a large bowl, beat the egg whites until stiff but not dry. Fold the whites into the hominy mixture. Pour into the prepared dish and bake for 45 minutes. Serve immediately.

CORN SOUFFLÉ

SERVES 6

2 tablespoons butter
2 tablespoons all-purpose flour
1 cup milk, scalded
2 cups fresh corn kernels cut from cob, or frozen (thawed) or canned whole corn kernels, drained

1 teaspoon salt
¼ teaspoon freshly ground black pepper
2 pimento slices, finely chopped
2 eggs, separated

METHOD:

1. Preheat oven to 350°F.

2. In a saucepan, melt butter, add flour and blend well. Add scalded milk, stirring constantly until mixture thickens and is smooth. Remove from heat.

3. Add corn, salt, pepper and pimento.

4. Beat egg yolks and stir into corn mixture. Beat whites until stiff and fold in gently.

5. Pour into a well-buttered casserole. Bake for 25 to 30 minutes and serve immediately.

PARSNIP SOUFFLÉ WITH LEMON SAUCE

SERVES 8

4 tablespoons butter
4 tablespoons whole wheat flour
2 cups milk
salt, freshly ground black pepper
    and cayenne
¼ teaspoon freshly grated nutmeg
4 cups (approximately 1½ pounds
    uncooked) cooked parsnip puree
5 eggs, separated
pinch of salt

FOR THE LEMON SAUCE:
2 tablespoons arrowroot
½ cup water
juice of 1 lemon, strained
peel of 1 lemon, grated
¼ teaspoon freshly grated nutmeg
2 cups (1 pint) heavy cream,
    whipped

watercress for garnish

METHOD:

1. Preheat oven to 350°F.

2. Make cream sauce base by melting butter in a saucepan; add flour and cook, while stirring, over low heat for 2 minutes, until smooth. Add milk slowly and cook to thicken. Stir in salt, pepper, cayenne and nutmeg. Add parsnip puree. Let cool.

3. Beat in egg yolks one at a time.

4. Beat egg whites with salt until stiff but not dry. Fold one third of the whites into mixture, continuing to fold in gently until all the whites are incorporated. Fold in remaining whites. Pour into buttered 2-quart soufflé dish or casserole and bake 40 to 50 minutes, until high and top is firm.

5. *Prepare the Lemon Sauce:* In a saucepan, blend arrowroot in water until dissolved. Add lemon juice, grated lemon peel, and nutmeg, and cook to thicken. Add ¼ teaspoon nutmeg and more lemon juice at this point if a more pronounced flavor is desired. Cool. Fold into whipped cream.

6. Serve soufflé immediately with Lemon Sauce spooned over each serving and garnished with watercress.

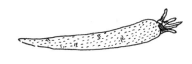

PEA SOUFFLÉ

SERVES 6

two 10-ounce packages frozen peas,
    thawed
1 teaspoon granulated sugar
½ teaspoon salt
freshly ground black pepper
4 thin slices white onion

few pinches of thyme
2 tablespoons softened butter
3 egg yolks
1 cup dry bread crumbs
1 cup milk
4 egg whites

METHOD:

1. Preheat oven to 350°F.

2. Place peas in a mixing bowl. Add sugar, salt, pepper to taste, onion slices, thyme and butter. Mix well.

3. Add egg yolks and beat rapidly.

4. Add bread crumbs and milk. Correct seasoning if necessary.

5. Fold in stiffly beaten, but not dry, egg whites.

6. Turn mixture into a 1½-quart buttered soufflé dish. Bake for 35 minutes, or until a knife blade comes out clean when inserted in the center. Serve immediately.

SPINACH SOUFFLÉ

SERVES 6

3 tablespoons butter
1 tablespoon chopped shallots
3 tablespoons all-purpose flour
1 cup milk
¾ cup chopped cooked spinach,
    fresh or frozen and thawed, well
    drained

½ teaspoon salt
dash of freshly ground black pepper
nutmeg to taste
5 egg yolks
6 egg whites, stiffly beaten

METHOD:

1. Preheat oven to 375°F. Butter a 1½-quart soufflé dish and set aside.

2. Melt 3 tablespoons butter in a saucepan, add shallots and cook 3 minutes or until limp. Blend in the flour until smooth and allow mixture to cook until bubbling and golden—2 to 3 minutes.

3. Remove from heat and add milk all at once. Return to stove and cook, stirring, until thick.

4. Add well-drained spinach and seasonings.

5. Allow to cool slightly and stir in egg yolks. Add stiffly beaten whites, folding in carefully. Pile lightly into soufflé dish and bake 25 to 30 minutes or until knife inserted in the center comes out clean. Serve hot.

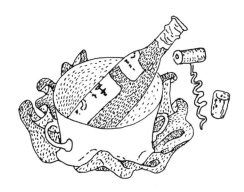

RICE

BLUSHING RICE (RICE WITH TOMATO SAUCE)

SERVES 6–8

3¾ *cups water*
1¼ *cups tomato juice*
1¼ *cups tomato ketchup or tomato*
   puree
2 *cups long grain rice*
2 *teaspoons salt or to taste*

2 *tablespoons chopped onions*
2 *tablespoons butter or more*
2 *tablespoons chopped fresh*
   parsley (reserve 1 tablespoon
   parsley for garnish)

METHOD:

1. In a heavy pot with a tightly fitting cover, put water, tomato juice and ketchup or puree. Bring to a boil.

2. Slowly add the rice and other ingredients, reserving 1 tablespoon fresh parsley.

3. Cover pot tightly, and reduce heat to let rice simmer. Cook rice 20 minutes or until tender. Remove from heat. Add more butter if desired.

4. Place rice in a hot serving dish and sprinkle the tablespoon of reserved parsley over the top.

CARIBBEAN RICE

SERVES 6

1 *cup coconut milk (see Note)*
1½ *cups water*
1 *cup long grain rice*
2 *tablespoons butter*

1 *medium onion, chopped*
salt and freshly ground black pepper
1½ *cups frozen peas, slightly*
   thawed

METHOD:

1. Place coconut milk and water in a large saucepan (about 2 quarts) with tightly fitting cover. Bring to boil and add the rice, butter, onion, salt and pepper.

2. Return to a boil and then reduce heat and simmer, covered, for about 20 minutes, when rice should be almost done.

3. Add partly thawed peas to rice. Cook for another 5 to 8 minutes, when all moisture should be absorbed and rice cooked. Serve immediately.

Note: Coconut milk can be bought in some stores—just make sure you get the unsweetened milk. It can also be made as follows: grate half a fresh coconut and add 1 cup of water. Let stand for about 20 minutes and then squeeze in a cheesecloth or drain in fine sieve. The liquid remaining is the coconut milk.

ORANGE-FLAVORED RICE

SERVES 6

This is an excellent accompaniment to ham, pork and poultry.

¾ cup thinly sliced celery	2 cups orange juice
¼ cup finely chopped onions	4 tablespoons orange rind
8 tablespoons (1 stick) butter	salt and freshly ground black pepper
3 cups water	2 cups long grain rice

METHOD:

1. In a heavy saucepan cook the celery and onions in the butter until tender and translucent.

2. Stir in water, orange juice, orange rind, salt and pepper. Bring to boil.

3. Sprinkle in rice and cover pan with tight-fitting cover. Cook over low heat for 25 minutes or until rice is tender.

SAVORY BROWN RICE

SERVES 8

This rice dish is a fine accompaniment to duck or other fowl.

4½ cups water
3 teaspoons powdered chicken-
  stock base
2 cups brown rice
1 cup mushrooms, stems removed,
  sliced if large

5⅓ tablespoons (⅓ cup) butter
one 5-ounce can water chestnuts
½ cup chopped scallions
3 tablespoons chopped pimento

METHOD:

1. Bring water and chicken-stock base to boil.

2. Stir in brown rice. Lower heat, cover, and simmer until tender and water is absorbed, about 45 minutes. Keep hot.

3. Melt butter in a skillet and sauté mushrooms until done. Set aside.

4. Drain water chestnuts and cut in half. Add mushrooms, with their drippings, water chestnuts and all remaining ingredients to rice. Stir gently until combined. Serve hot.

WILD AND WHITE RICE

SERVES 12

8 tablespoons (1 stick) butter
1 cup chopped celery
1 cup chopped onions
10 chicken bouillon cubes
10 cups boiling water
2 cups wild rice, washed and

  picked over
3 teaspoons seasoned salt
¼ teaspoon freshly ground black
  pepper
2 cups long grain white rice
chopped fresh parsley for garnish

METHOD:

1. Preheat oven to 400°F.

2. Melt butter in dutch oven and sauté celery and onions until tender, about 5 minutes. Remove from heat.

3. Dissolve bouillon cubes in water and add this bouillon, along with wild rice, seasoned salt, and pepper, to the celery-onion mixture; stir well.

4. Bake, covered, 30 minutes. Add white rice and stir with a fork. Bake 30 minutes longer or until rice is tender and all liquid absorbed.

5. Fluff up with fork. Turn onto serving platter and sprinkle with parsley before serving.

SAVORY WILD RICE WITH RAISINS

SERVES 6

1½ cups wild rice
1¼ cups minced onions
1 tablespoon butter
4 or 5 beef bouillon cubes mixed

with 4 or 5 cups boiling water
¾ cup seedless raisins, soaked in
water until plumped, then
drained

METHOD:

1. Wash rice well and pick over, then drain thoroughly.
2. Sauté onions in butter until translucent; set aside.
3. Combine rice and boiling beef bouillon in a saucepan. Simmer, covered, until rice is tender and bouillon has been completely absorbed—about 40 minutes.
4. Add raisins and onions and mix well. Serve hot.

MAGIC WHEAT GOURMET STYLE

SERVES 6

Brill's Magic Wheat is a type of grain, packaged in a box, which can be purchased at most gourmet food stores.

4 tablespoons (½ stick) butter
1 small onion, finely chopped
1 cup finely chopped celery
4 medium mushrooms, finely
chopped

1 teaspoon salt
2 cups Brill's Magic Wheat
5 cups hot unsalted chicken stock
2 tablespoons chopped fresh
parsley for garnish

METHOD:

1. Melt butter in a heavy pot that has a tight-fitting cover and sauté onion, celery and mushrooms until light gold. Add Magic Wheat and salt, and mix well; add hot chicken stock and bring to a boil.

2. Cover, reduce heat and simmer until all moisture is absorbed, about 12 minutes.

3. Serve hot in an attractive dish, garnished with chopped parsley.

CHAPTER SEVEN

VEGETABLES

ARTICHOKE HALVES WITH BUTTER

water
½ cup lemon juice
½ cup olive oil

1 teaspoon salt
3 large artichokes
4 tablespoons butter, melted

METHOD:

1. In large kettle, combine water (enough to cover artichokes), lemon juice, olive oil and salt and bring to a boil.

2. Meanwhile trim stems from artichokes; cut a 1-inch slice from each top. Remove discolored leaves from base. With scissors, trim thorny tips off remaining leaves. Cut each artichoke in half lengthwise and carefully scoop out the fuzzy chokes in the center with a spoon and discard. Wash the artichokes well.

3. Add to the boiling liquid and return to boil; then reduce heat and let simmer, covered, 35 to 40 minutes, or until bases of artichokes feel soft.

4. Drain and serve hot with melted butter.

Note: As artichokes discolor quickly, rub cut surfaces with lemon or lemon juice as they are cut.

BAKED STUFFED ARTICHOKES

SERVES 12

12 medium artichokes
1 cup (2 sticks) butter
1 pound mushrooms, thinly sliced
1 cup thinly sliced green onions
    (scallions)
4 tablespoons chopped fresh
    parsley

2 teaspoons salt
¼ teaspoon freshly ground black
    pepper
bread cubes made from 6 slices of
    white bread, crusts removed
1 cup hot water
2 cups boiling water

METHOD:

1. Rinse artichokes. With sharp knife, cut off stems and 1 inch straight across the tops. With scissors, trim thorny tips off remaining leaves. Remove loose and discolored leaves around the base. Gently spread leaves apart and remove leaves from center to expose fuzzy and

prickly portion (choke). With spoon, carefully scrape choke from the center of each artichoke.

2. Preheat oven to 400°F. In a 10-inch skillet over medium heat melt half the butter and sauté mushrooms, green onions and parsley for 5 minutes or until onions are tender. Season with salt and pepper. Add bread cubes and 1 cup hot water and toss until stuffing is well mixed.

3. Stuff each artichoke center and between leaves with equal amounts of the stuffing. Place in 1 large baking dish or 2 smaller ones. Pour 2 cups boiling water around artichokes; cover dish or dishes tightly with foil and bake for 1¼ hours or until leaves can be pulled off easily.

4. Melt the remaining butter. To serve, cut each artichoke in half from top to bottom with a sharp knife and spoon about 1 teaspoon melted butter over each half.

ASPARAGUS WITH LEMON BUTTER

SERVES 12

4 pounds medium-size fresh asparagus	freshly ground black pepper
salt	5 teaspoons lemon juice
	¾ cup (1½ sticks) butter, melted

METHOD:

1. Cut off and discard the tough whitish woody bottom of each stalk.

2. Peel with a vegetable peeler to remove the little scales, and wash the asparagus.

3. Bring a large pot of lightly salted water to a boil. Six to 10 minutes before ready to serve, plunge asparagus in the boiling water and cook until just tender. Do not overcook.

4. Remove with slotted spoon and drain well. Place in a rectangular or oval heated dish. Sprinkle very lightly with pepper.

5. Blend lemon juice with melted butter and pour over asparagus to serve.

ASPARAGUS WITH CREAM, BUTTER AND EGGS

SERVES 6

¾ cup crème fraîche (or ¼ cup
  dairy sour cream and ½ cup
  whipping cream—see below)
3 pounds asparagus

salt
¾ cup (1½ sticks) butter, melted
6 hot soft-cooked eggs

METHOD:

1. If you don't have crème fraîche, combine sour cream and whipping cream and let stand for 6 hours before using.

2. Break or cut off the tough woody white parts of the stalks. With a vegetable parer, remove the small scales. Wash the asparagus. Place asparagus in skillet.

3. Add ½ inch water to skillet. Sprinkle with salt and cook, covered, for 5 minutes or until crisp-tender. Drain and place on a warmed platter wrapped in a clean towel to keep warm.

4. To serve, place asparagus on hot individual plates with a small dish of melted butter and a small dish of crème fraîche on the side. Place egg in egg cup beside each portion of asparagus. Dip asparagus in butter, then in cream, and eat the eggs along with the asparagus.

GREEN BEANS WITH PIMENTO BUTTER

SERVES 6

For this dish I prefer fresh red peppers to canned or bottled pimentos.

1½ *pounds young green beans, ends snipped off*
1½ *cups boiling water*
1 *teaspoon light-brown sugar*

FOR THE PIMENTO BUTTER:
3 *sweet red peppers, halved, with ribs, stems and seeds removed*
8 *tablespoons (1 stick) unsalted butter, melted*
1 *teaspoon salt*
½ *teaspoon freshly ground black pepper*

1 *tablespoon cider vinegar or 2 tablespoons lemon juice*
1 *teaspoon sugar*
½ *teaspoon sweet paprika, preferably imported*

½ *cup heavy cream, whipped*
6 *strips roasted red pepper, ½ inch wide (reserved from peppers for pimento butter) for garnish*

METHOD:

1. Put the beans into boiling water, add the sugar, and stir once. Cook briskly, covered, for 4 or 5 minutes, or until beans are just slightly crunchy. Drain the beans and run cold water over them to set the bright green color and to cool them. Drain.

2. *Prepare the Pimento Butter:* Preheat oven to 400°F. Cover a baking pan with foil and lay the pepper halves in the pan, cut side down. Cover with another layer of foil. Roast for 30 minutes, until the peppers are soft and the skins will slip off easily. Remove from the oven, peel off the skins (over a bowl to catch the pepper juice if there is any). Cut 6 strips of pepper, ½ inch wide, and reserve for garnish. In a blender or food processor, place the roasted peppers, with whatever juice they have given up, butter, salt, pepper, vinegar, sugar and paprika. Puree until smooth and light. Correct all seasonings. Place in a saucepan.

4. When ready to serve, heat pimento butter over very low fire until warm and reheat the beans by dipping them briefly in boiling water. Fold the whipped cream into the butter and spoon over the beans. Garnish with the reserved strips of roasted pepper.

GREEN BEANS WITH TOMATOES

SERVES 6

1/4 cup olive oil
3/4 cup minced onions
3 garlic cloves, minced
one 16-ounce can (or two 8-ounce
    cans) plum tomatoes, including
    juice

3/4 cup chopped fresh flat-leaf
    parsley, leaves only
1 teaspoon dried marjoram
1 1/2 pounds green beans, trimmed
    and cut into 2-inch pieces
about 1 cup boiling water
lemon juice to taste (optional)

METHOD:

1. In a stainless steel or enamel 4-quart saucepan heat olive oil over moderate heat until it is hot. Add onions and garlic and cook, stirring, until the onion is softened.

2. Pass the tomatoes with juice through a sieve. Add the tomatoes, parsley and marjoram to the onion mixture.

3. Add the green beans and the boiling water to the tomato-onion mixture (the liquid should cover the beans halfway) and salt and pepper to taste. Cook, covered, over moderate heat, stirring occasionally, for 5 to 10 minutes or until beans are tender (this depends on the age and toughness of the beans). If necessary, add a little more water. Add lemon juice to taste if desired.

4. To serve, transfer the vegetables to a heated serving dish.

CREAMED GREEN BEANS

SERVES 6

two 9-ounce packages frozen
    French-style green beans or
    1 1/2 pounds fresh green beans,
    frenched (cut in half length-
    wise)

1/2 cup light cream or half-and-half
1/8 teaspoon freshly ground black
    pepper
lettuce leaves

METHOD:

1. Cook frozen beans according to directions on package until barely tender. If fresh beans are used, cook them in lightly salted boiling water for no more than 4 minutes. Drain.

2. Add cream and pepper.

3. Bring to a slow boil, stirring constantly, until cream reduces and thickens and coats beans.

4. Serve on a bed of lettuce leaves.

HERBED LIMA BEANS

SERVES 6

3½ pounds fresh lima beans,
   unshelled
3–3½ quarts boiling water
dried or fresh rosemary to taste

6 tablespoons butter
salt and freshly ground black pepper
2 tablespoons chopped fresh
   parsley

METHOD:

1. Shell the lima beans and rinse briefly.

2. Put the beans in a large saucepan of boiling water, cover and cook until tender, 10 to 15 minutes. Drain thoroughly.

3. In a saucepan, melt the butter and stir in the rosemary. (Add enough rosemary for a distinctive, but not overpowering, flavor.)

4. Pour sauce over the beans. Season with salt and pepper to taste, sprinkle with chopped parsley and serve hot.

PUREED LIMA BEANS

SERVES 6

3 cups dried lima beans
6 tablespoons butter
2 medium onions, chopped

2 tablespoons chopped parsley
salt and freshly ground black pepper

METHOD:

1. Wash beans, drain, and soak overnight in fresh water, using 3 to 4 times as much water as beans. If any beans float to the top, discard them.

2. Bring beans and their soaking water to a boil and cook slowly until tender in about 40 minutes. Then drain off liquid, leaving a small amount for simmering later.

3. Add butter, onions, 1 tablespoon of the parsley, salt and pepper.

4. Simmer until onions are cooked and liquid has been absorbed. Puree beans in a blender or food mill until smooth. Place in serving dish and garnish with remaining tablespoon of chopped parsley.

HOME STYLE VIRGINIA BAKED BEANS WITH HAM

SERVES 6

1 *pound dried navy beans*	1/8 *teaspoon ground cloves*
1 *quart water*	1/2 *cup dark unsulphured molasses*
1/2 *cup chopped onion*	2 *tablespoons light brown sugar*
1/2 *teaspoon salt*	1 *tablespoon dry mustard*
3/4 *pound cooked Virginia ham*	6 *slices cooked Virginia ham*
with some fat, cut into cubes	1 *ounce (2 tablespoons) Bourbon*
1 *tablespoon Worcestershire sauce*	*or dark rum*

METHOD:

1. Wash beans, cover with water and refrigerate overnight.

2. The next day place beans, with their soaking water, in a large heavy-bottomed pot with a cover. Add onion and salt. Cover and cook over low flame until tender but not mushy, about 45 minutes to 1 hour, adding more water if needed.

3. Preheat oven to 350°F.

4. Remove beans to a bake-and-serve casserole and add cubed ham. Mix the remaining seasonings together and add to beans, blending in well.

5. Place in oven and bake about 45 minutes. When ready to serve, place a ham slice on each serving plate. Heat rum or Bourbon, pour over beans in the casserole, ignite (be careful) and serve, spooning a portion over each ham slice.

SOUTHERN BAKED BEANS

SERVES 10

4 *cups dried navy beans*	4 *ounces ham or salt pork, cubed*
1/4 *cup Bourbon*	1 *can (8 1/4 ounces) chunk pine-*
1/2 *cup molasses*	*apple, drained, or 1/2 cup fresh*
1/2 *cup strong black coffee*	*pineapple cubes*

METHOD:

1. Wash beans, cover with water and soak overnight (discarding any that float to the top). Next day, simmer in soaking water 45 minutes to 1 hour, or until tender. Drain, reserving the cooking liquid.

2. Preheat oven to 300°F.

3. Combine cooked beans, Bourbon, molasses, coffee and ham or salt pork and some of the bean-cooking liquid in a baking crock or dish.

4. Bake, covered, 1 to 1½ hours, adding some of the reserved bean-cooking liquid if the beans become dry. Add pineapple, placing it around the edge of crock, during the last 15 minutes of cooking time.

PINK BEANS WITH HERBS

SERVES 8

3 *cups dried pink beans*	4½ *tablespoons lemon juice*
¼ *cup olive oil*	2 *teaspoons dried oregano*
1 *cup chopped onions*	2 *teaspoons dried rosemary*
4 *tablespoons butter*	*salt and freshly ground black pepper*

METHOD:

1. Wash beans. Soak overnight in water to cover. Discard any that float to top.

2. Next day place beans in a pot and simmer in their soaking water for 2 to 2½ hours, or until tender. When cooked, drain off any excess liquid.

3. Preheat oven to 325°F.

4. In a skillet, heat the oil and in it sauté the onions until soft. Add the onions and all other ingredients to the beans and mix well.

5. Place bean mixture in a buttered oven-proof dish and bake for 15 to 20 minutes. Serve hot.

BAKED WHOLE BABY BEETS WITH CREAMED FRESH HORSERADISH

SERVES 6

Beets, also known as beetroot, have their origin in the Mediterranean. They are served as a pickle and a relish more often than as a vegetable. However, beets baked in their skins are one of the most tantalizing of vegetables. Most of the taste of the earth is lost when they are boiled.

12 *tender young beets (2 or 3 bunches depending on size), green tops removed*
4 *tablespoons vegetable oil*

FOR THE CREAMED FRESH HORSE-
   RADISH:

2 *tablespoons freshly grated horse-radish or 2 tablespoons prepared horseradish*
salt
1 *cup heavy cream, whipped, or* ¾ *cup sour cream*

METHOD:

1. Preheat oven to 350°F.

2. Scrub the beets, leaving root and top ends on to prevent loss of flavor. Rub with vegetable oil.

3. Place beets on a rack placed over a roasting pan, add 1 cup water to pan and bake until crunchy tender, about 30 minutes to 1 hour, depending on size.

4. Remove skins and root and top ends while still warm. Scoop out a groove in the center of each beet with a small spoon.

5. *Prepare the Creamed Fresh Horseradish:* Season horseradish lightly with salt and fold in whipped heavy cream or sour cream.

6. If necessary, reheat beets in a few teaspoons of water in the top of a double boiler over hot water and then set in center of a large serving platter. When ready to serve, spoon creamed horseradish onto the groove of each beet, letting some run down the sides.

BAKED CREAMY BEETS ON A BED OF STEAMED HONEY-FLAVORED BEET TOPS

SERVES 6

1 pound tender beet tops, washed
  and drained (from about 6
  beets)
1 cup water
1 tablespoon apple cider vinegar
2 tablespoons clover honey
sea salt and freshly ground black
  pepper

3 ounces cream cheese at room
  temperature
½ cup plain yogurt
2 tablespoons chopped onion
6 medium-size baked beets
  (page 194), each sliced into
  3 pieces
sweet paprika

METHOD:

1. Preheat oven to 400°F.

2. Chop beet tops into ½-inch pieces. Place in heavy-bottomed pot; add water. Cover and cook until tender, approximately 10 to 12 minutes. Using a slotted spoon, remove tops from liquid and drain well. Place tops in a serving casserole.

3. Stir vinegar and honey together and add to tops, tossing to coat. Add salt and pepper to taste.

4. Beat yogurt into cream cheese and add onion.

5. Lay beet slices over tops and spoon cheese and yogurt over. Dust with paprika and place in oven to heat, about 15 minutes.

GALE BEETS

SERVES 6

12 medium beets, peeled and sliced
  ¼ inch thick
½ cup orange juice
1 tablespoon cornstarch
½ teaspoon salt

⅛ teaspoon freshly ground black
  pepper
2 tablespoons sugar
3 tablespoons butter

METHOD:

1. Preheat oven to 400°F.

2. Arrange sliced beets in baking dish.

3. Mix together orange juice, cornstarch, salt, pepper and sugar until cornstarch dissolves. Pour over beets.

4. Place in oven to bake for 30 minutes, turning the beets over once or twice.

5. Remove from oven and dot with butter cut into bits. Return to oven briefly until butter is melted. Serve hot.

BROCCOLI WITH HERB BUTTER

SERVES 6

3 *pounds broccoli*
1 *cup (2 sticks) butter*
4 *tablespoons fresh lemon juice*

1/4 *teaspoon oregano*
1/4 *teaspoon salt*
freshly ground black pepper

METHOD:

1. Wash broccoli. Trim the coarse bottoms from the broccoli stalks and discard, then cut the tough skin away from the remaining stalks. Remove the large leaves and cut the broccoli into spears.

2. Place broccoli on a vegetable steamer in a deep pot, add about ½ inch water, cover and steam the broccoli spears for 20 minutes or until tender. Combine and heat the other ingredients until the butter melts, and pour over broccoli.

3. Serve very hot.

GARLIC-SEASONED BROCCOLI

SERVES 6

3 *pounds very fresh, green*
   broccoli
4 *ounces fat pork, cut into 2 or 3*
   pieces

salt and freshly ground black pepper
2 *garlic cloves*
1/3 *cup (5 1/3 tablespoons) butter*

METHOD:

1. Wash broccoli thoroughly, and cut off the thick ends of the stalks, leaving just a small portion of stalk. Pare the tough outer skin away from the thick part and cut into 1½-inch pieces and break or cut the remaining stalks into flowerets. Remove the large leaves.

2. Bring a large pot of water to a boil and drop in the fat pork. Boil for a few minutes, then add salt and pepper to taste.

3. Add cubed broccoli pieces and cook for 4 or 5 minutes. Then add the broccoli flowerets and cook an additional 4 or 5 minutes (do not overcook). Remove with a slotted spoon, put into a serving dish and keep warm. Discard the pork.

4. Crush garlic and blend with butter in a saucepan. When butter is melted, strain through a fine sieve to remove bits of garlic. Season with more salt and pepper, if desired. Pour over broccoli and serve.

BRUSSELS SPROUTS WITH PEANUTS

SERVES 6–8

Brussels sprouts, the favorite vegetable of the English and one of their specialties, becomes a Southern standby when combined with peanuts.

2 *pounds Brussels sprouts*	*salt and freshly ground black pepper*
4 *tablespoons butter*	¼ *teaspoon ground mace*
3 *ounces peanuts, coarsely*	1 *teaspoon lemon juice*
broken up and toasted	

METHOD:

1. Wash sprouts, pick over and score stem end. Cook sprouts in boiling water to cover until just crisp-tender—5 to 7 minutes. Remove from heat, drain in colander, and then plunge sprouts in cold water to set the green color.

2. When ready to serve, heat butter until frothy and sauté peanuts until light golden. Add the sprouts, together with salt, pepper, mace and lemon juice, and reheat briefly.

Note: Do not cook the sprouts too far ahead of serving time as they lose their texture and flavor if allowed to stand.

BRUSSELS SPROUTS ON A BED OF TOASTED BREAD CUBES

SERVES 6

2 *pounds Brussels sprouts,*
  trimmed, washed, stem ends
  scored
4 *tablespoons butter*
2 *teaspoons salt*
¼ *teaspoon freshly ground black*
  pepper

1 *teaspoon mace*
2 *teaspoons lemon juice*

FOR THE TOASTED BREAD CUBES:
8 *slices day-old bread*
4 *tablespoons butter, melted*
1 *tablespoon chopped fresh parsley*
salt and freshly ground black pepper

METHOD:

1. Cook sprouts in boiling water to cover just until crisp—5 to 7 minutes. Don't overcook. Drain and plunge into cold water to set the color. Drain again.

2. *Prepare the Toasted Bread Cubes:* Preheat the oven to 350°F. Cut the crusts from the bread and cut bread into ½-inch cubes. Toss cubes in 4 tablespoons melted butter, then add parsley, salt and pepper. Place on baking sheet and toast in oven until golden.

3. Heat 4 tablespoons butter until frothy, add sprouts with other ingredients, toss lightly and cook until heated through. Serve on a bed of Toasted Bread Cubes.

RED CABBAGE AND CHESTNUTS IN RED WINE

SERVES 8

½ *pound salt pork, rind removed,*
  blanched in boiling water 5–10
  minutes, and then plunged
  quickly into cold water and
  drained
2½ *pounds chestnuts, shells scored*
  in a cross, parboiled for about
  2 minutes, peeled and chopped
⅔ *cup finely chopped onions*
2 *cups beef stock*

2 *cups dry red wine*
3 *tablespoons vinegar*
¼ *teaspoon ground nutmeg*
¼ *teaspoon ground cloves*
4 *pounds red cabbage cut in*
  medium-size wedges
salt and freshly ground black pepper
2 *tablespoons melted butter*
lettuce leaves (optional)

METHOD:

1. Dice prepared salt pork and fry in a skillet until it is crisp and golden and all fat has been rendered. Add the chopped chestnuts and onions. Sauté until onions are transparent; set aside.

2. In a large saucepan, place stock, wine, vinegar, nutmeg and cloves. Bring to boil, add cabbage and cook until tender, 10 to 15 minutes (do not overcook).

3. Drain well. Add salt and pepper to taste, toss lightly.

4. Combine chestnut mixture with cabbage, add melted butter and toss again very lightly. Serve hot, on a bed of large lettuce leaves if you wish.

STEAMED WHOLE CARROTS IN PARSLEY BUTTER

SERVES 6

Carrots, of Near East origin, are truly great world travelers as evidenced in their use in a variety of cuisines. The ancient medical men believed they had great therapeutic value, even though they were not aware of their high vitamin and mineral content. Their sweet goodness should not be destroyed by allowing them to stand in water for any length of time.

Nutritional researchers have discovered that carrots with tops left on while in storage or in the market lose more nutrients than the carrots packaged in plastic bags, because the green tops continue to draw nutrients from the carrot root.

When steaming vegetables such as carrots, adding a few grains of light brown sugar helps to retain their flavor and color.

6 *medium-size young carrots,*	4 *tablespoons butter*
uniform in size, unpeeled	2 *tablespoons chopped fresh*
1 *cup chicken stock*	*parsley*

METHOD:

1. Scrub carrots, run the tip of a sharp knife down the center of each carrot and place on a vegetable steamer in a pan with a tight cover. Add chicken stock and steam until crunchy-tender—approximately 30 minutes.

2. Remove from pan and drain the stock. Holding carrots with a

fork, remove skins with the point of a peeling knife. If skins do not remove easily, use paper towels and rub gently.

3. Melt butter in the pan and add parsley; turn carrots in butter to coat all sides. Serve hot.

STEAMED CARROTS WITH LEMON BUTTER GLAZE

SERVES 2

3 or 4 fresh carrots (2 cups), cut
  in 1/4-inch slices
1 tablespoon butter

2 or 3 teaspoons sugar
1 tablespoon lemon juice
1/2 teaspoon grated lemon rind

METHOD:

1. Steam carrots in vegetable steamer over water in pan with tight-fitting cover for 5 to 10 minutes, or until tender. Drain and return carrots to pan.

2. Melt butter in another pan; add sugar and lemon juice. Cook for 2 or 3 minutes, pour over carrots and toss lightly. Sprinkle with lemon rind and serve hot.

FRESH BABY CARROTS AND FRESH PEAS

SERVES 6

3 or 4 dozen fresh baby carrots
  (or frozen, if fresh are
  unavailable)
1 1/2 pounds fresh peas or 2 ten-ounce
  packages of frozen

8 tablespoons (1 stick) hot melted
  butter
1/2 teaspoon celery seed or dried
  oregano or 1 tablespoon chopped
  fresh parsley or dill
salt and freshly ground black pepper

METHOD:

1. Wash carrots well and scrape lightly.

2. Cook carrots in a vegetable steamer over a small amount of water in a pot with a tight-fitting cover, about 5 minutes or just until tender (do not overcook). If using frozen, follow directions on package.

3. Shell fresh peas, wash and cook in the same manner. If using frozen, follow directions on package.

4. Mix carrots and peas together, toss in hot melted butter and season with any of the herbs and salt and pepper to taste. Serve hot.

JULIENNE CARROTS AND SNOW PEAS

SERVES 8

2 cups chicken stock or water
4 cups julienned carrots
3 cups snow peas (green beans
  may be substituted if snow peas
  are not available)
1 cup water

4 tablespoons butter
1½ tablespoons sugar (optional)
1 teaspoon salt or to taste
3 tablespoons chopped fresh
  parsley

METHOD:

1. Bring stock or water to a boil in a heavy saucepan. Add carrots and simmer for 5 to 6 minutes, or just until tender. Drain the carrots.

2. Prepare the snow peas by removing strings (if any) from sides, and slicing each pea in half (or prepare the green beans the same way).

3. In another pot, bring the cup of water to a boil, add snow peas and cook for 1 minute. If you are using green beans, cook for an extra 2 minutes. Drain.

4. Melt the butter, adding sugar if desired. Combine carrots and snow peas and toss lightly in butter mixture. Add salt and parsley. Place in an attractive dish and serve at once.

PUREED GINGER CARROTS

SERVES 12

4 pounds carrots
4 cups water
2½ teaspoons salt

12 tablespoons (1½ sticks) butter,
  melted
2 teaspoons ground ginger
freshly ground black pepper

METHOD:

1. Peel carrots and slice in 1-inch pieces. Place them in a heavy saucepan with water and half the salt. Bring to a boil over medium heat, then cover, reduce heat and cook the carrots for 20 to 25 minutes or until soft.

2. Remove from heat and drain off the water. Puree the carrots in a food mill, electric blender or food processor until completely smooth.

3. Place carrot puree in a saucepan or top part of a double boiler. Add butter, ginger, the remaining salt and pepper to taste. Reheat over boiling water until carrots are piping hot. Serve immediately.

CAULIFLOWER WITH CRISP BACON AND A GREEN BEAN GARNISH

SERVES 6

1 medium head fresh white
  cauliflower
2½ cups milk, scalded
2 tablespoons fresh lemon juice
1 teaspoon salt
freshly ground black pepper
½ cup shelled, toasted sunflower
  seeds

6 tablespoons butter, melted
1 roasted sweet red pepper
  (page 245), cut in 1-inch strips
  (or ½ small jar pimentos)
1 cup crumbled crisp bacon
  (approximately 8 strips)
1 pound whole green beans,
  steam-cooked

METHOD:

1. Wash and trim cauliflower, leaving the core and some of the fresh green leaves on. Place bottom down in a heavy pot. Sprinkle cauliflower with lemon juice and pour hot milk over it. After milk returns barely to a boil, reduce heat and simmer until tender (approximately 25 minutes).

2. Remove cauliflower from pot, drain well (if desired, save milk to make a soup) and place on a large preheated serving platter. Sprinkle with salt, dust generously with pepper, and then scatter sunflower seeds over top. Arrange the pepper strips attractively over the cauliflower. Spoon melted butter over the entire head and sprinkle bacon over all. Surround with hot beans and serve.

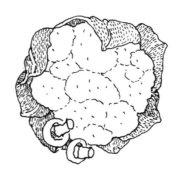

CAULIFLOWER FLOWERETS WITH MUSHROOMS AND SWEET PEPPER STRIPS

SERVES 12

6 cups cauliflower flowerets
boiling water
salt
4 cups sliced mushrooms
⅓ cup lemon juice

⅔ cup butter
1½ large sweet red peppers, cut
into thin strips
1½ large sweet green peppers, cut
into thin strips

METHOD:

1. Cook cauliflower flowerets in pot in small amount of boiling salted water (about 1 inch) for 5 minutes or until tender. Remove from pan with slotted spoon and set aside to keep warm.

2. Meanwhile, sprinkle mushrooms with lemon juice. Melt half the butter and sauté the mushroom slices: keep warm.

3. In another pan melt the remaining butter and sauté the pepper strips. Don't overcook; try to retain their color.

4. Place the flowerets in the center of a large bowl or platter, surround with mushroom slices and toss the pepper strips lightly over the top. Serve hot.

STEAMED CAULIFLOWER WITH HOLLANDAISE SAUCE

SERVES 8

1 large or 2 medium cauliflowers
1½ cups milk
salt

FOR THE HOLLANDAISE SAUCE:
2 tablespoons butter
1 tablespoon all-purpose flour

1 cup boiling water
2 eggs, well beaten
1 tablespoon onion juice
1 teaspoon salt
1 teaspoon freshly ground black
pepper
1 teaspoon chopped fresh parsley

METHOD:

1. Wash cauliflower and remove the hard stem and the leaves.

2. Heat milk in a saucepan, add cauliflower and salt. Cook 15 to 20 minutes, until just tender. Drain.

3. *Meanwhile, prepare the Hollandaise Sauce:* Cream butter and flour in a bowl. Add water and stir well.

4. Place ingredients in double boiler over hot water and cook, stirring. Remove from heat when thickened. Add the well-beaten eggs gradually, mixing as you add. Stir in onion juice, salt, pepper and parsley.

5. Serve the cauliflower hot with the sauce poured over.

CELERY ROOT WITH CREOLE MUSTARD BUTTER

SERVES 6

1 tablespoon olive oil
3 large cooked celery roots, peeled and thickly sliced (Celery Root Soup, page 57)
½ lemon
1 cup Creole Mustard Butter (Deviled Oysters, page 37)

1 cup soft whole wheat bread crumbs
¼ cup chopped chives or tender green tops of scallions
sweet paprika
2 tablespoons chopped chives for garnish

METHOD:

1. Preheat oven to 350°F.

2. Brush a baking sheet with olive oil.

3. Squeeze lemon juice over slices of celery root. Brush all surfaces with the Creole Mustard Butter. Place on baking sheet.

4. Combine crumbs with the ¼ cup chives or scallions. Spread crumb mixture, using the back of a spoon, over buttered celery root, pushing the crumbs into the mustard butter. Dust top lightly with paprika.

5. When ready to serve, bake for 10 to 15 minutes or until heated through and surface is a light golden color. Sprinkle with the 2 tablespoons chopped chives.

STEWED CREAMY CHESTNUTS

SERVES 12

3 pounds chestnuts
4 cups milk
4 tablespoons butter

¼ cup all-purpose flour
salt and freshly ground black pepper

METHOD:

1. Score a cross in the hard shell of the chestnuts. Bring a large quantity of water to a boil and cook the chestnuts in the boiling water for a few minutes and then drain. This blanches them, making it possible to remove the shells. Remove shells and furry inner skins.

2. Place the nuts in a large saucepan, add milk and salt and cook thoroughly, 15 to 20 minutes or until tender. Do not allow chestnuts to get soft and mushy.

3. Pour off the milk, strain and reserve. Set chestnuts aside. Melt butter over low heat, blend in the flour, stirring, and stir in milk slowly. Simmer and stir sauce with a wire whisk until thickened and smooth. Season with salt and pepper. Pour sauce over chestnuts and serve hot.

FRESH CORN PUDDING

SERVES 6

2½ *cups fresh corn kernels, cut off the cob*
2 *tablespoons all-purpose flour*
1 *teaspoon salt*

¼ *teaspoon freshly ground black pepper*
1½ *tablespoons butter*
2 *eggs, beaten*
1½ *cups milk*

METHOD:

1. Preheat oven to 325°F.

2. Mix flour, salt and pepper and sprinkle over the corn.

3. Add the butter and mix well with a wooden spoon.

4. Whip eggs, add milk and mix with corn mixture.

5. Pour into a greased baking dish. Place on center rack in oven. Bake slowly for 1 hour and 10 minutes.

6. Insert knife in center; if it comes out clean the pudding is done. Serve hot.

CORN AND CHEESE "PIE"

SERVES 6–8

This is actually more a pudding than a pie, as there is no pastry crust—just a browned crust formed while baking.

4 cups (two 17-ounce cans)
  cream style corn
1 cup (8¾-ounce can) whole corn
  kernels, drained
6 tablespoons all-purpose flour
2 tablespoons butter, melted
2 tablespoons grated onion

3 tablespoons grated Cheddar
  cheese
salt and freshly ground black pepper
3 eggs
2 cups undiluted evaporated milk
  or rich cream

METHOD:

1. Preheat oven to 350°F.

2. Grease casserole dish, set aside.

3. In a mixing bowl combine cream style corn and corn kernels. Blend in flour, melted butter, onion, cheese, salt and pepper.

4. Beat eggs well and add evaporated milk or cream. Combine with corn mixture and blend very well.

5. Pour mixture into casserole dish and bake for 45 to 50 minutes or until "pie" is set and golden brown.

GOLDEN DANDELION BLOSSOMS SAUTÉ

SERVES 10–12

Dandelions, native to Greece, grow abundantly all over Europe and the United States. The tender green leaves of the wild dandelion (which grows in fields and among uncut grasses, and is not the same variety found in mowed lawns) are delicious in salads when picked in the spring, but the blossoms and roots are also eminently edible.

6 cups dandelion blossoms in full bloom (see Note)
6 cups water
½ cup apple cider vinegar
8 tablespoons (1 stick) butter or ½ cup vegetable oil
¾ cup unbleached all-purpose flour
¼ cup water-ground cornmeal (or substitute 1 full cup flour)

½ teaspoon sweet paprika
salt and freshly ground black pepper to taste
mace
12 fresh, tender, green dandelion leaves, washed and dried, 6 lemon wedges, 6 toast points, 6 large dandelion blossoms for garnish

METHOD:

1. Add vinegar to water and pour over blossoms; reserve 6 blossoms for the garnish. Let stand 5 minutes; drain in sieve and run cold water over blossoms to remove all vinegar flavor and any insects. Toss well and dry with paper towels but do not break apart.

2. Melt butter or oil in a large sauté pan.

3. Mix flour, cornmeal and paprika in a large brown bag; shaking bag to mix well.

4. Put blossoms in the bag and shake to coat with flour-cornmeal mixture.

5. Heat melted butter or oil until bubbling hot, add blossoms, toss gently with the tongs of a large fork, turning to brown all blossoms lightly. Dust with salt and pepper and a little mace to taste.

6. To serve, place cooked blossoms in center of a large hot serving platter. Surround with the dandelion leaves and toast points, lay the lemon wedges on the fresh leaves, and bunch the 6 fresh blossoms in the center of the platter, on top of cooked blossoms.

Note: Gather blossoms in the morning hours, as they close tightly at noon. Also, gather them in a nonpolluted area where they have *not been sprayed.*

MIXED GREENS SAUTÉ

SERVES 8

3 pounds mixed greens (mustard,
escarole, chicory, Swiss chard,
spinach, dandelion leaves or
other seasonal greens)
4 garlic cloves, minced

5½ tablespoons olive oil
1¼ teaspoons dried oregano
2 lemons, cut in wedges, for
garnish

METHOD:

1. Remove coarse stems from greens and wash greens thoroughly. Parboil them in 2 quarts boiling salted water in a covered kettle. Cook for 3 minutes. Drain well.

2. In large skillet sauté garlic in oil, add drained greens and oregano and cook 5 or 10 minutes longer, shaking pan, until greens are tender but still crisp. Serve garnished with lemon wedges.

ICED JERUSALEM ARTICHOKE SLICES

SERVES 6

The Jerusalem artichoke, a member of the sunflower family, is pale, asymmetrical and knobby. When served raw it has excellent flavor, the texture of water chestnuts, and it does not need to be peeled. Cooked, it resembles boiled potatoes and loses most of its sweet taste and crisp texture.

One of my earliest food memories is of my mother digging with the prongs of a large fork at the root of a tall green plant and pulling out these dirt-covered, knobby potatolike vegetables. She rubbed them with a towel and sliced them right there in the garden for us to eat. To this day I have never had enough to satisfy my taste for this earthy, crunchy root.

1½ pounds medium Jerusalem
artichokes

METHOD:

1. Scrub artichokes well, trim off all spots (do not peel). Slice thin and let stand in ice water for 1 hour before serving.

2. To serve, drain well, dry on paper towels and serve as a healthy snack or as part of the Vegetarian Dinner on page 384.

HEAVENLY BAKED MUSHROOMS

SERVES 6

2¼ pounds mushrooms
5 tablespoons dry sherry
4 tablespoons melted butter
4 tablespoons all-purpose flour
2 cups light cream, heated

salt to taste
½ teaspoon sugar
1 teaspoon marjoram
sweet paprika
toast points for 6 servings

METHOD:

1. Preheat oven to 400°F.
2. Wash mushrooms under running water, drain well and dry thoroughly with paper towels.
3. Slice mushrooms very thin and place in a 2-quart casserole. Add sherry and toss well.
4. To make sauce: Melt butter, then blend in flour, stirring, until smooth. Add hot cream and cook over a low fire until it thickens. Stir in salt, sugar and marjoram.
5. Pour cream sauce over mushrooms, sprinkle top lightly with paprika.
6. Bake for 15 to 20 minutes. Serve spooned over toast points.

CURRIED MUSHROOMS

SERVES 12

3 pounds medium-to-large
  mushrooms
2 tablespoons curry powder (or
  to taste)

1½ cups (3 sticks) butter
1 cup finely chopped onions
½ cup chopped chives
salt and freshly ground black pepper

METHOD:

1. Wipe mushrooms clean. Remove stems and discard or save for another dish.
2. Melt butter in a large skillet or saucepan with a cover and blend in curry powder.

3. Add onions and chives, cook for 3 to 5 minutes, then add mushrooms. Cover and simmer for 5 more minutes. Remove from heat and add salt and pepper to taste.

ROASTED WHOLE HONEY-GLAZED ONIONS WITH TOASTED CURRIED WALNUT HALVES

SERVES 6

Onions have been known throughout history and are popular in almost every country. Their skins should have a papery texture, and, if cooked whole, they should be uniform in size for best results.

6 *large yellow onions*
3 *tablespoons vegetable oil or butter*
2 *tablespoons pure clover honey*

FOR THE TOASTED CURRIED WALNUT HALVES:
18 *walnut halves*
3 *tablespoons butter*
½ *teaspoon curry powder*

METHOD:

1. Preheat oven to 375°F.

2. Cut root end off but leave skin on onions. Place each onion in a piece of foil, fold foil to prevent juices from escaping, and roast 45 minutes or until tender. Remove from oven and lower heat to 350°F. for the Toasted Curried Walnut Halves.

3. Remove onions from foil, peel off skin and set onions in a saucepan.

4. Mix vegetable oil (or butter) and honey together. Spoon glaze over the top of the onions while heating them over a low flame, until glazed on top.

5. *Meanwhile, prepare the Toasted Curried Walnut Halves:* Blend butter with curry powder. Add walnut halves and toss together to coat well. Place walnuts on baking sheet and toast in the oven until crisp. *Do not let them burn.*

6. Arrange 3 walnut halves over the top of each onion and serve as a side dish or as part of the platter in the Vegetarian Dinner on page 384.

BAKED ONIONS STUFFED WITH PECANS OR PEANUTS

SERVES 6

6 *large onions*
2 *tablespoons vegetable oil*
2 *tablespoons butter*
1 *tablespoon honey*
½ *cup coarsely chopped pecans*
    or peanuts

2 *tablespoons chopped fresh*
    parsley
¼ *teaspoon dried basil*
salt and freshly ground black pepper
½ *cup bread crumbs*

METHOD:

1. Preheat oven to 350°F.

2. Pull off all the layers of skin, (including the slippery membrane beneath the skin). Place each onion on a large square of aluminum foil and spoon 1 teaspoon of vegetable oil over each. Fold foil into a twist at top to seal loosely. Bake for about 45 minutes or until soft to touch (keep oven on after removing onions).

3. Open foil carefully and pull out centers of onions.

4. Blend butter, honey, nuts and seasonings. Toss with the crumbs.

5. Fill centers of onions, pushing stuffing down well. Place on a baking sheet.

6. Bake 20 minutes and serve.

CREAMED SILVER ONIONS

SERVES 8

36 *silver onions, peeled*
2 *cups chicken stock*
1–2 *tablespoons cornstarch or*
    arrowroot
1 *cup milk*

½ *cup heavy cream*
3 *tablespoons butter*
salt and freshly ground black pepper
a pinch of mace
sweet paprika

METHOD:

1. Boil onions in stock until tender but not mushy, 15 to 20 minutes. Remove from stock and keep warm.

2. Drain stock off into a heavy-bottomed skillet. Cool. Mix corn-

starch or arrowroot with a little water until dissolved. Beat the cornstarch or arrowroot into the stock and cook over low heat until it thickens to a smooth cream. Stir in milk and cream.

3. Stir in butter, season with salt, pepper and mace.

4. Pour over onions and sprinkle with paprika. Serve immediately.

WINE GLAZED ONIONS

SERVES 8

24 *medium onions*
4 *tablespoons vegetable oil*
¾ *cup dry red wine*

3 *tablespoons sugar*
salt and freshly ground black pepper
1–1½ *cups chicken broth*

METHOD:

1. Put oil in heavy, wide pan with a cover, just large enough to hold onions in a single layer.

2. Peel skin off onions, including the thin slippery membrane underneath, and place in pan. Cook over medium heat until oil sizzles. Add wine, sugar, salt, pepper and enough broth to cover bottom of pan 1 inch deep.

3. Cover and simmer for 1 hour, or until onions are tender, turning them a few times while cooking. Serve in a hot dish with wine-broth liquid poured over.

BRAISED PARSNIPS ROLLED IN CHIVE CRUMBS

SERVES 6

Parsnips should be creamy white and free of blemishes. They will be sweeter and more flavorful if left in the ground until after a frost. If harvested early, freezing (as done here), seems to enhance their flavor and natural sweetness. They can be mashed or cut in strips after removing the core if it seems tough.

1½ *pounds medium parsnips*
1 *cup water*
4 *tablespoons peanut or vegetable oil or butter*
salt and freshly ground black pepper

1 *cup whole wheat bread crumbs sautéed in 2 tablespoons oil or butter*
2 *tablespoons chopped chives*

METHOD:

1. The day before serving, scrub, trim and peel parsnips. Cut in 2-inch strips, removing the core with a sharp, pointed knife, if necessary. Place in a plastic bag and freeze overnight.

2. Next day, defrost and parboil in 1 cup of water about 7 minutes. Drain. Heat oil or butter in a pan with tight-fitting cover, add parsnips, cover and reduce to low heat. Braise until tender, approximately 10 minutes, stirring occasionally. Season with salt and pepper to taste.

3. To serve, add chives to sautéed crumbs and sprinkle over parsnips, turning to coat all sides. Serve as a side dish or as part of the vegetable platter in the Vegetarian Dinner on page 384.

CANDIED PARSNIPS WITH PINEAPPLE

SERVES 12

12 *medium parsnips, peeled*
fresh lemon juice to taste
salt and freshly ground black pepper
12 *slices pineapple*
8 *tablespoons (1 stick) butter*

6 *tablespoons honey*
1 *cup pineapple juice*
¼ *teaspoon freshly grated nutmeg*
sweet paprika
½ *cup dark rum (optional)*

METHOD:

1. Preheat oven to 350°F.

2. Pour a little lemon juice over parsnips before cooking to help them keep their color. Cook parsnips in boiling water until tender, about 12 minutes; drain well. Cut in half and remove core if tough. Lay parsnips in a well-buttered bake-and-serve casserole. Dust lightly with salt and pepper, then arrange pineapple slices in between the parsnips.

3. Melt butter in a saucepan, stir in honey and then add pineapple juice. Pour over parsnips.

4. Bake 30 minutes, basting frequently with the juice. Remove from oven. Dust with the grated nutmeg, or grate it on directly, and sprinkle on a little paprika. Place under broiler to brown lightly, checking to see that parsnips don't burn.

5. Warm the rum, flame (stand back) and pour over parsnips (this is optional) just before serving. Serve directly from casserole.

GREEN PEAS WITH RED SWEET PEPPER STRIPS AND ONION RINGS

SERVES 12

2½ pounds shelled fresh green peas
  or four 10-ounce packages
  frozen peas
1¼ cups water
1 large or two medium red sweet
  peppers, cut into strips

2 medium onions, cut in rings
4 tablespoons butter
salt and freshly ground black pepper
½ teaspoon chopped fresh dill

METHOD:

1. Place water in covered pot and bring to boil, add salt and peas. Cook, covered, 6 to 8 minutes or until peas are just tender (don't overcook). Follow package directions for frozen peas.

2. Remove from heat and drain in colander.

3. In skillet, melt butter and lightly sauté sweet pepper strips and onion rings.

4. Add the drained peas, salt, pepper to taste and dill. Toss lightly to blend and serve in a heated dish.

HOSTESS PEAS

SERVES 8

6 strips bacon
⅓ cup minced onion
1¼ tablespoons water
3 tablespoons butter
4 cups cooked frozen peas

½ cup shredded lettuce
½ teaspoon salt or less, if desired
1 teaspoon chopped pimento
  (optional)

METHOD:

1. Dice bacon and sauté until crisp; remove from sauté pan and drain on paper towels. Pour off all but 1 tablespoon of bacon fat and sauté onion in the same pan until soft. Remove and drain on paper towels.

2. Put the water and butter in a saucepan, add peas and lettuce and cook until lettuce is wilted.

3. Add bacon, onion and seasonings and mix. If you use the pimento, add just before serving.

PUREE OF GREEN PEAS WITH CAPERS

SERVES 8

6 *pounds fresh green peas (weight*
unshelled) or four 10-ounce
packages frozen peas, partially
thawed
1 *cup boiling water*
¼ *teaspoon light brown sugar*

salt and freshly ground black pepper
4 *tablespoons butter or more*
2 *tablespoons very small capers,*
drained
8 *strips of pimento for garnish*

METHOD:

1. Shell the peas and place them (or the partially thawed frozen peas) in a heavy saucepan with a tight-fitting cover. Add the boiling water, brown sugar and a light sprinkling of salt and pepper. Cover and steam peas until tender, about 5 minutes.

2. Drain the peas in a colander placed over a saucepan, reserving the cooking liquid. Puree the peas in a food processor or blender, working in small batches, until very smooth. Add the 4 tablespoons butter, increasing the amount if desired. Correct seasoning if necessary. If the puree is too thick, blend in a little of the cooking liquid, a spoonful at a time. Reheat the puree.

3. Rinse capers in a strainer and gently pat dry with paper towels. Stir capers into the puree and turn it into a serving dish. Garnish with strips of pimento.

FRENCH POTATO SOUFFLÉ

SERVES 12

Potatoes retain their everlasting appeal whether puffed delightfully in a soufflé, served Austrian style in a cake, in a casserole, in their own brown jackets—there are ways to cook potatoes galore! So let's eat them up!

4 *pounds medium potatoes*
4 *tablespoons bacon fat*
4 *tablespoons all-purpose flour*
2 *cups milk*
½ *cup heavy cream*

salt
1 *cup grated mild cheese*
6 *eggs, separated, yolks lightly*
beaten
freshly grated horseradish

METHOD:

1. Preheat oven to 375°F.

2. Wash the potatoes, place in a pot and cover with boiling salted water. Cook uncovered until tender, peel and mash.

3. Melt bacon fat in saucepan. Stir in flour until well blended.

4. Add milk and cook gently, stirring constantly, until smooth and thick. Remove from heat.

5. Stir in cream, salt to taste, cheese and lightly beaten yolks.

6. Beat egg whites until stiff and fold into potato mixture. Pour into 2 greased 1-quart baking dishes. Bake for 45 minutes. Serve piping hot with horseradish.

POTATOES ANNA

SERVES 6

The lowly potato is raised to culinary eminence when thin slices, generously bathed in butter, are arranged in layers, baked and then unmolded like an upside-down cake. Crusty outside, soft and creamy inside, Pommes Anna—created for a gourmandizing beauty at the court of Napoleon III—are the ultimate delight of potato lovers. The dish is easy to make if you use a cast-iron skillet and my trick of sautéing the potatoes lightly before baking so they will brown evenly and unmold without collapsing.

¾ cup (1½ sticks) butter
2½–3 pounds large, uniform-size
    potatoes, peeled

salt and freshly ground black pepper
paprika

METHOD:

1. Preheat oven to 475°F. Melt butter in small saucepan. Skim foam from top. Pour the clear yellow liquid (this is clarified butter) carefully from saucepan into small dish. Discard the milky liquid left at bottom of saucepan. Slice potatoes thinly and evenly, and dry with paper towels.

2. Heat ½ cup of the clarified butter in a large skillet over medium heat. Add potatoes and sauté 2 or 3 minutes, using a spatula to separate slices and keep them from sticking to bottom of skillet. Remove from heat; let cool until easy to handle. Heat remaining clarified butter in a heavy cast-iron or aluminum skillet, making sure sides of skillet are well buttered. Remove from heat. Start at center and overlap potatoes in

circles until bottom of skillet is covered. Sprinkle lightly with salt and pepper. Arrange overlapping slices around sides of skillet. Layer the potatoes, overlapping the slices, until all are used, sprinkling each layer lightly with salt and pepper. Press potatoes down firmly with small plate or large spatula.

3. Set skillet on upper rack of oven; place pan underneath on lower rack to catch any drippings. Bake 20 minutes. Again press potatoes down. Bake an additional 35 to 40 minutes. Remove from oven. Hold potatoes down firmly with small plate and pour off excess butter. Run knife around the edges of the potatoes. Place a warm plate over skillet. Invert. The potatoes should slide onto the plate. If desired, light sprinkle of paprika may be added before serving.

POMMES SOUFFLÉS

SERVES 6–8

These French fries are glorious indeed. They are fried in fat twice— first at a lower temperature and then in hotter fat. The result—delicate puffed potatoes—suitable for a king! (The legend goes that they were accidentally invented by a cook for Louis XIV.)

3–4 *pounds mature Idaho or large*	*fat or oil for frying*
Maine potatoes	*salt*

METHOD:

1. Cut potatoes into even, ⅛-inch-thick, lengthwise slices with a knife or slaw cutter. Slices must be even for potatoes to puff. Soak in ice water for 20 to 30 minutes.

2. Dry thoroughly between two clean towels or several paper towels.

3. Half-fill two large kettles or heavy saucepans with fat or oil. Heat the fat in one pan to 300°F. Heat fat in the second to 375°F. or 400°F. Drop slices, one at a time, into first pan. Put in only enough for a single layer—don't crowd them. Stir with a slotted spoon or skimmer to keep potatoes moving constantly. Keep fat temperature between 275° and 300°F. while potatoes are cooking. Cook 4 to 6 minutes.

4. Remove potatoes with spoon or skimmer and plunge into fat in second pan. They will puff at once and rise to the surface. When the potatoes turn a golden brown, remove and drain on paper towels. Sprinkle with salt. Serve immediately.

CREAMY CHEESE POTATOES

SERVES 6

2¼ pounds potatoes, peeled, sliced
   paper thin
5 tablespoons butter or vegetable
   oil
4 ounces Parmesan cheese, grated
4 ounces Gruyère cheese, grated

3 tablespoons chopped fresh chives
salt and freshly ground black pepper
1¼ cups heavy cream
3 tablespoons chopped fresh
   parsley

METHOD:

1. Preheat oven to 400°F.

2. Soak potatoes for 5 minutes in ice-cold water and drain on paper towels.

3. Grease the bottom and sides of a 12- by 10-inch casserole well with the butter or oil.

4. Arrange the potatoes in a layer in the casserole, then sprinkle with the grated cheeses and chopped chives mixed together, and dust with salt and pepper. Repeat the layers until all the potatoes are used up, topping with the cheese-chive mixture.

5. Pour cream over the potatoes.

6. Bake the potatoes until tender and golden brown on top, about 45 minutes. Sprinkle with chopped parsley and serve.

MOUSSELINE POTATOES

SERVES 12

6 pounds potatoes, preferably
   Idaho
¾ cup (1½ sticks) butter, melted
12 egg yolks

1 cup heavy cream
¼ teaspoon grated nutmeg
salt and freshly ground black pepper
6 egg whites

METHOD:

1. Preheat oven to 400°F.

2. Boil potatoes in water to cover until soft; drain, peel and mash until smooth. Beat in half the melted butter then lightly beaten egg yolks. Beat in enough cream to make the mixture smooth and fluffy, but still thick enough to hold its shape. Season with nutmeg, salt and pepper.

3. Beat egg whites until stiff, but not dry, and fold into potato mixture.

4. Mound mixture into 12 buttered baking dishes, brush tops with the remaining butter and bake about 10 minutes, or until the tops are well browned.

POTATO PUFFS

SERVES 8

2 pounds cooked, then mashed,
potatoes, preferably Idaho
(makes about 4 cups)
2 tablespoons all-purpose flour
2 eggs, beaten
1 garlic clove

2 teaspoons chopped chives
salt and freshly ground black pepper
2 cups grated Cheddar cheese
sweet paprika
1 tablespoon melted butter

METHOD:

1. Preheat oven to 325°F.

2. Add rest of ingredients, except paprika and melted butter, to mashed potatoes and blend well.

3. Using a tablespoon, drop the batter in small puffy mounds on a well-greased cookie sheet.

4. Dust lightly with paprika. Bake for about 11 minutes. Then place under broiler to brown for 1 minute, careful not to let them burn.

5. Spoon melted butter over tops. Serve hot.

BAKED POTATOES TOPPED WITH CREAMED LEEKS

SERVES 6

6 large baking potatoes, scrubbed,
rubbed with peanut oil, pierced
with a fork
12 medium leeks, white part only,
washed (trim and reserve 1½
inch of each tender green top
for garnish)
2 cups hot chicken or vegetable
broth

1½ cups (¾ pint) heavy cream
2 egg yolks, lightly beaten
salt and cayenne
6 tablespoons butter
⅔ cup grated Parmesan cheese
(optional)
paprika
½ cup chopped leek tops for
garnish

METHOD:

1. Preheat oven to 375°F. Bake potatoes until done, about 1 hour.

2. While the potatoes are baking, cut white parts of leeks in 1½-inch pieces and place in a shallow, heavy-bottomed pot. Pour broth over. Cover and cook until tender, approximately 15 minutes.

3. Remove leeks with slotted spoon. Reduce pan liquid to ½ cup, add ⅔ cup heavy cream, and bring to just below boiling—but do not let it boil. Season with salt and cayenne. Remove from heat.

4. Beat egg yolks into the remaining cream. Add a tablespoonful of the hot sauce to cream-yolk mixture, then beat cream-yolk mixture slowly into the sauce. Reheat, again being careful not to let mixture boil.

5. When the potatoes are done, remove from oven and split each down the center to release steam. When cool enough to handle, scoop out the insides carefully and spoon them into a bowl. Mash potatoes with butter until smooth. Season lightly with salt, refill shells and place on a hot ovenproof platter.

6. To serve, pour sauce over leeks and spoon mixture over potatoes. If cheese is used, sprinkle over tops. Dust potatoes with paprika. Place in oven to heat, sprinkle chopped leek tops over and serve piping hot.

DOUBLE-BAKED POTATOES

SERVES 6

6 *large baking potatoes, scrubbed and pierced with a fork*	2 *tablespoons butter*
2 *eggs, lightly beaten*	1½ *tablespoons finely chopped onion*
3 *tablespoons milk*	1½ *teaspoons crushed dried thyme*
3 *tablespoons grated Parmesan cheese*	⅛ *teaspoon freshly ground black pepper*
	sweet paprika

METHOD:

1. Preheat oven to 425°F.

2. Bake potatoes 45 minutes to 1 hour, or until tender to touch.

3. When ready, cut a thin slice off the top of each baked potato and reserve.

4. Carefully scoop out the pulp from the potatoes and place in a large bowl. Add the eggs, milk, cheese, butter, onion, thyme and pepper.

5. Beat until smooth. Spoon potato mixture into potato shells. Sprin-

kle lightly with paprika. Place on a baking sheet along with the cut tops (they'll be nutritious and delicious crunchy chips in about 15 minutes).

6. Return the filled potatoes to the oven and continue to bake for 30 minutes at 350°F. or until thoroughly heated.

BAKED CREAMED POTATOES

SERVES 6

6 *large baking potatoes*
¾ *cup (1½ sticks) butter*
salt and freshly ground black pepper
1 *cup heavy cream*

⅔ *cup grated Parmesan cheese*
⅔ *cup finely minced scallions*
3 *egg whites*
1 *cup grated Gruyère cheese*

METHOD:

1. Preheat oven to 375°F.

2. Wash and scrub the potatoes well. Make a slit in the tops of the potatoes for the steam to escape and bake for 1 hour, or until tender to touch.

3. Remove potatoes, cut in half and scoop pulp into large bowl. Mash with a potato masher or electric hand beater.

4. Add half the butter in small amounts, beating well with each addition to blend until smooth. Add the cream, the Parmesan cheese and the scallions and beat until mixed in.

5. Beat egg whites until foamy, add to potato mixture and blend well. Put into a greased ovenproof dish, shaping the top and sides with a spatula to make a mound toward the center.

6. Melt the remaining butter in a saucepan. Sprinkle the grated Gruyère over the potatoes and spoon the melted butter on top.

7. Place under a preheated broiler, about 4 inches from heat, for about 5 minutes. Be careful not to let the potatoes burn—just broil until the top acquires a glazed and golden look. Serve hot.

BAKED POTATO-VEGETABLE SQUARES

SERVES 6

6 *large Idaho potatoes, grated*
½ *pound mushrooms, minced*
2 *medium pimentos, minced*

2 *medium green peppers, minced*
salt and freshly ground black pepper
4 *ounces (1 stick) butter, melted*

METHOD:

1. Preheat oven to 325°F.

2. Mix all ingredients together with salt, pepper and melted butter.

3. Spread evenly over bottom of a well-buttered shallow baking pan, smooth top and press down to a flat mass.

4. Place a slightly smaller pan and then a weight over mixture. Bake for 1½ hours and remove from oven.

5. Remove weight and smaller pan, place a plate on top of vegetable mixture and invert onto the plate. Return the mixture to pan (bottom will now be on top), and press down again with smaller pan and weight. Bake until bottom is golden—approximately 45 minutes.

6. To serve, cut into squares.

Note: This dish may be prepared ahead and reheated.

DOUBLE-BAKED SWEET POTATOES

SERVES 8

8 *sweet potatoes, uniform size*
4 *tablespoons butter*
6 *tablespoons cream*

6 *tablespoons Madeira*
pinch of mace

METHOD:

1. Preheat oven to 375°F.

2. Scrub potatoes and remove the stemlike end (or pierce the potatoes with a fork) which will provide a little opening for the steam to escape while baking. Bake for about 1 hour or until tender to touch.

3. Cut potatoes in half lengthwise and scoop the potato pulp into a bowl, leaving a shell.

4. Mash the pulp with a fork or potato masher. Blend in the butter, cream and Madeira. Add salt to taste and a pinch of mace.

5. Fill the potato shells but do not pack down. The filling should come up over the edge just a bit.

6. Place on a baking sheet, and then under a hot broiler until they become a light golden brown and a crust forms.

SWEET POTATO ORANGE PUFF
(SOUTHERN STYLE)

SERVES 6

The flavor of the orange shell gives the sweet potato a most exotic and piquant taste.

3 cups boiled, mashed sweet
  potatoes (see Note)
3 egg yolks, slightly beaten
3 tablespoons melted butter
½ cup milk
1 scant teaspoon salt
a small pinch of freshly ground
  black pepper

2 tablespoons, rum, brandy or
  orange juice (optional)
3 egg whites
2 tablespoons sugar
6 orange shells (3 large oranges
  cut in half, pulp removed and
  reserved for another dish)

METHOD:

1. Preheat oven to 425°F.

2. In a large bowl combine the mashed sweet potatoes with the egg yolks, butter, milk, salt and pepper. Blend well. If you like the flavor of rum or brandy or want a stronger orange taste, add the liquor or orange juice to the potato mixture.

3. Beat one egg white until stiff and fold into potato mixture. Fill the orange shells with this mixture. Then place in a baking dish and bake for 15 minutes.

4. Meanwhile, prepare a meringue: In a mixing bowl, beat the remaining 2 egg whites until stiff. Then add sugar a little at a time, while continuing to beat, until peaks form. Remove orange shells from oven and top each potato-filled shell with a large dollop of meringue. Bake again for 5 minutes or until meringue is lightly browned. (As a substitute for the meringue, a marshmallow can be used for the topping of each puff.) Serve hot.

Note: To prepare the boiled mashed sweet potatoes, cook about 1½ pounds of unpeeled potatoes in boiling water for 25 to 30 minutes; then peel and mash.

DRESSED SPINACH

SERVES 8

4–5 *pounds fresh spinach*
pinch of nutmeg (or to taste)
salt and freshly ground black pepper
  ¼ *cup grated horseradish*

2–4 *tablespoons butter*
  ½ *cup slivered almonds and 3*
    hard-boiled eggs, sieved, for
    garnish

METHOD:

1. Preheat oven to 350°F.

2. Trim off the tough ends of the spinach. Wash in plenty of cold water, changing the water several times, until all the sand and grit is removed.

3. Cook spniach in a covered pot, with only the water that remains on the leaves, for 10 to 15 minutes. (No additional water is necessary as there is enough moisture on the leaves.)

4. Drain the spinach well and chop fine. Place in a bowl, add nutmeg, and season with salt and pepper to taste. Blend in the horseradish.

5. Pack the spinach into a buttered ovenproof dish and set in oven for 5 to 10 minutes.

6. Meanwhile, glaze the almonds for the garnish. Melt butter on low heat, add almonds and toss lightly until well-coated with butter.

7. Remove the spinach from the oven. Garnish the top with the sieved yolks and the glazed slivered almonds.

SEASONED SPINACH

SERVES 6

4 *pounds fresh spinach*
8 *tablespoons (1 stick) butter*
2 *tablespoons chopped onion*
1 *cup chopped sweet red pepper*

1 *teaspoon dried oregano (or to*
  taste)
salt and freshly ground black pepper

METHOD:

1. Trim tough stems off spinach and wash well in cold water, changing the water several times, until all the sand and grit are removed. Place in a skillet or heavy saucepan with only the water that clings to the leaves. Cover and cook for about 10 minutes and drain well.

2. With a sharp knife, chop the spinach into shreds and set aside.

3. In another saucepan melt butter, add onion and sweet pepper and sauté 3 to 5 minutes, until vegetables are just soft.

4. Add the well-drained spinach, oregano, salt and pepper to taste. Blend well and cook until heated thoroughly. Serve hot.

ACORN SQUASH BAKED WITH PINEAPPLE

SERVES 6

3 acorn squash, halved
2 tablespoons dry sherry
2 tablespoons brown sugar
6 tablespoons butter

½ cup crushed pineapple, drained
¼ teaspoon ground nutmeg
1 teaspoon salt

METHOD:

1. Preheat oven to 425°F.

2. Scoop out the squash seeds and fibers and discard. Place squash in greased baking dish.

3. Put 1 teaspoon each of sherry, brown sugar and butter in each squash half.

4. Cover and bake for 30 minutes or until tender.

5. Scoop squash out of shells, leaving wall about ¼ inch thick.

6. Mash squash and combine with remaining 4 tablespoons butter, pineapple, nutmeg and salt, beating well to blend.

7. Spoon back into shells and return to oven to bake for 15 minutes more.

BUTTERFLY SQUASH ON TOMATO RINGS

SERVES 6

6 green butterfly squash (called
   "patty pan" in some areas)
   about 3 inches in diameter
1 quart chicken stock, boiling
3 large, firm, ripe tomatoes, cut
   in half
4 ounces (1 stick) butter

¾ cup soft bread crumbs
3 tablespoons snipped fresh chives
   or chopped parsley
salt, freshly ground black pepper
   and sweet paprika
¼ teaspoon marjoram, crushed

METHOD:

1. Scrub squash, leaving stems on, and place in a heavy-bottomed saucepan. Pour in chicken stock and bring to a high boil. Cover, reduce heat and simmer until tender. Drain, retaining liquid for another dish, if desired.

2. Melt half the butter in a sauté pan and sauté tomatoes 2 to 3 minutes, turning once. Place tomatoes in center of a flat, round serving platter.

3. Melt the remaining butter in sauté pan, add the bread crumbs and toss. Season with salt, pepper, paprika and marjoram while continuing to toss crumbs. Spoon half of the crumb mixture over tomatoes.

4. Remove stems from squash, drain well and place on top of the tomato halves. Sprinkle remaining crumbs over squash. If desired, heat in oven preheated to 350°F. for 10 minutes and run under broiler to brown lightly.

VEGETABLE SPAGHETTI

SERVES 6–8

1 *large spaghetti squash (3–3½ pounds)*
3 *tablespoons olive oil*
1 *cup chopped onion*
1 *garlic clove, chopped*
1 *cup diced celery*
1 *cup chopped green pepper*
1 *small carrot, diced*

1½ *pounds tomatoes, peeled and chopped*
2 *tablespoons tomato paste*
1 *bay leaf*
basil, oregano and freshly ground black pepper to taste
1 *cup chopped zucchini squash*
freshly grated Parmesan cheese

METHOD:

1. Preheat oven to 400°F.

2. Wipe spaghetti squash and pierce with fork to let steam escape. Bake for 1 to 1¼ hours, until just tender to touch. When still warm but cool enough to handle, halve squash, remove seeds and fibers and, using a fork, scrape out the long strands of flesh.

3. Meanwhile, heat olive oil in a skillet or saucepan over moderate heat, and sauté onion and garlic until golden. Add celery, green pepper, carrot, tomatoes, tomato paste, and seasonings; simmer, covered, about 10 minutes.

4. Add zucchini and continue simmering for an additional 15 minutes. If sauce is too watery, cook, uncovered, for a few more minutes.

5. Spoon sauce over spaghetti squash and serve with Parmesan cheese.

BAKED CURRIED TOMATOES

SERVES 6

6 *large ripe tomatoes, skinned*
and stem ends removed
1 *cup tomato sauce*
2 *teaspoons curry powder*
2 *tablespoons currant jelly*

4 *tablespoons sharp Cheddar*
cheese
3 *tablespoons fresh bread crumbs*
crisp-cooked bacon bits (optional)

METHOD:

1. Preheat oven to 400°F.

2. Cut deep, narrow holes in the tomatoes (be careful not to go all the way through). Place the tomatoes in a buttered baking dish.

3. Combine the tomato sauce, curry powder and currant jelly in saucepan. Heat 5 minutes, pour over tomatoes (particularly inside the hollows) and bake 15 minutes.

4. Remove tomatoes from oven. Then turn on broiler.

5. Sprinkle cheese, bread crumbs and bacon (if used) over tomatoes and place under broiler to brown.

HERBED SCALLOPED TOMATOES

SERVES 6

3 *pounds firm ripe tomatoes,*
skinned and sliced 1/4 inch thick
1 *cup minced onions*
2 *cups soft bread cubes*
2 *tablespoons minced fresh*
parsley

1 *teaspoon dried oregano*
8 *tablespoons (1 stick) butter*
1 *cup unflavored yogurt*
(optional)

METHOD:

1. Preheat oven to 350°F.

2. Place a layer of sliced tomatoes on bottom of a heavy, well-buttered casserole.

3. Mix onions, bread cubes and seasonings and sprinkle over to-

matoes. Then make another layer of tomatoes and bread cubes; continue the layers until tomatoes are used up and top with the bread cube mixture.

4. Dot with butter and bake for 20 minutes. Remove from heat and place under broiler to brown top. If using yogurt, heat it in the top part of a double boiler over hot water. Serve at once, on the side, with scalloped tomatoes.

BAKED TOMATOES STUFFED WITH LEEKS

SERVES 6

6 *medium tomatoes*	¾ *cup grated Swiss cheese*
1 *large or 2 small leeks*	6 *tablespoons dry bread crumbs*
4 *tablespoons butter*	3 *teaspoons butter*
salt and freshly ground black pepper	3 *tablespoons chopped parsley*
Tabasco sauce	

METHOD:

1. Preheat oven to 400°F.

2. Grease a shallow baking dish or pan large enough to hold the 6 tomatoes.

3. Wash tomatoes and cut off stem end (not too close). Using a teaspoon, scoop out seeds and pulp and discard. Turn tomatoes upside down on paper towels to drain and place in baking dish.

4. Wash leeks very well and pat dry. Cut away the tough green tips. Lay the leek pieces flat on a cutting board and slice crosswise very fine.

5. Melt the 4 tablespoons butter in sauté pan, add leeks and cook until soft (do not overcook). Season with salt, pepper and Tabasco.

6. Spoon ⅙ of the cooked leeks into each tomato, then a tablespoon of cheese and a tablespoon of bread crumbs over the cheese. Place a half-teaspoon of butter on top of each tomato. Lower oven to 350°F. and bake for 12 minutes.

7. Sprinkle tops with chopped parsley and serve.

BAKED TOMATOES STUFFED WITH RICE

SERVES 12

⅓ *cup plus 1 tablespoon butter*
1½ *cups uncooked white rice*
⅓ *cup chopped onions*
2 *garlic cloves, chopped*
1½ *cans chicken broth (13¾-ounce*
   size)

1½ *cups water*
12 *medium tomatoes*
salt
⅓ *cup chopped fresh mint*
mint sprigs for garnish

METHOD:

1. Melt butter in large skillet and sauté rice, onions, and garlic until rice is golden brown.

2. Add chicken broth and water and bring to a boil. Lower heat and simmer, covered, 25 minutes, or until rice is tender. Remove cover and cook until any remaining liquid is absorbed.

3. Meanwhile, cut a slice from stem end of each tomato. With spoon, scoop out centers and remove seeds. Chop centers coarsely; set aside. Sprinkle inside of each tomato with about ⅛ teaspoon salt and invert them on paper towels to drain.

4. Preheat oven to 350°F.

5. Combine chopped tomato and mint with cooked rice and stuff tomatoes with mixture. Place in shallow, well-buttered baking dish.

6. Bake 15 minutes, or until tomatoes are just tender and hot. Garnish with mint sprigs.

Note: If desired, the tomatoes may be prepared several hours ahead and refrigerated until ready to bake.

PURPLE-TOP TURNIPS WITH CANDIED GINGER ROOT

SERVES 6

The turnip is an ancient vegetable that originated in Western Asia. Like the beet, there are numerous varieties. However, the purple-top and the rutabaga are the most popular. They are cooked in their skins here because boiling the turnips peeled dilutes their goodness and flavor.

12 *small purple-top turnips*
1½ *cups chicken stock*
½ *teaspoon dried crushed rosemary*
salt and freshly ground black pepper

3 *tablespoons butter*
4 *tablespoons chopped candied*
  ginger root

METHOD:

1. Scrub turnips, cut off top end and bottom root. Cook, covered, in chicken stock with the rosemary until just tender and the skins slip off easily—about 5 minutes.

2. Drain, retaining the liquid for other uses, if desired. Remove skins while still warm. Melt the butter, add the turnips and heat. (If preparing the Vegetarian Dinner on page 384, place in a circle around the beets.) Dust lightly with salt and pepper and add a teaspoon of ginger over each turnip to serve.

GLAZED CUBED YELLOW TURNIPS

SERVES 6

The lowly turnip acquires a touch of class when served glazed. This dish goes well with both meats and poultry.

2 *pounds yellow turnips, peeled*
water to cover
salt

2 *tablespoons sugar*
3 *tablespoons butter*

METHOD:

1. Dice turnips into bite-size cubes and place in a saucepan.
2. Cover with water. Add salt, sugar and butter.

3. Cook uncovered about 25 minutes or until tender and water has evaporated. The sugar and butter will form a glaze.

4. If served with poultry, add a little of the pan drippings or sauce from the poultry to heighten the flavor.

A SUPERB VEGETABLE CASSEROLE OF FRESH YAMS, BEETS, LIMAS AND TOMATOES

SERVES 8 AS SIDE DISH OR 4 AS LUNCHEON ENTREE

6 *medium-size young tender beets*
3 *medium yams, approximately*
  1 pound
½ *lemon, seeds removed*
1½ *cups fresh lima beans (butter beans)*
1½ *cups canned tomatoes, or 2 pounds fresh tomatoes, skinned*

1 *tablespoon clover honey*
3 *drops hot pepper sauce*
¾ *teaspoon dried crushed basil, or 2 teaspoons chopped fresh basil*
salt and freshly ground black pepper
8 *tablespoons (1 stick) butter*

METHOD:

1. Preheat oven to 350°F.

2. Boil beets until just tender, about 25 minutes. Skin and slice ¼ inch thick.

3. Pare yams and slice into ½-inch pieces. Squeeze lemon juice over the yams and toss to prevent discoloring. Set aside.

4. Cook lima beans, covered, 5 minutes. When done, drain in colander, run cold water over and shake dry.

5. Push tomatoes through sieve into a saucepan to make 1½ cups.

6. Add honey and seasonings to strained tomatoes and simmer 10 minutes to blend seasonings and turn tomatoes into a sauce.

7. Butter the sides and bottom of a heavy casserole and place a layer of yams first, then a layer of lima beans, a layer of beets and repeat until all vegetables are used, ending with a layer of beets.

8. Add half the butter to the tomato-sauce mixture and pour over the vegetables.

9. Bake for 30 minutes. Check to see if there is any liquid remaining—if so, bake another 10 to 15 minutes. Remove from oven and spread the remaining butter over the entire top. Let stand 10 minutes and serve.

ZUCCHINI GRATIN

SERVES 6

1½ cans (1-pound 2-ounce size)
   whole, peeled Italian plum
   tomatoes
4 tablespoons unsalted butter
2 tablespoons olive oil
2 cups chopped onion
1 pound zucchini
2 garlic cloves, finely minced

½ teaspoon dried basil, crumbled
a pinch of freshly grated nutmeg
salt and freshly ground black pepper
3 eggs
1½ cups ricotta cheese, sieved
1½ cups (1¼ pints) heavy cream
1 cup grated Parmesan cheese

METHOD:

1. Preheat oven to 450°F.

2. Slice tomatoes. Drain in colander or sieve and discard tomato liquid or save for another use.

3. Heat 2 tablespoons butter and the oil in a large skillet over medium heat. When foam subsides, add onion and sauté until soft— about 8 minutes.

4. Trim and rinse zucchini; cut into thin slices—there should be about 3 cups. Heat remaining 2 tablespoons butter in another large skillet and sauté zucchini 5 to 7 minutes and drain well on paper towels.

5. Add garlic to sautéed onion and sauté 2 minutes. Stir in tomatoes, basil, nutmeg, salt and pepper to taste. Cook over medium-high heat, stirring occasionally until moisture evaporates—about 8 minutes.

6. Beat eggs lightly in large bowl with wire whisk. Whisk in ricotta, cream, and Parmesan. Arrange half the zucchini slices in layer on bottom of 9-inch pie plate. Top with tomato mixture, spreading evenly. Arrange remaining zucchini slices over tomato layer. Pour ricotta mixture over all.

7. Bake 10 minutes at 400°F. Reduce heat to 375°F. and continue baking until top is brown and slightly puffed, about 25 minutes longer. Cut into wedges to serve.

ZUCCHINI WITH TOASTED SLICED ALMONDS

SERVES 6

6 *medium zucchini*
3 *tablespoons butter*
3 *tablespoons water*
1 *teaspoon salt*
1 *teaspoon onion juice*

½ *teaspoon sugar*
¼ *cup toasted sliced almonds*
½ *pint sour cream*
sweet paprika

METHOD:

1. Wash zucchini (do not peel) and slice very thin.

2. Melt butter in heavy pan with tight-fitting cover. Toss zucchini in butter, add water, cover and simmer until tender—about 6 minutes.

3. Add salt, onion juice and sugar. Toss until seasonings are blended.

4. Pour into a serving casserole and sprinkle the toasted almonds over. Top with sour cream, dust with paprika and serve.

CHAPTER EIGHT
SALADS, SALAD DRESSINGS AND RELISHES

SALADS AND SALAD DRESSINGS

ARTICHOKE HEARTS WITH FLAMINGO DRESSING

SERVES 6

two 9-ounce packages frozen
    artichoke hearts
2 tablespoons olive oil
2 teaspoons lemon juice

FOR THE FLAMINGO DRESSING:
  2 medium beets, cooked

6 tablespoons sour cream
4 tablespoons mayonnaise,
    preferably homemade

2 hearts of chicory, washed and
  dried

METHOD:

1. Cook artichoke hearts according to directions on package; drain well. Marinate in olive oil and lemon juice; refrigerate until chilled.

2. *Prepare the Flamingo Dressing:* Slice beets and put in blender or food processor with sour cream and mayonnaise. Cover and blend until smooth, about 30 seconds. To make by hand, sieve beets, add sour cream and mayonnaise and mix well. Arrange artichoke hearts on a bed of crisp chicory and serve with a spoonful of Flamingo Dressing in center of each heart.

STUFFED ARTICHOKE PETALS

APPROXIMATELY 40 PETALS

2 large artichokes, washed,
  trimmed and rubbed with ½
  lemon, then cooked, drained
  well
1 cup cooked, mashed beets
8 ounces cream cheese at room
  temperature
1½ tablespoons grated fresh

  horseradish
1 tablespoon fresh lemon juice,
  strained
1 tablespoon French Dressing
  (see below)
salt, freshly ground black pepper
  and cayenne
parsley for garnish

METHOD:

1. Mix beets with cheese and all the seasonings; beat until smooth.

2. Remove petals from the choke and arrange around the outer edge of a large well-chilled platter, leaving a 3-inch circle in the center.

3. Spoon cheese mixture into artichoke petals. Slice artichoke hearts in half, removing the fibrous hairy choke with a spoon. Lay in center of platter and dust lightly with freshly ground pepper. Refrigerate until chilled. Garnish with parsley.

FRENCH DRESSING

MAKES 1 CUP

½ *teaspoon salt*
1 *tablespoon dry mustard*
½ *teaspoon freshly ground black*
  pepper

3 *garlic cloves cut in half*
¼ *cup red wine vinegar*
¾ *cup olive oil (a brand of fine*
  French virgin oil is Old Monk)

METHOD:

1. Blend well half the vinegar with dry ingredients and add garlic.

2. Then add oil and remaining vinegar and mix until homogenized.

Note: Always shake well before serving as the seasonings settle to bottom and vinegar tends to separate from oil. Remove the garlic in the dressing after several hours; if left longer, the garlic flavor will be too intense for most tastes.

ASPARAGUS TIPS, ZUCCHINI, RED PEPPER AND WATERCRESS SALAD, WITH FRENCH DRESSING MADE WITH HORSERADISH

SERVES 12

36 *asparagus tips*
2 or 3 *medium zucchini*
¼ *cup salad oil*
¼ *teaspoon salt*
1½ *teaspoons finely chopped dill*
1 *large red pepper, cut into thin strips*
1 *large bunch watercress, washed and dried*

¼ *cup dry white wine*
¼ *cup wine vinegar*
1½ *teaspoons salt*
1 *teaspoon pepper*
½ *teaspoon sugar*
2 *teaspoons onion juice*
a few drops of Tabasco sauce
3 *tablespoons prepared horse-radish, well drained*
½ *cup vegetable oil*

FOR FRENCH DRESSING WITH
HORSERADISH (makes 1 cup):

METHOD:

1. Try to select asparagus that are about the same size. Wash well, and cut off the tips about 1½ inches long (reserve the rest of asparagus stalk for another use, such as asparagus soup).

2. Place asparagus in vegetable steamer in pot with tight-fitting cover, place and pour in 1 or 2 inches water. Steam for about 10 minutes (test after 8 minutes), just until tender. Remove from heat and let cool.

3. Wash zucchini and lightly pare off some of the skin, leaving stripes of green on the zucchini. Cut the zucchini into very thin rounds and place in large bowl. Add salt to the oil, pour over the zucchini slices and toss lightly until well coated. Sprinkle on dill, add the sweet pepper strips, and toss lightly.

4. Arrange the asparagus tips in clusters around the rim of a salad plate with the watercress sprigs, and then place the zucchini and sweet pepper mixture in the center.

5. *Prepare the French Dressing with Horseradish:* Add all ingredients to screw-top jar, cover and shake well to blend. Chill until quite cold. Shake again before serving.

AVOCADO SUPREME

SERVES 6

3 *cups diced avocado*
2 *tablespoons lemon juice*
2 *cups chopped celery*
4 *teaspoons chopped chives*

½ *cup mayonnaise, preferably homemade*
1 *cup crisply cooked bacon, crumbled*

METHOD:
1. Place avocado in a bowl and sprinkle on lemon juice.
2. Add all other ingredients except bacon, and mix lightly.
3. Serve on lettuce leaves, with bacon crumbs sprinkled on top.

AVOCADO, ENDIVE, MUSHROOM AND TOMATO SALAD

SERVES 12

FOR THE VINAIGRETTE DRESSING (makes 1 cup):
¼ *cup red wine vinegar or lemon juice*
¾ *cup olive oil*
1 *teaspoon Dijon mustard*

salt and freshly ground black pepper

4 *ripe avocados*
4 *Belgian endives*
½ *pint cherry tomatoes*
1 *pound mushrooms, sliced*

METHOD:
1. *Prepare the Vinaigrette Dressing:* Place all ingredients in a screw-top jar or other suitable container, cover and shake well to blend.
2. Peel, pit and cube avocados, and place in a bowl. Toss the avocado cubes gently with ¼ cup of the vinaigrette. Set aside.
3. Trim, core and cut Belgian endives lengthwise. Wash them in a bowl of cold water and then plunge into another bowl of cold water. Drain and dry on paper towels or in lettuce dryer. Place in a shallow dish with ¼ cup vinaigrette and toss lightly. Set aside until ready to serve. Just before serving add the mushrooms to the same dish and toss lightly.
4. Arrange the marinated avocado, endive and mushrooms alternately with the cherry tomatoes on a serving dish and drizzle the remaining vinaigrette over.

GUACAMOLE

SERVES 12 AS APPETIZER OR SALAD

3 *ripe avocados, peeled, seeds removed*
2 *tablespoons fresh lemon juice, strained*
1½ *tablespoons onion juice*
2 *teaspoons salt*
½ *teaspoon white pepper*
½ *teaspoon Tabasco sauce*
3 *tablespoons mayonnaise, preferably homemade*
4 *small, firm ripe tomatoes, skinned, seeds removed, diced into ¼-inch dice*
lettuce cups for 12
watercress for garnish

METHOD:

1. In a bowl, mash avocados (or cut into small cubes if you prefer that texture). Add lemon juice and mix to blend.

2. Combine onion juice, salt, pepper and Tabasco with the mayonnaise and mix into avocado.

3. Add the diced tomatoes and toss in gently. Do not mash them.

4. To serve, spoon onto a platter lined with crisp, dry lettuce cups. Garnish with watercress.

GUACAMOLE-FILLED TOMATOES

SERVES 10

10 *medium tomatoes*
2 *ripe avocados*
2 *tablespoons finely chopped, canned green chili peppers*
2 *tablespoons grated onion*
2 *tablespoons lemon juice*
½ *teaspoon salt*
dash of pepper
about 1½ teaspoons seasoned salt
lettuce leaves
mayonnaise

METHOD:

1. Wash tomatoes. Cut a thin slice across blossom end, core and scoop out pulp, reserving only ⅓ cup of pulp. The rest may be used for another dish. Turn hollowed-out tomatoes upside down on paper towels to drain.

2. Peel avocados, halve crosswise and remove pits. Put in large mix-

ing bowl, along with reserved tomato pulp, chili peppers, onion, lemon juice, salt and pepper. Mash until well combined.

3. Sprinkle insides of tomatoes with a pinch of seasoned salt. Fill with avocado mixture. Refrigerate until well chilled, about 4 hours.

4. Serve on a platter with lettuce leaves, each tomato topped with a little mayonnaise.

JELLIED BEET SALAD

SERVES 6

1 tablespoon unflavored gelatin
¼ cup cold beet juice
½ cup hot beet juice
2 tablespoons sugar
1 teaspoon honey

¼ cup lemon juice
2 cups shredded cooked beets
¾ cup chopped celery
lettuce leaves and parsley for
   garnish

METHOD:

1. Soak gelatin in cold beet juice, then add to hot beet juice and stir until dissolved.

2. Add sugar, honey and lemon juice. Mix well.

3. Mix in shredded beets and celery. Pour into a lightly greased mold. Refrigerate until firm. To serve, wrap a warm, damp towel around the mold and invert onto a large salad plate; garnish with lettuce and/or parsley.

RAW BEET, PEANUT AND TOMATO SALAD

SERVES 6–8

2¼ cups shredded raw beets
2 or 3 shallots, coarsely chopped
3 or 4 tomatoes, seeds removed,
   cut into small cubes
1½ cups chopped roasted peanuts
1 tablespoon lemon juice

5 tablespoons French Dressing
   (p. 237)
salt and freshly ground black pepper
12–16 lettuce leaves
¾ cup mayonnaise, preferably
   homemade

METHOD:

1. Place shredded beets in bowl. Add shallots, tomatoes, peanuts, lemon juice and dressing.

2. Toss lightly to blend. Season with salt and pepper. Place on a bed of lettuce leaves. Serve with the mayonnaise in a small dish in the center of the plate.

RAW BROCCOLI SALAD

SERVES 8

2 bunches fresh, crisp broccoli	½ cup sour cream
salt and freshly ground black pepper	2 teaspoons mustard, preferably
⅔ cup salad oil	Dijon
3 tablespoons fresh lemon juice	1 cup heavy cream
4 ripe tomatoes, cut into quarters	lettuce leaves

METHOD:

1. Wash broccoli, trim off the leaves and an inch or so from the bottom of stalks. Discard these. Peel the tough outer skin from the remaining stalks with a sharp knife. Cut off the flowerets from the tops of the stalks. Slice peeled stalks into thin rounds—about ⅛ inch thick.

2. Sprinkle the broccoli flowerets and sliced stalks with salt and pepper, add oil and lemon juice, toss, and let marinate for 15 minutes or more. Add tomatoes and toss lightly to mix.

3. In a bowl, blend the sour cream, mustard and cream together. Pour over the broccoli and toss gently until well coated.

4. Serve on lettuce leaves.

RED CABBAGE SALAD

SERVES 6

1 medium head red cabbage, shredded	1 tablespoon honey
1 apple, peeled, cored and cut into small cubes	1 teaspoon sugar
	salt and freshly ground black pepper
1 medium onion, chopped fine	3–4 tablespoons mayonnaise,
1 garlic clove, crushed	preferably homemade
1½ tablespoons vinegar	lettuce leaves or parsley for garnish

METHOD:

1. In a large, deep mixing bowl, place shredded cabbage, apple and onion.

2. In a small bowl, place crushed garlic, vinegar, honey, sugar, salt and pepper. Mix well and pour over cabbage mixture. Mix with a fork until all ingredients are well blended.

3. Add mayonnaise and blend in until all the cabbage is well coated. Correct seasoning to your taste with sugar, salt and pepper.

4. Place in center of salad bowl and surround with fresh crisp lettuce leaves or parsley.

CAULIFLOWER SALAD

SERVES 8

4 pounds cauliflower (about 2
   medium heads), outer green
   leaves and tough skin removed
½ teaspoon salt
¼ cup lemon juice, strained
1 cup vegetable or olive oil

2 tablespoons chopped onion
2 garlic cloves, mashed
1 cup tomato puree
½ cup dry white wine
2 teaspoons honey
salt and freshly ground black pepper

METHOD:

1. Add cauliflower to a large pot of salted boiling water. Cover and steam just long enough to blanch califlower—about 5 minutes. Do not overcook; the cauliflower should remain crisp.

2. Drain and separate into flowerets. Sprinkle with lemon juice.

3. In another saucepan, heat 1 tablespoon of oil and sauté onions slightly. Remove from heat. Add garlic, tomato puree, wine, honey and remaining oil. Blend well and add salt and pepper to taste.

4. Add cauliflower and toss until well coated.

5. Refrigerate and serve cold.

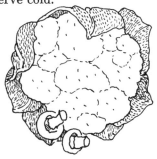

CELERY ROOT VINAIGRETTE TOPPED WITH ROASTED GARLIC CLOVES

SERVES 6

3 *large or 6 small celery roots*
  (*celeriac*)
boiling water to cover
  1 *small onion stuck with 2 cloves*
  2 *garlic cloves, crushed*
  ½ *lemon, cut in slices*

1 *cup Vinaigrette Dressing*
  (*see Avocado Endive Salad,*
  page 239)

FOR THE ROASTED GARLIC CLOVES:
  3 *heads garlic*
  3 *tablespoons vegetable oil or*
  butter
freshly ground black pepper

METHOD:

1. Scrub celery roots with a stiff brush. Trim off all spots and stems. Place in a pot, cover with boiling water and add the onion stuck with the 2 cloves, garlic and lemon. Bring to a brisk boil. Boil gently, covered, until just *crunchy* tender—about 20 minutes. Drain, cool slightly until roots can be handled. Remove outer peel. Slice large roots into 6 slices each and small ones into 4.

2. While roots are still warm, pour vinaigrette over them, toss to coat, and marinate several hours in refrigerator.

3. *Prepare the Roasted Garlic Cloves:* Preheat the oven to 350°F. Remove the outer skin from the heads of garlic. Pull cloves apart slightly but let them remain on the stems. Set each head of garlic clove on a separate square of heavy-duty foil. Spoon 1 tablespoon oil or butter over cloves in each package and grate fresh black pepper over them. Bring corners of foil up over top and fold to seal in. Place in oven and roast 45 minutes. Let cool 10 minutes before serving over chilled celery root.

COLE SLAW WITH SOUR CREAM DRESSING

SERVES 8

Vary your cole slaw with this fabulous Southern dressing. The follow-ing easy-to-make basic dressing will keep for several weeks, so double or triple the amount if you'll be using it later in other dishes.

FOR THE SOUR CREAM DRESSING
  (makes about 4 cups):
  1 *cup apple cider vinegar*
  1 *tablespoon salt*
  1 *tablespoon dry mustard*
  4½ *tablespoons sugar*
  3 *cups sour cream*

2 *pounds (approximately 6 cups) cabbage, outer leaves removed, finely shredded*
lettuce leaves
  2 *or 3 sweet red peppers, halved, with ribs, stems and seeds removed, for garnish*

METHOD:

1. *Prepare the Sour Cream Dressing:* Put first 4 ingredients in screw-top jar or other suitable container, cover and shake until well blended.

2. Put sour cream in a bowl, pour vinegar mixture in and blend well. Add cabbage and toss until well coated with dressing.

3. Prepare the roasted sweet red peppers: Preheat oven to 400°F. Cover a baking pan with foil and lay the pepper halves in the pan, cut side down. Cover with another layer of foil. Roast for 20 to 30 minutes, until the skins will slip off easily and the peppers are soft. Remove from the oven, peel or rub off the skins and cut peppers into ½-inch-wide squares.

4. Place cole slaw on a bed of crisp leaves of lettuce and decorate top with squares of roasted sweet red pepper.

CAESAR SALAD

SERVES 6

1 garlic clove
½ cup olive oil
1 head romaine lettuce
1 small bunch curly endive
  (chicory)
1 cup croutons
one 2-ounce can oil-packed anchovy
  fillets, drained, rinsed, patted
  dry, cut into pieces

3 or 4 tomatoes, diced
1 egg, beaten
1 tablespoon Worcestershire sauce
¼ cup lemon juice
½ teaspoon freshly ground black
  pepper
½ teaspoon salt
½ cup grated Parmesan cheese

METHOD:

1. Mash garlic clove with fork and add to oil in a bowl or jar. Wash lettuce and endive in cold water and dry thoroughly. Tear these greens into bite-size pieces and place in large wooden salad bowl.

2. Add croutons, anchovies and tomatoes to the bowl. Strain oil to remove garlic and pour over salad.

3. Combine remaining ingredients in a bowl; beat well. Pour over salad, toss lightly and serve.

CHEF'S SALAD BOWL

SERVES 8

1–2 medium heads lettuce (Boston,
  romaine or leaf)
2 cups shredded cabbage
6 radish roses
1½ pounds Virginia ham, julienned
1¼ pounds Swiss cheese, julienned
4 large tomatoes, peeled, cut in
  wedges

1 cucumber, thinly sliced
1 cup Garlic Cheese Croutons
  (page 251)
1 bunch watercress, trimmed,
  washed and dried
French Dressing (page 237)
French bread

METHOD:

1. Wash and dry all salad greens, tear into bite-sized pieces and add cabbage and radish roses.

2. Toss together. Place in one large salad bowl or 8 individual bowls. Arrange julienned ham and cheese on top.

3. Add tomato wedges and cucumber slices. Sprinkle on the croutons.
4. Garnish sides of bowl with watercress.
5. Serve wth French Dressing and French bread.

PEPPERED SLICED RINGS OF CRUNCHY CUCUMBER AND ZUCCHINI

SERVES 6

1 *long, thin cucumber (preferably seedless English or Burpless varieties)*
2 *small tender zucchini*

freshly ground black pepper
salt
6 *cherry tomatoes for garnish*

METHOD:

1. Wash cucumber carefully to remove wax, if any. Dry and score down its length with a fork. Slice paper thin and place in bowl.
2. Scrub the zucchini, dry well and slice paper thin. Place in bowl with cucumber slices.
3. Dust generously with pepper and add a few grains of salt, tossing well.
4. Serve in 6 individual bowls; garnish each with a cherry tomato.

CUCUMBER AND ONION SALAD WITH HORSERADISH CREAM DRESSING

SERVES 8

3 *medium cucumbers*
salt
2 *medium red onions*
½ *head Boston lettuce*
1 *tablespoon chopped fresh parsley*
¾ *cup grated Swiss cheese*
¼ *cup sesame seeds*

FOR THE HORSERADISH CREAM DRESSING (makes approximately 1½ cups):

2 *tablespoons prepared horse-radish, or 1 tablespoon grated fresh horseradish*
⅔ *cup heavy cream, whipped*
¾ *teaspoon salt*
2 *teaspoons finely granulated sugar*
1 *cup mayonnaise, preferably homemade*
Tabasco and Worcestershire sauce

METHOD:

1. Wash the cucumbers and remove some of the peel in strips, cut cucumbers in half and scoop out all the seeds. Cut each half in 2 lengthwise, then cut into 1-inch cubes. Sprinkle a little salt over the cucumbers and let stand for about 5 minutes. Then place in a large, coarse strainer, and rinse under cold running water. Drain well. Refrigerate for 30 minutes to chill.

2. Peel the red onions, cut into quarters, then into thin slices. Set aside.

3. Wash lettuce leaves and pat dry. Arrange on a flat salad platter or salad bowl.

4. Toss cucumber, onions and parsley together lightly and place in the center of the lettuce bed. Mix grated cheese and sesame seeds together and sprinkle over salad.

5. *Prepare the Horseradish Cream Dressing:* Fold the horseradish into the cream, add salt and sugar and fold in the mayonnaise. Season with Tabasco and Worcestershire sauce to taste. Serve the salad with the dressing on the side.

Note: This tangy horseradish dressing is also delicious on a watercress and tomato salad.

ENDIVE AND HEART OF ROMAINE SALAD WITH MANGO WEDGES AND CHEDDAR CHEESE FINGERS WITH RED WINE DRESSING

SERVES 6

3 *tablespoons sugar*
1 *quart ice water*
6 *large heads Belgian endive,*
   outer leaves removed if
   discolored
1 *large head romaine lettuce,*
   washed and drained
2 *large ripe mangos, peeled, cut*
   in large wedges
½ *pound Vermont or other aged*

Cheddar cheese, cut into 3-by-
½-inch fingers
watercress for garnish

FOR THE RED WINE DRESSING
   (makes 1 cup):
1 *teaspoon salt*
½ *teaspoon dry mustard*
¼ *teaspoon pepper*
⅓ *cup good red wine*
⅔ *cup olive or vegetable oil*

METHOD:

1. Stir sugar into ice water until dissolved. Place endive in water and refrigerate 2 hours (this removes any bitterness). Drain, rinse with cold water and dry well with paper towels. Cut off bases and separate spears.

2. Remove the outer leaves from the romaine (reserve them for another dish if desired). When ready to serve, arrange the romaine in a circle on a large, chilled salad platter. Lay spears of endive over the romaine leaves.

3. Pile the mango wedges in the center of the platter and arrange the cheese fingers around the outside. Garnish with watercress.

4. *Prepare the Red Wine Dressing:* Blend salt, mustard and pepper with wine. Very slowly beat in the oil, continuing to beat until creamy. Serve the dressing separately.

Note: For a variation, try this Sour Cream Dressing. Mix together ½ cup sugar, 2 teaspoons salt, ½ teaspoon freshly ground black pepper, ½ teaspoon celery salt, 2 teaspoons dry mustard, 1 teaspoon sweet paprika. Stir in 4 tablespoons each of lemon juice and vinegar. Blend in 2 cups (1 pint) of sour cream. If desired, beat 4 egg yolks until thick and fold into the sour cream mixture. Serve separately with the salad.

ENDIVE AND ROMAINE SALAD
WITH KIWI DRESSING

SERVES 2

2 *Belgian endives*
2 *teaspoons sugar*
2 *cups ice water*
6–8 *leaves romaine lettuce*
½ *cup sliced sweet pickle*

FOR THE KIWI DRESSING
  (makes about 1 cup):
  2 *kiwis, peeled and sliced*

3 *tablespoons lemon or lime juice*
¼ *cup dry white wine*
a pinch of salt
½ *teaspoon dry mustard*
1 *tablespoon chopped preserved ginger*
2 *tablespoons ginger syrup (from preserved ginger)*
½ *cup vegetable or safflower oil*

METHOD:

1. Wash the endives and remove any discolored leaves. Dissolve sugar in ice water in a bowl and add the endives. Let stand about 2 hours in refrigerator.

2. Drain endives and rinse in fresh cold water. Cut off the base and separate the spears carefully. Pat dry.

3. Wash romaine leaves, pat dry and arrange on a platter with endive leaves and sweet pickle slices.

4. *Prepare the Kiwi Dressing:* Put all ingredients into a blender container and puree until smooth, then force through a strainer. Serve with the salad.

Note: This dressing can also be used on a fresh fruit salad.

ENDIVE, HEART OF ROMAINE AND WATERCRESS SALAD WITH RED WINE DRESSING

SERVES 10–12

2 tablespoons sugar
3 cups ice water
6 heads Belgian endive, discolored
    outer leaves removed

1 head romaine lettuce
1 bunch watercress, tough stems
    removed
Red Wine Dressing (page 248)

METHOD:

1. Combine sugar and ice water. Place endives in sugar water and refrigerate at least 2 hours. Place in colander, rinse in cold water and drain well. Cut off bases and open spears. Dry with paper towels.

2. Remove outer leaves from the romaine and save for another salad. Wash the heart of the romaine and drain well. Arrange the heart leaves on a chilled salad platter. Then arrange endive spears around and over the romaine and the sprigs of watercress around the outside of the platter. Serve with Red Wine Dressing.

STUFFED ENDIVE SALAD

SERVES 6

2 tablespoons sugar
3 cups ice water
6 heads Belgian endive, bases cut
    off, separated into spears
4 ounces cream cheese, room

temperature
12 pitted black olives, chopped
2 teaspoons lemon juice
hot sauce to taste

METHOD:

1. Dissolve sugar in ice water and soak endives in it for 30 minutes, rinse off, drain and dry well. Set aside.

2. Blend olives into cream cheese. Add lemon juice and hot sauce.

3. Stuff into endive leaves and serve.

ESCAROLE SALAD WITH RUSSIAN DRESSING AND GARLIC CHEESE CROUTONS

SERVES 6

1 *large or 2 small heads escarole*

FOR THE GARLIC CHEESE CROUTONS:
1½ *cups bread cubes*
3 *tablespoons melted butter*
½ *teaspoon garlic powder*
¼ *cup grated Parmesan cheese*

FOR THE RUSSIAN DRESSING
(makes about 1½ cups):
1 *tablespoon minced celery*
1 *tablespoon minced green pepper*
1 *tablespoon minced pimento*
½ *cup chili sauce*
1 *cup mayonnaise*
1 *teaspoon onion juice*

METHOD:

1. Trim base away from the escarole and discard the tougher outer leaves. Separate the rest of the leaves and wash them well in a bowl of cold water, plunging them down several times. Transfer to another bowl of cold water and repeat process, or wash under cold running water, until all dirt and sand are removed. Dry thoroughly. Tear into convenient pieces and place in a large bowl.

2. *Prepare the Garlic Cheese Croutons:* Preheat oven to 375°F. Toss bread cubes in butter. Add garlic powder and cheese. Toast on a baking sheet or pan in oven until a light golden brown.

3. *Prepare the Russian Dressing:* Blend all ingredients together and refrigerate until ready to use.

4. Pour the Russian Dressing over the escarole and toss to coat leaves. Scatter croutons on top and serve. (If you prefer, serve the dressing separately.)

GREEN SALAD WITH FRESH HERB DRESSING

SERVES 6

FOR THE FRESH HERB DRESSING:
½ cup salad oil, preferably olive
¼ cup tarragon vinegar
1 tablespoon snipped chives
1 tablespoon snipped fresh dill, or
   1 teaspoon dried dill weed
½ garlic clove, crushed
1 teaspoon sugar
1 teaspoon salt

dash freshly ground black pepper

1 small head Boston lettuce,
   washed, dried and chilled
2 Belgian endives, discolored
   outer leaves removed, washed,
   dried and chilled
2 tablespoons chopped fresh
   parsley
6 sprigs watercress for garnish

METHOD:

1. *Prepare the Fresh Herb Dressing:* In a jar with tight-fitting lid combine oil, vinegar, chives, dill, garlic, sugar, salt and pepper. Shake well. Refrigerate until well chilled—at least 1 hour.

2. Tear the lettuce leaves and endives into bite-size pieces and place in a salad bowl. Add parsley.

3. Shake dressing vigorously; pour over salad. Toss until greens are well coated. Garnish with watercress.

LETTUCE AND WATERCRESS WITH SPICY SALAD DRESSING

SERVES 6

1 large or 2 small heads lettuce
   (romaine, Boston, Bibb or a
   combination)
1 bunch watercress, tough stems
   removed

FOR THE SPICY SALAD DRESSING
   (makes 2 cups):
1 teaspoon anchovy paste or

3 chopped canned anchovy
   fillets
2 tablespoons tarragon vinegar
1 cup mayonnaise, preferably
   homemade
1 cup chili sauce
½ tablespoon Tabasco sauce
2 tablespoons Worcestershire
   sauce

METHOD:

1. Wash and dry the lettuce and watercress.

2. *Prepare the Spicy Salad Dressing:* Mix vinegar and anchovy paste or anchovies together, then add all other ingredients and mix well. Keep in refrigerator in covered jar until needed. Stir or shake well before serving.

3. Pour desired amount of dressing over lettuce and watercress, toss until the leaves are coated, and serve.

TOSSED SALAD WITH ROQUEFORT DRESSING

SERVES 8

2 *large or 3 medium heads lettuce*
   (*romaine, Boston, Bibb or a*
   combination)

FOR THE ROQUEFORT DRESSING
   (makes 1 cup):
½ *cup olive oil*
2 *tablespoons white wine vinegar*
2 *tablespoons lemon juice*
salt, if necessary

½ *teaspoon celery seed*
⅛ *teaspoon freshly ground black*
   pepper
½ *teaspoon sugar*
½ *teaspoon sweet paprika*
⅓ *cup crumbled Roquefort cheese*

2 *medium tomatoes, cut in*
   wedges

METHOD:

1. Trim the lettuce, wash carefully and pat dry. Place in a salad bowl.

2. *Prepare the Roquefort Dressing:* Combine all ingredients in jar with tight-fitting lid. Shake vigorously to combine. Refrigerate until ready to use. Shake dressing again before using.

3. Pour the dressing over lettuce and toss gently until leaves are coated. Serve in bowls or plates and arrange tomatoes around the outside.

Note: For Tossed Salad with Shredded Beets, use the same amount of lettuce and substitute about 2 cups of cooked shredded beets for the tomatoes.

HEARTS OF ROMAINE WITH PICKWICK CAFÉ ROQUEFORT CHEESE DRESSING

SERVES 6

3 *heads romaine*

FOR THE PICKWICK CAFÉ ROQUEFORT
  CHEESE DRESSING (makes 2
  cups):
½ *pound imported Roquefort
  cheese or blue cheese*
1 *cup mayonnaise, preferably
  homemade*

1 *cup French Dressing (page
  237)*
2 *tablespoons Worcestershire
  sauce*
2 *tablespoons white or wine
  vinegar*
salt, if needed
cayenne pepper

METHOD:

1. Remove the outer leaves from the romaine and save for another use. Wash the hearts, cut them in half and dry thoroughly.

2. *Prepare the Pickwick Café Roquefort Cheese Dressing:* Mash the cheese with a fork in a bowl. Add mayonnaise slowly, beating to make a stiff paste. Add other ingredients, and salt only if necessary. Add a dash of cayenne. The mixture should be thick; if a few lumps of cheese remain, it's all right.

3. Arrange the hearts of romaine on separate plates and spoon over them about 1 cup of the dressing, serving the extra dressing on the side.

CREOLE POTATO AND SHRIMP SALAD

SERVES 8

1½ *pounds potatoes, not too large,
  well scrubbed*
2 *tablespoons grated onion*
2 *tablespoons minced green
  pepper*
2 *tablespoons chili sauce, strained*
¼ *cup apple cider vinegar*
2 *tablespoons salad oil*
1 *teaspoon hot mustard, such as
  Creole*

1 *cup mayonnaise, preferably
  homemade*
*salt, freshly ground black pepper,
  cayenne*
1½ *pounds cooked shrimp, shelled
  and deveined*
lettuce leaves
  2 *hard-boiled eggs, sliced, and
  1 large sweet red pepper, cut
  into ¼-inch strips, for garnish*

METHOD:

1. Cook potatoes with skins on in boiling water to cover until tender—about 20 to 30 minutes depending on size; peel and cube while warm. Place in a bowl. Add onion, green pepper, chili sauce, vinegar and oil; let stand 30 minutes.

2. Add mustard to mayonnaise and stir into the potatoes, tossing to coat. Season with salt, pepper and cayenne to taste.

3. Split shrimp down center and arrange cut side up in bottom of a large round bowl. Spoon potato salad over shrimp, pressing down well. Chill 2 hours. When ready to serve, place lettuce on a large platter, turn shrimps and potato salad out on the lettuce and garnish with egg and sweet red pepper strips.

HOT POTATO SALAD

SERVES 6

1½ *pounds potatoes*
4 *tablespoons chutney or pickle*
   relish
4 *tablespoons heavy cream*
1 *tablespoon white wine or* ¾
   tablespoon apple cider vinegar

½ *teaspoon freshly ground black*
   pepper
salt to taste
6 *dry whole wheat toast squares*

METHOD:

1. Place potatoes in their skins in a pot with boiling water to cover and cook until tender—about 20 to 30 minutes, depending on size. Peel, cut into 1-inch cubes and set aside.

2. Preheat oven to 350°F.

3. Add remaining ingredients to potatoes (except toast), toss together and place in casserole. Heat 6 to 8 minutes. Serve hot with dry whole wheat toast squares.

Note: If very small new potatoes are used for this salad they should be cooked only 15 minutes, then peeled and served whole.

SPRING POTATO SALAD

SERVES 6

2 pounds small new potatoes
½ cup sliced scallions
¼ cup chopped fresh parsley
¼ cup olive oil

2 tablespoons vinegar
¼ teaspoon salt
1 garlic clove, minced

METHOD:

1. Wash potatoes and cook them in their skins in boiling salted water to cover for 15 minutes or until just tender.

2. Peel (or the skin can be left on if you like) and place in a bowl. Add scallions and parsley to potatoes and toss.

3. Combine olive oil and remaining ingredients. Pour over potatoes and toss. Serve warm.

RADISH AND CARROT SALAD WITH LOW CALORIE EGGLESS "MAYONNAISE"

SERVES 12

3 heads iceberg lettuce
12 radishes, sliced
4 carrots, shredded

FOR THE LOW-CALORIE EGGLESS
   "MAYONNAISE" (makes 2 cups):
2 cups low-fat cottage cheese

¼ cup vegetable or safflower oil
2 tablespoons water
2 tablespoons cider vinegar
2 teaspoons dry mustard
1 teaspoon sweet paprika
dash of pepper

METHOD:

1. Wash and dry lettuce; cut into small wedges.

2. Add radish slices and shredded carrot. Toss lightly.

3. *Prepare the Low-Calorie Eggless "Mayonnaise":* Blend all ingredients in a blender to a smooth cream.

4. Serve the salad in salad bowls with the dressing spooned over.

SPINACH SALAD BOWL

SERVES 6

1 *pound young fresh spinach,*
  picked over
1 *garlic clove, slivered*
½ *cup salad oil*
¼ *cup red wine vinegar*
¼ *cup lemon juice*

¼ *teaspoon salt*
dash of freshly ground black pepper
2 *tablespoons grated Parmesan*
  cheese
2 *hard-cooked eggs, chopped*
6 *slices bacon, crisply cooked*

METHOD:

1. Remove stems and wash spinach thoroughly in plenty of cold water until all sand and grit are removed; dry spinach completely. Tear leaves into bite-size pieces. Refrigerate 2 hours. Combine garlic and oil in bowl; let stand 1 hour. Discard garlic.

2. Just before serving, make the dressing: Combine vinegar, lemon juice, salt, pepper and cheese. With portable electric mixer or wire whisk, gradually beat in garlic oil in a thin stream.

3. In a salad bowl, lightly toss spinach with dressing, coating well. Sprinkle egg around the edge, crumble bacon in center and serve.

CRUNCHY VEGETABLE SALAD WITH GINGER WINE DRESSING

SERVES 6

½ *pound tender spinach leaves*
¾ *pound fresh white button*
  mushrooms
1 *tablespoon lemon juice*
½ *pound Jerusalem artichokes*
4 *small Belgian endives, or 1*
  large, discolored outer leaves
  removed
2 *tablespoons sugar*
3 *cups ice water*

FOR THE GINGER WINE DRESSING
  (makes about 1¼ cups):
½ *cup sauterne*
2 *tablespoons ginger syrup from*
  preserved ginger
¼ *cup chopped preserved ginger*
¼ *cup fresh lemon juice*
¼ *cup salad oil, preferably peanut*
salt and freshly ground black pepper

METHOD:

1. Wash spinach thoroughly in several changes of cold water until all sand and grit are removed. Trim off stems, shake dry (or spin in lettuce dryer) and refrigerate.

2. Wash mushrooms in a sieve under running water and pat dry with paper towel. Cut off stems (save for another dish) and slice the mushrooms. Place in well-chilled glass salad bowl, spoon lemon juice over and toss gently to coat.

3. Scrub artichokes with a brush in cold water and dry. Cut into thin slices. Place on a cutting board, shred and then add to mushrooms.

4. Wash endives well, then soak in a mixture of sugar and ice water for 1 hour. Drain and rinse well with cold water. Dry on paper or linen towels. Cut off the bases and then slice in 1-inch pieces. Add to the mushrooms and artichokes. Scatter spinach over vegetables and toss to mix well.

5. *Prepare the Ginger Wine Dressing:* Place wine, ginger syrup, preserved ginger and lemon juice in blender container. Blend on low speed for a few turns, then add oil slowly, beating until creamy. Season with salt and pepper and refrigerate until ready to use. (If there is any dressing left over, it will keep for some time under refrigeration.)

6. Spoon ¼ cup of the dressing over the salad and toss gently to coat. Serve with the remaining dressing on the side.

SPINACH AND APPLE SALAD WITH RICE WINE VINAIGRETTE DRESSING

SERVES 8

1½ *pounds young, tender spinach*
2 *medium-size red Delicious*
  apples
¾ *cup ripe olives*
½ *cup grated Swiss cheese*

FOR THE RICE WINE VINAIGRETTE
  DRESSING (makes 1⅓ cups):
⅓ *cup rice wine*
1 *teaspoon prepared Dijon*
  mustard
1 *cup olive oil*
salt and freshly ground black pepper

METHOD:

1. Wash spinach very well in plenty of cold water until all the sand and grit are removed. Discard tough stems and any blemished leaves. Pat dry. Place in lettuce crisper for a few hours.

2. *Prepare the Rice Wine Vinaigrette Dressing:* In a bowl combine

mustard and wine and blend well. Add the olive oil in a stream, whisking until well combined. Add salt and pepper to taste and whisk again.

3. When ready to serve salad, peel and shred the apples quickly; combine with spinach, olives and grated cheese. Place in a salad bowl, toss with the dressing and serve.

VEGETABLE SALAD BOWL

SERVES 6

2 *tomatoes, sliced*	¼ *cup sliced raw mushrooms*
½ *cup snap beans, cooked*	6–8 *raw broccoli flowerets*
½ *cup lima beans, cooked*	2 *raw carrots, cut in thin strips*
1 *cup French Dressing (p. 237)*	1 *cup radish slices*
½ *cup sliced cucumber*	1 *onion, sliced*
1 *raw zucchini, sliced*	*mixed greens*

METHOD:

1. In a large bowl, combine tomatoes and cooked vegetables. Pour on dressing, toss to coat, and marinate in the refrigerator for at least 4 hours.

2. Drain and save marinade. Arrange the marinated and raw vegetables on mixed greens.

3. To serve, use the marinade as dressing.

MARINATED VEGETABLE SALAD

SERVES 6–8

½ *pound green beans*	¼ *cup finely chopped onion*
2 *medium celeriac (celery root)*	1 *garlic clove, peeled and finely*
2 *medium zucchini*	*chopped*
1 *small eggplant (about 1 pound)*	1 *tablespoon salt*
2 *cups boiling water*	1 *tablespoon mixed pickling spice*
1 *cup white wine vinegar*	6 *whole black peppercorns*
½ *cup olive oil*	¼ *teaspoon dill seed.*

METHOD:

1. Wash green beans and trim ends. Wash celeriac; peel; cut into ½-inch-thick slices, then cut each slice into strips about ½ inch wide. Scrub zucchini with vegetable brush and cut into ¼-inch slices. Wash eggplant but do not peel.

2. Place beans and celeriac in medium-size saucepan. Add the 2 cups boiling water and simmer, covered, for 5 minutes. Drain, reserving cooking water, and set both aside.

3. In another saucepan, combine the 2 cups reserved water used to cook beans and celeriac, the vinegar, olive oil, onion, garlic, salt, pickling spice, peppercorns and dill. Bring to a boil.

4. Cut eggplant into slices ½ inch thick; then quarter each slice. Add to boiling mixture along with zucchini, beans and celeriac, simmer (stirring once or twice) 3 minutes or until vegetables are just tender.

5. Turn into bowl; let cool. Then refrigerate, covered, overnight.

CRUNCHY VEGETABLE SALAD WITH GINGER LIME DRESSING

SERVES 6

3 large Jerusalem artichokes, scrubbed, trimmed well and shredded

2 celery hearts, washed, dried and shredded

2 large apples (Baldwin or Granny Smith), shredded

18 fresh mushrooms (stems removed) washed, dried, thinly sliced

2 tablespoons lemon juice

6 lettuce cups

FOR THE GINGER LIME DRESSING (makes about 1½ cups):

¼ cup candied ginger, shredded

3 tablespoons ginger syrup from jar

juice of 1 large lime, strained

1 large lime, peel on, washed and sliced paper thin

2 tablespoons lemon juice, strained

salt, freshly ground black pepper, hot sauce

¾ cup vegetable or safflower oil

6 very small pickled beets and 18 tender fresh spinach leaves (stems removed), washed and dried, for garnish

METHOD:

1. Gently toss together the artichokes, celery, apples and mushrooms with lemon juice.

2. *Prepare the Ginger Lime Dressing:* Mix together the ginger, syrup, lime juice, lime slices and lemon juice. Let stand at room temperature for 1 hour. Dribble the oil in slowly, beating until creamy thick. Season with salt, pepper and 1 or 2 drops hot sauce to taste.

3. When ready to serve, spoon half the dressing over salad and toss to coat. Fill each lettuce cup with salad and place a beet in center of each, with a spinach leaf (or leaves) sticking up in center of salad.

BLACK WALNUT, APPLE AND WATERCRESS SALAD WITH SESAME-VERMOUTH DRESSING

SERVES 12

6 *large tart apples, peeled, cored and diced*
2 *tablespoons lemon juice*
2 *cups California black walnuts, cut into pieces*
lettuce cups

2 *bunches watercress, trimmed, washed and dried*

FOR THE SESAME-VERMOUTH DRESSING (makes about 2¼ cups):
2 *teaspoons clover honey*
1½ *cups dry vermouth*
6 *ounces (¾ cup) pure cold-pressed sesame oil*

METHOD:

1. In a large bowl, toss apples with lemon juice to coat. Add nuts and mix again.

2. *Prepare the Sesame-Vermouth Dressing:* In a bowl, stir the honey into the vermouth and add oil, beating slowly. While beating oil, add salt and pepper to taste. Beat until blended.

3. Add desired amount of dressing to apple-walnut mixture and toss to coat. (Refrigerate any leftover dressing and use it again for another salad.) Arrange crisp cups of lettuce on a large salad plate and place salad on top in a mound. Place the bunches of watercress leaves in the center and serve.

WATERCRESS-MUSHROOM SALAD

SERVES 8

3 *bunches watercress*
½ *pound mushrooms*
1 *small garlic clove*
⅔ *cup olive oil*
¼ *cup white vinegar*

¼ *teaspoon dry mustard*
1 *teaspoon salt*
½ *teaspoon sugar*
¼ *teaspoon freshly ground black pepper*

METHOD:

1. Trim, wash and dry watercress. Trim stems from mushrooms and wipe caps with damp cloth. Crush garlic and wipe around the inside of bowl.

2. Slice mushroom caps thinly. Combine with watercress in salad bowl.

3. Combine remaining ingredients in screw-top jar or in blender container.

4. Shake or whirl to blend. Just before serving, add dressing to salad and toss to coat lightly.

WATERCRESS, ENDIVE AND BEET SALAD

SERVES 4

4 *medium beets*	2 *garlic cloves, crushed*
salt	4 *tablespoons red wine*
2 *bunches watercress*	4 *tablespoons olive oil*
4 *Belgian endives*	*freshly ground black pepper*
1 *teaspoon salt*	

METHOD:

1. Trim the leafy tops from the beets, leaving about 2 inches of stem on. Do *not* trim the root end. Wash the beets and place them in a saucepan. Add water to cover and salt to taste. Bring to a boil and simmer until tender—about 30 to 40 minutes. Drain. Refrigerate until chilled.

2. Rinse watercress. Cut off and discard stems. Cut endives in half lengthwise and rinse under cold water. Shake the greens dry in a salad basket or lettuce dryer.

3. Pare both ends of beets with a paring knife. Using the fingers, slip off the skins. Cut beets into julienne strips.

4. Add salt to a salad bowl. Rub bowl well with garlic. Add watercress, endives and beets and toss lightly together.

5. Mix the red wine, olive oil, salt and pepper to taste together in a screw-top jar. Shake well, pour over salad and toss to coat.

RELISHES

BEET AND HORSERADISH RELISH

one 16-ounce can beets or 2½ cups
   fresh beets, cooked
1 teaspoon (or to taste) grated
   horseradish, fresh if possible
1 tablespoon minced onion

2 teaspoons salt
⅛ teaspoon freshly ground black
   pepper
½ cup vinegar
about ½ cup canned beet juice

METHOD:

1. Drain beets reserving ½ cup of the juice. If using fresh beets, re-serve the water used to cook the beets.

2. Cut beets into small cubes. Add remaining ingredients and enough beet juice to cover. Mix well and refrigerate overnight.

CALIFORNIA RELISH

1 cup cooked beets, peeled and
   diced
1 cup canned, crushed pineapple,
   drained

¼ cup minced onion
2 tablespoons French Dressing
   (page 237)
lettuce leaves

METHOD:
1. Toss all ingredients together and chill.
2. Serve on top of lettuce leaves.

RADISH AND JERUSALEM ARTICHOKE RELISH

SERVES 6

6 *large red radishes, washed,*
trimmed, thinly sliced
6 *large Jerusalem artichokes,*
scrubbed, trimmed and grated
with peel on
½ *lemon*
salt and freshly ground black pepper

2 *tablespoons peanut or safflower*
oil
2 *tablespoons onion juice*
1 *cup sour cream or plain yogurt*
6 *lettuce cups*
sprigs of fresh parsley for garnish

METHOD:

1. Toss radish slices and shredded artichokes together. Squeeze lemon juice over and season lightly with salt and pepper. Add oil and toss to coat vegetables.

2. Stir onion juice into sour cream or yogurt; pour over vegetables, tossing to coat well. Refrigerate until chilled.

3. To serve, spoon relish into the lettuce cups. Garnish each with a sprig of fresh parsley.

TOMATO RELISH

MAKES 2 CUPS

1½ *pounds (about 3 or 4 large)*
tomatoes
1½ *small green peppers, minced*
1 *cup diced celery*
1½ *tablespoons minced onion*

1½ *teaspoons salt (or to taste)*
3 *tablespoons granulated sugar*
3½ *tablespoons red wine vinegar*
1 *cup cold water*
lettuce leaves

METHOD:

1. Remove stems from tomatoes and cut crosses at base. Put the tomatoes in boiling water for 30 seconds, drain and cool. Peel off the skin. Halve each tomato perpendicularly to stem end. Gently squeeze each half to remove seeds; cut into ½-inch cubes and place in bowl.

2. Add remaining ingredients except lettuce and toss gently. Refrigerate until well chilled; drain.

3. Spoon onto lettuce leaves and serve.

TURNIP-RADISH RELISH

MAKES 2½ CUPS

2 cups raw white turnips, pared
  and grated
½ cup sliced radishes
4 tablespoons sour cream

½ teaspoon salt or to taste
dash of freshly ground black pepper
2 tablespoons French Dressing
  (page 237)

METHOD:
1. Combine all ingredients and mix well together.
2. Refrigerate until ready for use.

CHAPTER NINE

BREADS, QUICK BREADS AND PANCAKES

BREADS

HERBED BREAD

MAKES 1 LOAF

1 *cake yeast*
¼ *cup warm water*
¾ *cup raw milk, scalded*
2 *tablespoons honey*
1½ *teaspoons salt*
2 *tablespoons soybean oil*

1 *egg, beaten*
½ *teaspoon nutmeg*
1 *teaspoon ground sage*
2 *teaspoons celery seeds*
3–3½ *cups stone ground whole
    wheat flour, unsifted*

METHOD:

1. Soften yeast in warm water. Combine hot milk, honey, salt and soybean oil. Cool to lukewarm.

2. Add yeast and mix well.

3. Add egg, nutmeg, sage, celery seeds and 2 cups of the flour. Beat until smooth.

4. Add more flour, if necessary, to make a moderately soft dough. Knead on a lightly floured surface for about 8 minutes. Place in lightly oiled bowl, turning once to oil surface of dough. Cover and let rise in a warm place (85°F.), free from drafts, until double in bulk (about 1½ hours).

5. Punch down and let dough rise again for about 10 minutes. Shape into a round loaf and place in oiled 9-inch glass pie plate. Cover and let rise again until double in bulk—about 60 minutes. Bake in hot oven (preheated to 400°F.) for 35 minutes or until done.

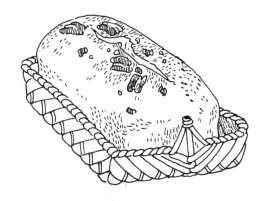

HERBED PARMESAN BREAD

MAKES 2 LOAVES

2 *cups warm water (105°–115°F.)*
2 *packages active dry yeast*
2 *tablespoons sugar*
2 *teaspoons salt*
2 *tablespoons softened butter*

½ *cup plus 1 tablespoon grated*
  Parmesan cheese
1½ *tablespoons dried oregano leaves*
4¼ *cups sifted all-purpose flour*

METHOD:

1. If possible, check temperature of warm water with a thermometer. Sprinkle yeast over water in large bowl of electric mixer, stirring until dissolved.

2. Add sugar, salt, butter, ½ cup cheese, oregano and 3 cups of flour. Beat at low speed until smooth—about 2 minutes. Scrape down the sides of bowl and the beater with rubber scraper.

3. Let rise in a warm place (85°F.) free from drafts for 45 minutes or until quite light and bubbly and more than double in bulk.

4. Preheat oven to 375°F. Lightly grease a 1½–2 quart casserole.

5. With wooden spoon stir down batter. Beat vigorously for 30 seconds—about 25 strokes. Turn into prepared casserole. Sprinkle evenly with 1 tablespoon of cheese.

6. Bake 55 minutes or until nicely browned. Turn out on wire rack. Let cool completely, or serve slightly warm, cut in wedges.

GRILLED MUSTARD HORSERADISH RYE BREAD

SERVES 4

8 *tablespoons (1 stick) butter,*
  slightly softened
1 *garlic clove*
1 *tablespoon prepared mustard*
  (Dijon is good)

1 *tablespoon prepared horseradish*
pinch of salt
1 *loaf (1 pound) round unsliced*
  rye bread

METHOD:

1. Make mustard-horseradish butter by combining all ingredients except bread in a bowl.

2. Cut rye bread into ½-inch-thick slices, being careful not to cut all the way through.

3. Spread butter mixture between bread slices. Wrap loaf in aluminum foil.

4. Prepare a charcoal grill and adjust grill 3 inches from prepared coals. Heat bread on grill 15 minutes, or until heated through.

Note: To cook indoors, bake foil-wrapped bread in a 375°F. oven 20 minutes.

SALLY LUNN BREAD

MAKES 2 RINGS (24 LARGE SLICES)

This is a wonderful light and buttery bread which, although it contains yeast, is not kneaded. Leftover bread is delicious toasted. Refrigerate to store.

¾ cup milk
⅓ cup sugar
1 teaspoon salt
1½ cups (3 sticks) butter
2¼ cups compressed yeast (to substitute dry yeast, use 2 teaspoons for each ⅔-ounce package of compressed)
5 eggs, beaten
2¼ pounds all-purpose flour, sifted

METHOD:

1. Scald milk and add sugar, salt and butter to saucepan. Cool to lukewarm and pour into a large mixing bowl. Crumble in the yeast and stir in the beaten eggs. Add flour and beat thoroughly for 5 to 7 minutes. Cover and let rise in a warm place until double in bulk.

2. Punch down dough and beat for 1 minute more. Place dough in two large Sally Lunn ring molds or two (10-inch) tubular pans. Cover lightly and let rise again in a warm place until double in bulk, about 1 hour.

3. Preheat oven to 450°F.

4. Bake for 1 hour. Serve warm with butter.

SAUSAGE CHEESE SPOON BREAD

SERVES 6

½ pound link sausages
½ quart (2 cups) milk
1 cup uncooked farina
2 teaspoons salt
½ teaspoon dry mustard

¼ pound grated Cheddar cheese
1 onion, grated
3 egg whites
3 egg yolks
1 pimento, chopped, for garnish

METHOD:
1. Preheat oven to 350°F.
2. Sauté sausages lightly. Drain.
3. Scald 1⅓ cups of the milk in a saucepan. Combine farina, salt and mustard, and gradually add to scalded milk, stirring constantly. Blend in cheese and onion. Cook for 5 minutes or until the mixture thickens and the cheese melts. Remove from heat. Cool.
4. Lightly blend in remaining cold milk.
5. Beat egg whites until stiff. Beat egg yolks. Add a little of the warm farina mixture to the egg yolks. Mix well and pour in the rest of the farina, stirring constantly. Fold in stiffly beaten egg whites.
6. Pour into greased baking pan. Lay sausages on top and garnish with chopped pimento.
7. Bake for 40 minutes or until top is puffy and golden brown and the center is firm.

SOUTHERN CORN STICKS

MAKES 24

solid vegetable shortening (to
    grease pans)
2 eggs
2 cups milk
⅔ cup unflavored yogurt or but-
    termilk
3 cups yellow cornmeal

4 teaspoons double-acting baking
    powder
1 teaspoon baking soda
2 teaspoons salt
8 tablespoons (1 stick) butter,
    melted and cooled slightly

METHOD:

1. Grease heavy cast-iron corn stick pans (or other pan—see Note) generously and evenly with the shortening.

2. Beat the eggs until light; beat in milk and yogurt or buttermilk.

3. Mix together thoroughly the cornmeal, baking powder, soda and salt. Stir these dry ingredients by hand into the egg mixture just until moistened. Fold in the melted butter. Let stand ½ hour.

4. Preheat oven to 400°F.

5. Place the greased pans (or pan) in the oven. Heat until sizzling hot and remove from oven. Stir the batter well and spoon it carefully into the indentations of the corn stick pans (if a skillet or other pan is used, smooth the top of the batter).

6. Bake in the lower third of the oven until the sides of the corn sticks come away from the pan and tops are lightly golden, 12 to 15 minutes. If, when pierced with a cake tester, the sticks are baked but the tops still not golden brown, run them under the broiler for a moment until lightly browned. Serve piping hot.

Note: If you do not have corn stick pans, cut the recipe in half and bake the batter in a 10-inch iron skillet or a 9- by 3-inch baking pan, heating the greased pan as directed for the corn stick pans. The top of the bread will be crisper if browned under a broiler briefly after baking. This batter may be frozen, then defrosted in the refrigerator. If, upon defrosting, the batter is too thick, thin it with a little milk.

SPIDER CORN BREAD

MAKES ONE 9- BY 5- BY 3-INCH LOAF

2 *eggs*	¼ *cup sugar*
4 *cups milk*	4 *teaspoons baking powder*
2⅔ *cups cornmeal*	2 *tablespoons butter or other*
⅔ *cup all-purpose flour*	*shortening*

METHOD:

1. Preheat oven to 350°F.

2. Beat the eggs and add the milk.

3. Sift together cornmeal, flour, sugar and baking powder. Add gradually to the egg-and-milk mixture and beat into a smooth batter.

4. Melt the shortening, let cool slightly, then blend into batter.

5. Grease a large loaf pan, pour in the batter and bake for 25 to 30 minutes, or until a knife inserted in the center comes out clean.

ZUCCHINI NUT BREAD

MAKES 2 LOAVES

3 *eggs*
1 *cup vegetable oil*
1½ *cups honey*
2½ *cups whole wheat flour*
¼ *cup wheat germ*
2 *tablespoons baking powder*

1½ *teaspoons cinnamon*
1½ *teaspoons ground nutmeg*
¾ *teaspoon salt*
2½ *cups shredded zucchini or other squash*
1½ *cups walnuts or pecans*

METHOD:

1. Preheat oven to 350°F.

2. Beat eggs well, then beat in oil and honey.

3. Mix together flour, wheat germ, baking powder, cinnamon, nutmeg and salt. Add to egg mixture. Stir until moist, then stir in zucchini and nuts.

4. Pour into 2 well-greased 8½-by-4½-inch loaf pans. Bake for approximately 1 hour.

MUFFINS

BRUNCH BERRY MUFFINS

MAKES 12 MUFFINS

8 *tablespoons (1 stick) butter,*
softened
4 *tablespoons clover honey*
2 *small eggs, lightly beaten*
1 *cup milk*

2½ *teaspoons double-acting baking*
powder
1¾ *cups all-purpose flour, sifted*
pinch of salt
1 *cup fresh blueberries, stems*
removed

METHOD:

1. Preheat oven to 375°F.

2. Combine butter and honey. Beat in eggs, milk, and dry ingredients.

3. Fill standard-size greased muffin tins half full of the batter. Spoon 1 heaping teaspoon berries into the center of each muffin and spoon a little more batter over the berries.

4. Bake 15 to 20 minutes, or until tops are a light golden color. Serve with butter and honey.

DARK BRAN MUFFINS

MAKES ABOUT 18 MUFFINS

2 *cups all-purpose flour*
2 *cups bran*
1 *teaspoon salt*
2 *teaspoons baking soda*

6 *tablespoons butter*
2 *eggs, beaten*
2½ *cups milk*
1 *cup dark molasses*

METHOD:

1. Preheat oven to 375°F.

2. Sift flour, bran, salt and baking soda together.

3. Cream the butter; add eggs, milk and molasses.

4. Combine flour mixture with butter-egg-milk mixture until the dry ingredients are absorbed, but do not overmix.

5. Pour batter into large well-greased muffin tins until ⅔ full and bake for about 20 minutes.

BANANA BRAN MUFFINS

MAKES 12 MUFFINS

1 *cup all-purpose flour*	2 *eggs, well beaten*
½ *teaspoon salt*	2 *cups all-bran*
½ *tablespoon baking soda*	½ *cup buttermilk*
4 *tablespoons butter, softened*	1 *banana, diced*
½ *cup sugar*	

METHOD:

1. Preheat oven to 375°F.

2. Sift the flour, salt and soda together.

3. Cream the butter and sugar, add the eggs, bran and buttermilk.

4. Add the banana and stir into the flour mixture until just mixed. Drop into standard-size greased muffin tins, filling them about ⅔ full, and bake for 20 to 25 minutes.

CORNFLAKE MUFFINS

MAKES 2½ DOZEN MUFFINS

3 *cups cornflake crumbs*	3 *cups all-purpose flour*
3 *cups milk*	½ *teaspoon cinnamon*
¾ *cup sugar*	1½ *teaspoons salt*
¾ *cup butter (1½ sticks)*	2 *teaspoons baking powder*
3 *eggs*	*marmalade, honey, apricot or*
2 *teaspoons vanilla*	*strawberry jam*

METHOD:

1. Preheat oven to 400°F.

2. Place cornflake crumbs in a bowl, pour milk over and let stand until moist, about 15 minutes.

3. Meanwhile, beat sugar and butter together until light and fluffy.

Add eggs, one at a time and beat well after each addition, then add vanilla. Blend in with soaked cornflake mixture.

4. Sift together the flour, cinnamon, salt and baking powder. Then blend into the cornflake mixture.

5. Spoon into standard-size well-greased muffin tins until ⅔ full. Bake 20 to 25 minutes. Serve with marmalade, honey, apricot or strawberry jam.

ORANGE MUFFINS

MAKES ABOUT 18 SMALL MUFFINS

12 *tablespoons (1½ sticks) softened*
   butter
1⅔ *cups sugar*
  3 *eggs, beaten*
  ½ *cup orange juice*
grated rind of 2 oranges

1 *teaspoon vanilla*
2½ *cups all-purpose sifted flour*
  2 *teaspoons baking powder*
  ½ *teaspoon salt*
confectioner's sugar

METHOD:

1. Preheat oven to 375°F.

2. Cream butter and sugar well, then add beaten eggs, orange juice, orange rind and vanilla.

3. Mix flour, baking powder and salt together and add to liquid ingredients. Stir lightly until batter is slightly moist and still lumpy.

4. Grease small muffin tins (1¾ inches in diameter) and dust lightly with flour. Pour batter into each until ⅔ full and bake 15 minutes or until tops are golden. Remove muffins from tins and dust with confectioner's sugar to serve.

RICE MUFFINS

MAKES ABOUT 24 MUFFINS

3 *cups all-purpose flour*
1 *heaping tablespoon baking*
  powder
½ *teaspoon salt*
2½ *cups milk*

2 *teaspoons sugar*
3 *eggs, well beaten*
2 *teaspoons butter, melted*
1 *scant cup cooked rice*

METHOD:

1. Preheat oven to 350°F.

2. Sift the flour with the baking powder and salt, then stir in about half the milk. Next add the sugar and remaining milk, then the well-beaten eggs and melted butter.

3. Add the rice and stir mixture well for about 5 minutes.

4. Butter standard-size muffin tins, fill ⅔ full with batter and bake for 20 to 30 minutes. Test by inserting a knife or skewer. If it comes out clean, they are done.

BISCUITS AND ROLLS

SOUR CREAM BISCUITS WITH SMOKED HAM BUTTER

MAKES 12 (1½-INCH) BISCUITS

1½ cups all-purpose flour
¾ teaspoon baking powder
½ teaspoon salt
¾ cup sour cream
1 small egg

melted butter (for brushing tops)

FOR SMOKED HAM BUTTER:
  8 tablespoons (1 stick) sweet
    butter
  1 cup ground smoked ham

METHOD:
  1. Preheat oven to 400°F.
  2. Sift flour, baking powder and salt together.
  3. Beat sour cream and egg together and stir into flour mixture.
  4. Mix the dough lightly by hand, turn it out onto a floured board, knead lightly for 30 seconds and roll it out about ½ inch thick.
  5. With a small biscuit cutter cut out biscuits. Brush tops with melted butter. Bake them on a lightly buttered baking sheet for about 25 minutes, until golden brown.
  6. *Meanwhile, prepare Smoked Ham Butter:* Soften butter and blend in ham. Split biscuits and fill with ham butter.

HOT POTATO SCONES

MAKES 2½ DOZEN

1½ cups sifted all-purpose flour
1 tablespoon baking powder
½ teaspoon cinnamon
pinch of salt
½ teaspoon grated lemon peel
5 tablespoons butter
1 cup mashed potato, freshly

cooked, then cooled
2 eggs, lightly beaten
2 teaspoons sugar
2 tablespoons milk
  (approximately)
butter
your favorite jam or marmalade

METHOD:

1. Have all ingredients ready, then set the oven at 400°F.

2. Place flour, baking powder, cinnamon and salt in the bowl of an electric mixer. Mix well with a fork and add grated lemon peel and the 5 tablespoons butter.

3. Then turn on mixer and mix at medium speed until all ingredients are incorporated; add mashed potato and blend in well.

4. Beat eggs slightly with sugar and about 2 tablespoons of milk. Add to potato-and-flour mixture, blending everything together at low speed. The dough should be short and biscuit-like; if necessary, add a little more milk to bind it together. With a tablespoon, cut into dough and drop it by spoonfuls on a greased cookie sheet. Gently shape the tops with light pats of the finger so they have a uniform, roundish shape.

5. Turn oven up to 425°F. and bake for about 10 minutes, then reduce heat to 400°F. and bake for another 5 to 10 minutes. Check while baking and don't let scones burn. Serve hot with butter and your favorite jam.

SOUTHERN POTATO BUNS

MAKES 2½ TO 3 DOZEN

3 *medium potatoes, boiled and*
  peeled
¼ *cup vegetable shortening*
8 *tablespoons (1 stick) butter*
2 *tablespoons honey*
2 *teaspoons salt*
2 *cups milk*

1 *egg, beaten*
8 *cups sifted enriched flour*
2 *tablespoons dry yeast*
¼ *cup warm water*
melted butter
1 *egg yolk or egg white, beaten*

METHOD:

1. Mash boiled potatoes until quite smooth.

2. Blend shortening, butter, honey, salt and milk together in a saucepan and bring to a boil. Remove from heat and cool slightly. Add beaten egg and 2 cups of the flour alternately to scalded milk, beating after each addition.

3. Dissolve yeast in ¼ cup warm water, then add to milk-egg-flour mixture. Cover and let rise in a warm place for 30 minutes.

4. Add remaining 6 cups of flour. Knead for 5 minutes. Cover and let rise in a warm place for 1½ to 2 hours, until double in bulk.

5. Roll out dough ½ inch thick. Cut into biscuit-size rounds. Fold over in half and pinch the edges together. Place in a well-greased pan. Brush with melted butter and either egg white or yolk. Let rise 2 hours. Preheat oven to 450°F., then bake for 20 to 30 minutes or until lightly browned.

HOT PUFFS FILLED WITH BUTTER

MAKES APPROXIMATELY 18 PUFFS

2 cups all-purpose flour, sifted
½ teaspoon salt
1 teaspoon melted butter

2 teaspoons dry granular yeast
1 cup warm milk
12 tablespoons (1½ sticks) unsalted butter

METHOD:

1. Mix flour and salt together in a bowl. Stir in the teaspoon of melted butter.

2. Dissolve yeast in ½ cup milk and add to flour mixture. Add the remaining milk and mix to form a dough. Knead lightly on floured board until dough is rounded and smooth.

3. Roll out dough ¼ inch thick and cut with 3-inch biscuit cutter. Lay biscuit rounds on buttered aluminum foil, cover with a towel and let rise until double in size—approximately 30 minutes.

4. Fry biscuits on a lightly buttered hot griddle for 3 to 4 minutes until bottoms are golden brown. Turn and brown the other side. Split and fill with the remaining butter.

WHOLE WHEAT HAM PUFFS

MAKES 1 DOZEN

1 cup warm water
¾ cup whole wheat flour
½ cup wheat germ
2 teaspoons dry yeast (1 envelope)
¼ cup lukewarm water
1 egg, beaten

2 teaspoons honey
1 tablespoon butter
½ teaspoon salt or to taste
¾ cup brown rice flour
6 ounces (approximately) lean,
    cooked country ham, minced

METHOD:

1. Preheat oven to 400°F.

2. Combine the cup of warm water with whole wheat flour and wheat germ, and beat well.

3. Dissolve yeast in the ¼ cup of lukewarm water and add to flour-wheat germ mixture.

4. Mix remaining ingredients, except the ham, and combine with first batter. Pour into greased muffin tins.

5. Place a spoon of the minced ham down into center of each muffin. Bake for 15 to 20 minutes until golden brown.

PANCAKES

OYSTER PANCAKES—EASTERN SHORE

SERVES 6

You can use either of 2 batters for these pancakes. The first is made with Bisquick and will turn out like a puff; the other is a traditional pancake batter, and the result will be much flatter.

BATTER NO. 1
  1 egg, beaten
  ½ cup liquid (oyster liquor from shucked oysters, milk or cream)
  1 cup Bisquick
  1 tablespoon chopped fresh parsley
  1 tablespoon chopped fresh chives
  1 tablespoon chopped shallots
salt and freshly ground black pepper
  1 pint shucked oysters, drained, cut into pieces

BATTER NO. 2
  2 eggs, well beaten
  1 cup milk or ½ cup milk and ½ cup oyster liquor from shucked oysters

  2 cups all-purpose flour
  1½ teaspoons baking powder
  1 tablespoon chopped fresh parsley
  1 tablespoon chopped fresh chives
  1 tablespoon chopped shallots
salt and freshly ground black pepper
  1 pint shucked oysters, drained, cut into pieces

FOR THE TARTAR SAUCE:
  1 cup mayonnaise, preferably homemade
  ¼ cup finely chopped onion
  ½ cup finely chopped sweet pickle
  1 tablespoon chopped fresh parsley
  2 teaspoons lemon juice
salt and freshly ground black pepper

METHOD:

1. Beat eggs very well and add liquid (oyster liquor, milk, cream or half oyster liquor and half milk).

2. Add Bisquick (or flour and baking powder) and mix well.

3. Add all seasonings and oysters and blend well.

4. *Prepare the Tartar Sauce:* Place mayonnaise in a bowl, add other ingredients and blend well.

5. Drop batter by spoonfuls on a lightly greased hot griddle. When bubbles appear on the surface, but before they break, lift the cakes with a spatula to see if they are browned. When they are, turn over and cook about half as long as first side.

6. Serve immediately with Tartar Sauce.

MASHED POTATO PANCAKES

SERVES 6

3 tablespoons vegetable oil or
  butter
3 large onions, chopped
2 eggs

2 cups mashed potatoes
6 tablespoons whole wheat flour
freshly ground black pepper and salt
1½ teaspoons water

METHOD:

1. Preheat oven to 375°F.

2. Heat the oil or butter in a skillet. Add the onions and sauté lightly until soft and golden.

3. Beat the eggs in a bowl (reserve 2 teaspoons for egg wash). Add sautéed onions, mashed potato, flour, salt and pepper.

4. Using your hands, shape dough into 18 pancakes and place on a greased cookie sheet. Add the 1½ teaspoons of water to reserved eggs and brush the top of each pancake.

5. Bake in preheated oven for 20 to 25 minutes or until golden brown.

FLUFFY YOGURT PANCAKES

SERVES 6–8

4 eggs
1 cup unflavored yogurt
½ cup milk
4 tablespoons vegetable oil or
  melted butter
2 cups unbleached all-purpose
  flour

2 tablespoons sugar or honey
2½ tablespoons baking powder
1 teaspoon baking soda
butter
maple syrup, honey or jam

METHOD:

1. Beat eggs in a large bowl. Add yogurt, milk, oil or butter, flour, sugar or honey, baking powder and soda. Blend well but do not overmix.

2. Heat a well-greased griddle until very hot, pour the batter from a large spoon into cakes and cook 2 or 3 minutes. Turn pancakes over just before bubbles break.

3. Place a small pat of butter on each pancake and stack 2 or 3 together. Serve hot with maple syrup, honey or jam.

APPLE PANCAKE

SERVES 2

⅓ cup sifted all-purpose flour
¼ teaspoon salt
1 teaspoon sugar
1 egg, well beaten
⅓ cup milk
2 tablespoons butter

2 apples, pared, cored and sliced
cinnamon, sugar and lemon juice
  to taste
2 tablespoons lingonberries mixed
  with 2 tablespoons raspberry
  juice

METHOD:

1. Preheat oven to 425°F.

2. Combine flour, salt and sugar in a bowl.

3. In another bowl, beat together egg and milk, add flour mixture and beat until smooth.

4. Melt butter in a 10-inch oven-proof frying pan. Sauté apples until soft but not mushy.

5. Pour the pancake batter over the apples.

6. Gently shake the pan over the heat until the pancake is set and brown on the bottom.

7. Sprinkle the top generously with cinnamon and sugar. Set the pan in the hot oven for 10 to 12 minutes until the top browns.

8. When finished, slip pancake onto a warm platter, sprinkle again with cinnamon and sugar, and with lemon juice. Spread with lingonberry-raspberry juice mixture, cut in half and serve.

ONION HUSH PUPPIES

MAKES ABOUT 20

2 cups white cornmeal
⅓ cup all-purpose flour
1 tablespoon plus 2 teaspoons
  baking powder
1 teaspoon salt
pinch of cayenne

3 large eggs, lightly beaten
1 cup buttermilk
⅔ cup minced onion
2 garlic cloves, crushed
vegetable shortening for frying

METHOD:

1. In a large bowl combine cornmeal, flour, salt, baking powder and cayenne and mix well.

2. In another bowl beat eggs and add buttermilk. Add to dry mixture and blend. Add onion and crushed garlic. Mix well and let stand for 20 minutes.

3. In a deep fryer heat 3 inches vegetable oil, and when very hot, fry heaping tablespoons of the batter, 6 at a time, for about 3 minutes, turning them as they brown until all sides are golden brown.

4. Transfer to paper towels with a skimmer.

5. Serve the hush puppies at once on a heated platter.

CORN FRITTERS I

SERVES 8

4 or 5 ears fresh corn (or
  substitute 2 cups frozen corn
  kernels if fresh is unavailable—
  but do not use canned)
2 tablespoons unsalted butter
3 eggs, separated
½ cup heavy cream
1 teaspoon salt

½ teaspoon freshly ground black
  pepper
pinch of cayenne
pinch of mace
1 tablespoon chopped parsley
  (no stems)
1 tablespoon snipped chives
unsalted butter and/or vegetable oil
  for frying, as needed

METHOD:

1. Using a sharp knife, cut the kernels from the ears of corn, without cutting too deeply; then, over a pie pan or bowl, with the back of the knife blade, scrape down the ears again to remove the hearts of the kernels and the "cream" remaining on the cobs. Reserve the corn cream separately. Measure 2 cups of the kernels, including no more than about 3 tablespoons of the corn cream.

2. Melt the butter in a skillet over medium heat until the foam subsides. Sauté the kernels with their cream in the butter for about 3 minutes, stirring. Reserve.

3. In a mixing bowl, whisk together the egg yolks, heavy cream, salt, pepper, cayenne, mace, parsley and chives. Add the sautéed corn kernels, stir, and correct seasonings.

4. Shortly before you are ready to fry the fritters, beat the egg whites to form stiff peaks and fold them gently into the corn mixture using a rubber spatula.

5. Heat a large, heavy skillet until quite hot, then add a small amount of butter or oil. Without removing the skillet from the heat, tilt

it to spread the fat in a thin layer. Spoon the fritter batter into the pan, using about 1½ tablespoons for each fritter; the batter should spread into rounds about 2½ to 3 inches across. Brown the fritters, then flip them gently with a spatula and brown the other side. Remove them to a platter lined with paper towels and keep warm while you cook the rest, adding fat to the pan as needed. Serve the fritters piping hot. You may reheat them briefly in the oven if necessary, but the sooner they are served after cooking, the better.

CORN FRITTERS II

SERVES 6

8 ears fresh corn
⅔ cup fine cracker crumbs
1 teaspoon baking powder
1 teaspoon salt
2 tablespoons sugar

2 eggs
¼–½ cup milk
unsalted butter and/or vegetable oil
for frying

METHOD:

1. Cut and scrape corn off the cobs.

2. Mix the corn together with the cracker crumbs, baking powder, salt, sugar and eggs and blend well. If necessary, add a little milk to make batter less stiff.

3. Heat a heavy skillet until quite hot, then add small amount of butter or oil. Without removing the skillet from the heat, tilt it to spread the fat in a thin layer. Using a tablespoon drop fritters onto the skillet and fry until brown, about 3 minutes. Turn to brown the other side. Drain on paper towels as fritters are done and serve hot.

CHAPTER TEN
DESSERTS

CAKES

ALMOND TORTE

10 *eggs, separated*
1¾ *cups sugar*
¼ *cup dry bread crumbs*
1 *teaspoon lemon rind*
¼ *cup lemon juice, strained*
8 *ounces blanched almonds, very*
finely ground

FOR THE CHOCOLATE BUTTER ICING:
3 *squares (ounces) unsweetened*
chocolate, melted
1 *cup (2 sticks) unsalted butter,*
softened

¼ *cup sliced toasted almonds*

METHOD:

1. Preheat oven to 350°F.

2. Beat the egg whites until stiff and gradually beat in one cup of sugar. Fold in the crumbs, lemon rind and juice, then fold in the ground almonds.

3. Divide the mixture among four 9- or 9½-inch layer pans that are lined on the bottom with parchment paper or unglazed brown paper and then greased. Bake 15 to 20 minutes or until lightly browned. Let cakes cool in the pan for about 5 minutes, then loosen with a metal spatula, remove from pan and place on racks to cool further. Leave until completely cool.

4. *Prepare the Chocolate Butter Icing:* Place the yolks, slightly beaten, and the remaining sugar in top of double boiler. Cook over hot water until sugar dissolves and mixture thickens. Do not allow to boil or it will curdle.

5. Remove top of double boiler from the hot water, beat in the melted chocolate and then gradually beat in the butter. Refrigerate until mixture reaches spreading consistency. Fill and frost the layers with icing.

6. Garnish with sliced almonds. Refrigerate again until firm.

APPLE CAKE

SERVES 8

2 cups sifted all-purpose flour
7 tablespoons sugar
4 teaspoons baking powder
½ teaspoon salt
8 tablespoons (1 stick) unsalted
  butter

1 egg, slightly beaten
½ cup milk
8 cups peeled, thinly sliced apples
¾ teaspoon cinnamon
2 teaspoons grated lemon rind
½–¾ cup apple juice

METHOD:

1. Preheat oven to 350°F.
2. Sift together flour, sugar, baking powder and salt.
3. Cut in pieces of butter until mixture is crumbly.
4. Make a well in center; pour in egg and milk and mix lightly until a smooth dough is formed. Roll or pat dough to fit bottom and sides of a 13-by-9-by-2-inch buttered baking pan or dish. Arrange apple slices on top so that they overlap.
5. Mix remaining sugar, cinnamon and lemon rind together. Sprinkle apples with sugar mixture. Bake for 1 hour, basting occasionally with apple juice. Let cake cool in the pan.

KENTUCKY BOURBON CAKE

MAKES ONE 10-INCH RING
SERVES 12

2 cups (about 1 pound) candied
  red cherries
1½ cups (about 8 ounces) white
  seedless raisins
1 cup Bourbon
1½ cups (3 sticks) unsalted butter
2⅓ cups granulated sugar

2⅓ cups firmly packed brown
  sugar
6 eggs, separated
5 cups sifted cake flour
4 cups (about 1 pound) pecans
2 teaspoons freshly grated nutmeg
1 teaspoon baking powder
Bourbon (for storing cake)

METHOD:

1. Preheat oven to 275°F.
2. Combine cherries, raisins and the cup of Bourbon in a bowl. Cover and let stand overnight. Drain fruit, reserving Bourbon, and set aside.

3. Cream butter and sugar together until light. Add egg yolks and beat well.

4. Combine ½ cup flour and the pecans and set aside. Sift remaining flour, nutmeg and baking powder together. Add flour mixture and reserved Bourbon alternately to butter-and-sugar mixture, beating well after each addition. Beat egg whites until stiff but not dry; fold whites into the mixture. Fold cherries, raisins and pecan-flour mixture into batter. Turn into buttered 10-inch tube pan lined with buttered wax paper. Bake in preheated oven for 3½ hours. Let cake cool in the pan, then remove.

5. Fill center of cake with cheesecloth saturated with Bourbon. This will help keep the cake moist. Wrap in heavy wax paper or foil and store in a tightly covered container. Keep in cool place (in refrigerator, if necessary).

CAROB-ALMOND TORTE WITH BUTTER CREAM FROSTING AND ORANGE ZEST

SERVES 12

This recipe was created to be served after a lecture on flowers and shrubs of Biblical times given by Audrey Jocely at the New York Garden Club. The basic ingredients used are mentioned in the Bible. Carob powder is milled from the pod of the tamarind tree (St. John's bread), and is used here in place of flour.

6 *large eggs, separated*
1 *cup plus 6 tablespoons raw sugar*
¾ *cup milk (plus 2 tablespoons, if necessary)*
1 *cup carob powder*
1 *pound (4 cups, approximately) almond meal or very finely ground almonds (see Note)*
pinch *of salt*
2 *well-buttered 9-inch spring-form pans (see Note)*

FOR THE BUTTER CREAM FROSTING:
1½ *cups light brown sugar*
1½ *tablespoons carob powder*
¾ *cup light cream*
⅓ *pound unsalted butter (at room temperature)*
2 *tablespoons orange liqueur*

FOR THE ORANGE ZEST:
2 *large California oranges*
1 *cup water*
1½ *cups granulated sugar*

METHOD:

1. Preheat oven to 320°F.

2. Beat the egg yolks until thick and pale in color. Add 1 cup raw

sugar and beat until mixture is light and creamy and forms a ribbon when the beater is lifted.

3. Slowly add the ¾ cup milk, beating to blend; set aside until needed.

4. Press the carob powder through a sieve and combine sieved carob with the almond meal or almonds, stirring to mix well.

5. Slowly add carob-almond mixture to egg mixture, beating till thoroughly combined. If the mixture is too thick, add 2 tablespoons milk.

6. Beat egg whites with a pinch of salt until frothy. Then add 6 tablespoons raw sugar, a little at a time, beating constantly until the whites are stiff.

7. Fold whites into batter and divide the mixture between the 2 pans. Bake for 25 minutes, or until firm when pressed in the center with the fingertips.

8. Remove cakes from the oven and cool on a rack (in their pans) for 10 minutes. Run a knife around the edges of the pans and remove the rings. To remove the cakes from the pan bottoms, run a long metal spatula under the cakes to loosen. Let them continue to cool on the racks and then place the layers on plates.

9. *Prepare the Butter Cream Frosting:* In a heavy saucepan, mix the light brown sugar and the carob powder together. Add the light cream and stir well to dissolve lumps. Simmer over a low flame, stirring frequently, until a soft ball forms in cold water. Remove from heat and set pan in a large bowl or basin of cold water. Stir until cool. Then beat in the softened butter and the orange liqueur.

10. *Prepare the Orange Zest:* Wash the oranges and cut the zest (the outer oily peel) from them. Be careful not to include the bitter white pith. Place zest and water in a blender or food processor and grind. Pour into a heavy saucepan and add granulated sugar. Cook slowly, stirring frequently, taking care not to scorch the mixture. Cool before using.

11. Spread half the frosting over the bottom cake layer, then spread on half the orange zest. Place the top layer on, and frost the top and sides of the torte smoothly. Spread remaining orange zest over the top and refrigerate. When cold, cover torte with plastic wrap.

Note: Almond meal can be purchased at health food stores or may be made from whole almonds by finely grinding them in a blender or food processor.

Two 9-inch cake pans can be substituted for the spring-form pans.

With regular cake pans, great care must be taken when removing the layers, as they are quite fragile.

DELIGHTFUL CHOCOLATE CAKE

SERVES 8–12

1 cup unsifted unsweetened cocoa
2 cups boiling water
2¾ cups sifted all-purpose flour
2 teaspoons baking soda
½ teaspoon salt
1 cup unsalted butter (2 sticks), softened
2½ cups granulated sugar
4 eggs
1½ teaspoons vanilla extract

FOR THE CHOCOLATE BUTTER CREAM FROSTING:

one 6-ounce package semisweet chocolate pieces
½ cup light cream
1 cup (2 sticks) unsalted butter
2½ cups unsifted confectioner's sugar

FOR THE WHIPPED CREAM:

1 cup (½ pint) heavy cream, chilled
¼ cup unsifted confectioner's sugar
1 teaspoon vanilla extract

METHOD:

1. In a medium bowl, combine cocoa with boiling water, mixing with wire whisk until smooth. Cool completely. Sift flour with soda, salt, and baking powder and set aside. Preheat oven to 350°F. Butter well and lightly flour three 9-by-1½-inch layer pans.

2. In large bowl of electric mixer, at high speed, beat butter, sugar, eggs and vanilla, scraping bowl occasionally, until mixture is light and creamy—about 5 minutes. At low speed, beat in flour mixture (¼ at a time), alternating with cocoa mixture (⅓ at a time), beginning and ending with flour mixture. Do not overbeat.

3. Divide evenly into pans and smooth the top. Bake 25 to 30 minutes, or until surface springs back when gently pressed with fingertips. Cool in pans for 10 minutes. Carefully loosen sides with spatula; remove from pans and cool on racks.

4. *Prepare the Chocolate Butter Cream Frosting:* In medium saucepan combine chocolate pieces, cream and butter and stir over medium heat until smooth. Remove from heat. In a bowl set over ice, blend in confectioner's sugar with a wire whisk; beat until mixture is thick and holds its shape.

5. *Prepare the Whipped Cream:* Whip cream with sugar and vanilla; refrigerate.

6. To assemble cake: Place 1 layer on a plate, top side down; spread with half of whipped cream filling. Place second layer on top, top side down; spread with rest of whipped cream. Then place third layer top side up.

7. To frost: With spatula, frost sides first, covering them completely; use rest of frosting on top, swirling decoratively. Refrigerate at least 1 hour before serving. To cut, use a thin-edged sharp knife; slice with a sawing motion.

CHOCOLATE ALMOND DREAM CAKE

SERVES 6

The delicate aroma of chocolate will be something for you to remember.

6 *ounces sweet chocolate*
¾ *cup (1½ sticks) unsalted butter*
¾ *cup sugar*
6 *eggs, separated*
6 *ounces blanched almonds,*
   chopped

FOR THE MOCHA FROSTING:

2 *ounces (squares) sweet chocolate*
2 *teaspoons instant coffee powder*
½ *cup heavy cream*

METHOD:

1. Preheat oven to 375°F.

2. Melt chocolate in the top of a double boiler over hot water. Let cool slightly.

3. In a mixing bowl, cream butter, add sugar and beat until light and fluffy. Beat in egg yolks one at a time. Stir in the cooled melted chocolate and beat in the chopped almonds.

4. Beat egg whites until stiff, fold into mixture. Turn into a buttered 9-inch spring-form pan.

5. Bake at 375° for 20 to 25 minutes, then reduce heat to 350° and bake for 20 to 30 minutes longer. Test for doneness by inserting a knife in center of cake. If it comes out clean, the cake is done.

6. Remove from oven, let cool in pan on a rack for 10 minutes, then run a spatula around edge of pan and remove the cake. Wrap in a damp towel and let stand for 15 minutes. Remove cloth and then cover lightly with wax paper. Leave for 24 hours before frosting.

7. *Prepare the Mocha Frosting:* Break chocolate into small pieces, and place with the coffee powder in the top of a double boiler over hot water. Heat until melted and remove from burner. Let cool for a little

while, then stir in the heavy cream slowly, until frothy and thick. Spread the frosting on top and sides of the cake.

MOTHER'S FUDGE CAKE

SERVES 12

This cake is so rich and fudgy that you may find that it doesn't need a frosting. But if you do want one, try the Chocolate Butter Cream Frosting in the Delightful Chocolate Cake recipe on page 292.

4 *ounces semisweet chocolate*
¼ *cup strong coffee*
8 *tablespoons (1 stick) unsalted butter at room temperature*
1 *cup sugar*
6 *egg yolks*
1 *teaspoon vanilla*
2½ *cups almond meal or finely ground almonds (see Note, page 290)*

1 *tablespoon baking powder*
2 *tablespoons dark rum*
6 *egg whites at room temperature*
⅛ *teaspoon salt*
6 *tablespoons fine dry bread crumbs*
one *10-inch spring-form pan, well buttered*

METHOD:

1. Preheat oven to 375°F.

2. Place chocolate and coffee in mixing bowl and set bowl over a basin of hot water to soften chocolate.

3. Add butter, beat well, then add sugar slowly, beating after each addition. Beat in egg yolks one at a time. Add vanilla and continue to beat until well blended.

4. Stir baking powder into almond meal and beat into batter slowly. Add rum, beating to mix in well.

5. Beat egg whites with salt until stiff but not dry. Stir ⅓ the whites into batter, stirring until completely incorporated. Fold in remaining whites and pour into the well-greased spring-form pan. Bake for 45 minutes, or until firm when pressed with fingertips. Cool on rack 30 minutes before removing from pan.

COCONUT AND SWEET CHERRY TORTE WITH BURGUNDY WINE SAUCE

SERVES 8

FOR THE BOTTOM CRUST:
1 *cup all-purpose flour*
¼ *cup sugar*
8 *tablespoons (1 stick) unsalted*
  butter
one 8-inch spring-form pan

FOR THE TOPPING:
2 *eggs*
½ *cup all-purpose flour*
1 *cup sugar*
1 *teaspoon baking powder*

1 *cup shredded coconut*
½ *cup pitted dark sweet (Bing)*
  cherries (canned), well drained
  (see Note)
1 *cup heavy cream, whipped*

FOR THE BURGUNDY WINE SAUCE:
1½ *cups cherry juice (from canned*
  cherries)
⅓ *cup Burgundy*
sugar to taste

METHOD:

1. Preheat oven to 350°F.

2. *Prepare the Bottom Crust:* Sift flour and sugar together. Cut butter into mixture and blend well. (It will be a light crumblike dough but will flatten into a pastry shell.) Press into bottom of spring-form pan. Bake for 15 minutes until light golden. Remove from oven and let cool in pan.

3. *Prepare the Topping:* Beat eggs. Blend flour, sugar and baking powder together and beat into eggs until thick and creamy.

4. Fold in coconut and cherries and pour over the prebaked bottom crust. Bake 15 minutes at 350°F. (top will be golden). Reduce heat to 250°F. and bake until center is firm when pressed with fingertips.

5. *Prepare the Burgundy Wine Sauce:* Heat cherry juice, wine and sugar together in saucepan and let simmer 5 minutes.

6. Serve torte topped with whipped cream and Burgundy Wine Sauce. This dessert tastes best when served at room temperature.

Note: Raisins and cut-up prunes may be substituted for the cherries. They must be precooked and well drained before adding. But add cherry juice or other fruit juice to the wine sauce in any case.

BROWN DERBY GRAPEFRUIT CAKE

SERVES 12

3 cups all-purpose flour
1½ cups sugar
1 tablespoon baking powder
1 teaspoon salt
½ cup water
½ cup vegetable oil
6 eggs, separated
4 tablespoons grapefruit juice,
   strained if necessary
1 teaspoon grated lemon rind
½ teaspoon cream of tartar

FOR THE CREAM CHEESE FROSTING:

1½ pounds cream cheese
4 teaspoons lemon juice
2 teaspoons grated lemon rind
1¼ cups confectioner's sugar
12–16 drops yellow food coloring
2 or 3 grapefruit sections, fresh or
   canned

two 1-pound cans grapefruit sections
   or about 24 fresh grapefruit
   sections and lemon leaves
   (optional) for garnish

METHOD:

1. Preheat oven to 350°F.

2. Sift together into a large bowl flour, sugar, baking powder and salt.

3. Make a well in center of dry ingredients and add water, oil, egg yolks, grapefruit juice and lemon rind. Beat until very smooth.

4. Beat egg whites and cream of tartar until stiff. Then fold, do not stir, yolk mixture into whites.

5. Divide batter into 2 ungreased 9½-inch pans. Bake for 25 to 30 minutes, or until cake springs back when touched with the finger.

6. Cool cakes in pans on a cake rack for about 5 minutes. Then loosen with a metal spatula and invert pans on cake rack until completely cool. Remove carefully.

7. With a serrated knife, gently cut layers in half to make 4 layers.

8. *Prepare the Cream Cheese Frosting:* Beat cream cheese until fluffy. Add lemon juice and rind. Gradually blend in sugar and food coloring. Beat until well blended. Crush enough grapefruit sections to make 4 teaspoons, then blend into cheese mixture.

9. Spread frosting on the 2 bottom halves of cake. Cover each with its top half and place 1 two-layer cake on top of the other. Cover tops and sides of entire cake with frosting. Garnish with the 24 grapefruit sections and the lemon leaves, if available. Refrigerate until ready to serve.

OLD FASHIONED 1–2–3–4 CAKE

1 cup (2 sticks) unsalted butter
2 cups sugar
½ teaspoon salt
4 eggs
3 cups all-purpose flour
3 teaspoons baking powder
¾ cup milk
2 teaspoons vanilla

FOR THE ORANGE FILLING:
¾ cup sugar
¼ cup all-purpose flour

grated rind of 1 orange
1 tablespoon lemon juice, strained
2 egg yolks, slightly beaten
⅛ teaspoon salt

FOR THE FROSTING:
4 tablespoons unsalted butter
1½ cups confectioner's sugar
2 egg whites
grated lemon rind or lemon essence
(optional)

METHOD:

1. Preheat oven to 350°F.

2. Combine butter, sugar and salt in a mixing bowl and beat until very light and fluffy.

3. Sift flour and baking powder together and set aside.

4. Beat eggs until thick and lemon-colored, then blend into butter-and-sugar mixture.

5. Add flour-baking powder mixture to batter alternately with milk, and blend very well. Add vanilla. Pour batter into 2 well-greased 9½-inch layer pans. Bake for 25 to 30 minutes. Cool cakes in pans placed on a rack for about 5 minutes. Then loosen with a metal spatula and invert on rack until completely cool.

6. *Prepare the Orange Filling:* Mix all ingredients in a heavy-bottomed pot. Cook over moderate heat, stirring constantly, until thick and smooth. Cool, then spread on top of one of the cake layers. Then place the other layer on top.

7. *Prepare the Frosting:* Cream butter until light. Gradually add ½ cup of the sugar; set aside. Beat egg whites until foamy, then slowly add the remaining cup of sugar and continue to beat until stiff. Combine the 2 mixtures and mix. Add more sugar if necessary to make frosting thick enough to spread. (A few drops of grated lemon rind or lemon essence may be added now.) With a spatula, spread the frosting over the top and sides of the cake.

ORANGE KISS ME CAKE

SERVES 6

1 *large seedless orange, washed*
  and cut up
1 *cup raisins*
⅓ *cup walnuts*
2 *cups all-purpose flour*
1 *teaspoon baking soda*
1 *teaspoon salt*
1 *cup sugar*
4 *tablespoons (½ stick) unsalted*
  butter

1 *cup milk*
2 *eggs*

FOR THE ORANGE NUT TOPPING:
¼ *cup of the reserved orange-*
  raisin-nut juice
⅓ *cup sugar*
1 *teaspoon cinnamon*
¼ *cup chopped walnuts*

METHOD:

1. Preheat oven to 350°F.

2. Grind the entire orange (both flesh and rind) in a blender or food processor until a pulp. With a slotted spoon, remove the pulp and reserve, add the raisins and walnuts to the juice that remains and grind briefly. Strain, reserving the orange-raisin-nut juice and raisin-nut mixture separately.

3. Sift flour, baking soda, salt and sugar together and set aside until needed.

4. Beat butter at low speed, add ¾ cup of the milk and beat until creamy.

5. Add unbeaten eggs, beat 2 minutes and then add remaining milk. Add flour mixture and blend well, then add orange pulp and raisin-nut mixture to the batter and mix well. Pour into a greased 8½-inch (2¼ inches high) round pan. Bake for 40 to 50 minutes. Let cool in pan on rack for about 5 minutes, then loosen with a metal spatula and turn cake out onto rack until completely cool.

6. *Prepare the Orange Nut Topping:* When ready to serve drip reserved orange-raisin-nut juice over the cake. Combine sugar, cinnamon and chopped walnuts and sprinkle on top.

BASIC SPONGE CAKE ROULADE

SERVES 10–12

This easily prepared basic roulade (rolled cake) is a thin but surprisingly resilient, firm, moist sponge cake. It may be spread before rolling with a wide variety of fillings—flavored pastry cream, ice cream or fresh fruit—or it may be rolled and covered with your favorite icing.

5 eggs	1 teaspoon vanilla
½ cup granulated sugar	grated rind of 1 lemon
½ cup all-purpose flour, sifted	

METHOD:

1. Cut a piece of wax paper 12 inches by 18 inches to fit a baking sheet or jelly-roll pan of the same size.

2. Butter paper, lay the buttered side up on baking pan and set aside.

3. Preheat oven to 400°F.

4. Separate the eggs, yolks in one large mixing bowl and whites in another. Add ¼ cup sugar to yolks and beat until light yellow. Add the remaining sugar to whites and beat until they form soft peaks. Fold half of the whites into the yolk mixture and blend in the flour, vanilla and grated lemon rind. Fold in the remaining whites.

5. With a spatula, spread the roulade mixture over the prepared paper on the baking sheet. Bake for 10 minutes, or until light brown but still moist.

6. Remove the roulade from the oven and let cool in the baking pan for at least 15 minutes. Then turn upside down onto another piece of wax paper which has been lightly sprinkled with sugar; carefully peel off the baked paper.

7. Fill roulade with filling of your choice, then roll up in the sugared paper and wrap in a dry kitchen towel until ready to serve; or roll up first, then cover with icing and refrigerate until ready to serve.

FROZEN SPONGE CAKE WITH ZABAGLIONE SAUCE

SERVES 12

½ recipe Basic Sponge Cake
  Roulade (page 299)
½ cup red currant jelly
¼ cup medium-dry sherry
 2 pints softened vanilla ice cream
 1 pint softened raspberry sherbet
 1 cup (½ pint) heavy cream,
  whipped

2 tablespoons chopped pistachio
  nuts

FOR THE ZABAGLIONE SAUCE:
 5 egg yolks
½ cup sugar
½ cup medium-dry sherry or
  Marsala

METHOD:

1. Follow the directions for preparing the batter and baking the Basic Sponge Cake Roulade, but use 2 round 8-inch cake pans lined with buttered wax paper, and if necessary increase the cooking time. Remove paper from cake when done and place layers back in pans.

2. Spread each layer with half the jelly; then sprinkle with half the sherry. Freeze until firm—about 1 hour.

3. Now spread 1 layer with ice cream, the other with sherbet.

4. Lift layers from pans. On a large piece of aluminum foil, place one layer sherbet-side-up; top with second layer, ice-cream-side up. Wrap cake in foil to hold layers in place. Then freeze cake again until firm—at least 2 hours.

5. *Prepare the Zabaglione Sauce* 1 hour or less before serving: In a 2-quart metal saucepan, over lowest heat possible, beat egg yolks with egg beater or electric beater. Gradually beat in sugar. Add sherry or Marsala; beat until very thick and fluffy and about double in bulk, about 10 minutes. Set saucepan in bowl of ice; continue beating until sauce is cool. Cover and refrigerate. To serve, beat again lightly with an egg beater or whisk.

6. Before you are ready to serve the cake, remove, unwrap and set on a plate or foil-covered cardboard to defrost. Spread top and sides with whipped cream. Sprinkle nuts around top edge. Serve with Zabaglione Sauce on the side.

PIECRUSTS

TIPS FOR A GOOD PIECRUST

To make a good piecrust the flour should always be sifted. Shortening may be vegetable shortening or half shortening and half lard, or part butter—but always cold and firm. In making piecrust, flour and shortening must be molded into a homogenized mixture. This is accomplished by gradually moistening the mixture with cold water, then chilling the dough before rolling. When a lightly mixed and lightly rolled pie dough is put in a very hot oven, the water it contains follows a law of physics: It expands and puffs the flour grains, while at the same time, the heat melts the shortening. When this takes place, the crust is tender and flaky. Although very nearly the same formula is used for making most of the piecrusts that follow, the pies may vary considerably in appearance and taste—because of subtle differences in ingredients *and* the techniques of the cook. Overmixing gives a smooth doughlike mass. This type of dough does not respond to the intense heat of the oven and the result is a piecrust that is neither tender nor flaky.

PROBLEMS AND SOLUTIONS

Soggy Crusts: If the bottom crusts of your fruit pies are soggy and soaked with fruit juice, next time try washing the bottom with beaten egg white before filling. If you have the same problem with custard pies, brush the bottom with melted shortening before filling.

For a light glaze on pies, wash the top with milk and melted butter mixed together. For a medium glaze, use egg whites and melted butter, mixed. For a rich brown glaze, use whole eggs and melted butter. For a flaky texture on top, wash with melted butter only. The best all-around wash mixture for two 8- or 9-inch piecrusts is: 1 egg beaten with 1 tablespoon melted butter and 2 tablespoons warm milk.

Fruit filling and piecrust should, ideally, be done at the same moment; that is, when piecrust has finished baking, filling should just have reached the boiling point. (Exact oven temperatures to achieve this happy result are, unfortunately, difficult to determine.) Too low a temperature causes the filling to boil before the crust is baked, and the filling will run out of the pie. Too high a temperature will brown the crust before it is thoroughly baked; this is often the cause of a soggy bottom crust. Too much sugar in the filling can also cause it to run over.

BASIC PIE DOUGH

FOR ONE 9-INCH OR 10-INCH BY 2-INCH BOTTOM PIE SHELL

1½ *cups sifted all-purpose flour*	4 *tablespoons shortening*
8 *tablespoons (1 stick) cold butter,*	3½ *tablespoons cold water*
cut into pieces	¼ *teaspoon salt*

METHOD:

1. Mound sifted flour on a floured pastry board. Make a well in the flour and place the butter and shortening in it. With your hands, mix the butter and shortening into the flour until it achieves a granulated texture.

2. Again make a well in this mixture. Add water and salt and mix in with fingers just until the water is absorbed. Do not overmix.

3. Form the dough into a ball, flatten out slightly with your hand, wrap in a damp towel or wax paper and refrigerate for 1 hour, or until chilled.

4. Preheat oven to 375°F. Lightly butter a pie plate. Roll out dough ⅛ inch thick and about 2 inches larger than the pan dimensions (to allow for shrinkage) and line the pie plate with the dough. Trim edges and press rim down with fingers. If the piecrust is to be baked before filling, prick the sides and bottom of the dough with a fork in several places.

5. Lightly butter the bottom of another pie plate and place on top of the dough inside the first one. Chill in refrigerator 15 minutes. Turn pans over and bake, bottom side up, for 25 minutes, until golden brown.

Note: If this recipe is to be used for quiche or other pies that need a partially baked crust at first, substitute the following baking time: Bake at 375°F. for 5 minutes, bottom side up. Turn pans over and bake for 10 minutes more, until crust is slightly browned.

SWEET PIE DOUGH

MAKES TWO 10-INCH BY 2-INCH PASTRY SHELLS

This is a pastry that can be used for making a flan—it is rich and tender.

2¾ cups all-purpose flour, sifted
¾ cup (1½ sticks) cold butter cut
   into pieces
4 tablespoons finely ground
   almonds

1 egg yolk
1 tablespoon heavy cream
½ cup granulated sugar
dash of vanilla
1 egg white, beaten (optional)

METHOD:

1. Preheat oven to 375°F.

2. Mound the sifted flour on a pastry board. Make a well in the flour and place butter in it and then the almonds. With your hands mix the butter and almonds into the flour until granulated in texture.

3. Beat the yolk, add cream and sugar, and beat well. Add vanilla and mix, then add to the flour-almond mixture until dough clings together. Work dough into a smooth round ball. Divide in half, wrap the dough in wax paper or aluminum foil and chill 1 or 2 hours.

4. Roll out each half separately on a floured board until dough is ⅛ inch thick and forms a circle about 2 inches larger than the pie pan. Make sure each circle of dough is well pressed into its pie pan, trim the edges and press rims with fingers or the tines of a fork. (The entire surface of the crust may be glazed with beaten egg white if you wish.) If the crusts are to be baked before filling, prick the bottoms and sides well. If they are to be partially baked, keep them in the oven for about 15 minutes; the edges should not brown. Cool and fill as desired and finish baking. If the shells are to be fully baked, bake for an additional 20 to 25 minutes or until golden brown.

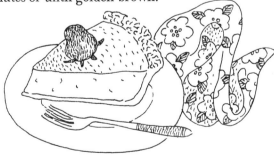

"WATER-WHIP" PASTRY

MAKES ONE 9-INCH PASTRY SHELL

A layered dough similar to Danish pastry in texture.

½ cup, less 1 tablespoon, solid
   homogenized vegetable
   shortening
3 tablespoons boiling water

1 teaspoon milk
1¼ cups all-purpose flour, sifted
   once before measuring
½ teaspoon salt

METHOD:

1. Preheat oven to 450°F.

2. Put shortening in medium-size bowl, add boiling water and milk.

3. Break up shortening with fork (it is easier if you tilt the bowl toward you). Beat until mixture is smooth and thick, like whipped cream.

4. Sift flour and salt into shortening mixture. Stir in the bowl with whipping strokes until the dough clings together. Work dough into a smooth round ball. Wrap in wax paper or aluminum foil and refrigerate 1 to 2 hours to relax the dough.

5. Roll between two 12-inch squares of wax paper into a circle ⅛ inch thick and 2 inches wider than pie pan. Fit pastry into 9-inch pie pan and prick sides and bottom with the tines of a fork if the shell is to be baked before filling. Flute rim.

6. Bake for 14 to 19 minutes, just before the edges turn brown, for a partially baked crust. Cool and fill as desired and finish baking. For a fully baked crust, bake the shell for an additional 20 minutes, until it is a light golden brown. Cool and fill.

PASTRY PIECRUST

MAKES ONE 8-INCH OR 9-INCH PASTRY SHELL

This short butter pastry is good for a custard pie if the shell is partially baked for 15 minutes first. The dough requires no kneading or chilling.

1 cup all-purpose flour
¼ teaspoon salt
6 tablespoons butter or shortening

1 teaspoon sugar
2 tablespoons ice water

METHOD:

1. Preheat oven to 375°F.

2. Sift flour into bowl, add salt and mix well. Add butter or shortening and cut in with pastry blender or knife.

3. Add sugar and ice water a little at a time, just enough barely to moisten, and blend to make a dough, still using pastry blender or knife (do not knead).

4. Roll out on lightly floured pastry board to about ⅛ inch thick and a circle 2 inches wider than the pan. Line the pie pan or tart pan with dough, trim and crimp the edges and prick all over with the tines of a fork if the crust is to be baked before filling. To partially bake the crust, bake for 15 to 20 minutes or just before the pastry is about to brown. Cool and fill as desired. For a fully baked crust, bake for an additional 20 minutes, until crust is light golden brown. Cool and fill.

PASTRY SHELLS

MAKES ONE 8-INCH AND ONE 9-INCH PASTRY SHELL

2¼ cups all-purpose flour
¾ cup granulated sugar
½ teaspoon salt
½ tablespoon cinnamon
¾ teaspoon freshly grated nutmeg

½ cup blanched, ground almonds
1½ tablespoons grated lemon rind
1 egg
2–3 tablespoons ice cold water
1¼ cups (2¼ sticks) butter

METHOD:

1. Preheat oven to 400°F.

2. Sift dry ingredients together into a large mixing bowl.

3. Blend in ground almonds, lemon rind, egg and butter. Mix ingredients well, adding a small amount of water to make mixture the consistency of cookie dough—but it should not be sticky.

4. Pat dough into 8-inch or 9-inch pie pans, which have been lightly floured. Shape dough with your fingers, pressing it into the pans to shape into pie shells about ⅜ inch thick. Use a little flour on your fingers if dough becomes sticky.

5. If the shells are to be baked before filling, prick the crust on the sides and bottom well with a fork. For a fully baked crust, bake at 400°F. for 15 minutes, reduce heat to 375° and bake 25 to 30 minutes longer, until lightly browned. Cool the crust and fill as desired. Remove from the oven after the first 15 minutes of baking and let pies cool for a partially baked crust.

Note: Leftover dough can be used to make an attractive lattice design and arranged on the pie after the shell has been filled with the desired filling. To make lattice top, roll out remaining pastry dough about ⅛ inch thick, and with pastry cutter or sharp knife cut strips about ½ inch wide. Arrange lattice strips on pie in one direction, then lay strips on top in opposite direction, interweaving them. Bake pie according to directions in recipe.

CORN OIL PASTRY SHELL

MAKES ONE 8- OR 9½-INCH PASTRY SHELL

½ cup corn oil
2–3 tablespoons milk
1½ cups sifted all-purpose flour

1½ teaspoons sugar
1 teaspoon salt

METHOD:
1. Preheat oven to 425°F.

2. Beat corn oil and milk together with fork until creamy; set aside.

3. Mix flour, sugar and salt. Pour oil-and-milk mixture all at once over flour mixture; mix with fork until flour is completely dampened.

4. Press dough evenly and firmly with fingers to line bottom of an 8-inch or 9½-inch pan then press dough up to line sides and partly cover rim of pan, until about ¼ inch thick. Be sure dough is pressed to uniform thickness.

5. To flute, pinch dough lightly, using the thumb and forefinger of

one hand and supporting dough on the inside with the forefinger of the other. Do not make the fluted edge too high.

6. If shell is to be baked before filling, prick sides and bottom well with a fork. Bake for about 12 minutes, or until just before the crust turns brown, for a partially baked crust. Cool and fill as desired. For a fully baked shell, bake the crust for an additional 20 to 25 minutes, until the crust is lightly browned. Cool and fill.

Note: For fillings such as custard, pumpkin and pecan, the unbaked crust can be filled and the pie then baked at 400°F. for 15 minutes; reduce heat to 350° and bake until crust is lightly browned. Test filling with a knife—if it comes out clean, the pie is done.

APRICOT PRESERVE CUSTARD PIE

SERVES 6–8

one 8-inch or 9-inch partially baked | *2 cups sugar*
shell of your choice in pie pan | *6 eggs*
(pages 305–6) | *2 teaspoons vanilla*
1 cup thick apricot preserves | *whipped cream*
8 tablespoons (1 stick) unsalted
butter

METHOD:

1. Preheat oven to 350°F.

2. Just before you are ready to prepare custard filling, line the bottom of the partially baked cooled pastry shell with apricot preserves.

3. To prepare custard filling, cream butter, add sugar and beat until light and fluffy.

4. Beat eggs until quite light and blend with butter-and-sugar mixture. Add vanilla.

5. Pour mixture into pastry shell.

6. Bake for 45 minutes at 350°F. Test with a knife; if it comes out clean, custard is set. If not, bake for 10 minutes longer. Let cool. Serve with a dab of whipped cream on top of each wedge.

APRICOT SOUR CREAM PIE

SERVES 8

1 cup light brown sugar (or less
    if jam is very sweet)
1 cup sour cream
1 cup apricot jam
1 teaspoon vanilla
⅛ teaspoon salt
2 tablespoons lemon juice, strained
3 eggs

one 9-inch unbaked pie shell of your
    choice in pie pan, brushed with
    1 beaten egg white (pages
    305–6)
2 tablespoons apricot brandy
1 cup heavy cream, whipped with
    sugar to taste

METHOD:

1. Preheat oven to 350°F.

2. In a mixing bowl, beat sugar and sour cream into jam; add vanilla, salt and lemon juice and mix well. Beat in eggs, one at a time, beating well after each addition. Set filling aside.

3. Pierce prepared pastry shell with a fork in several places. Place in oven and bake 10 minutes. Remove and fill. Bake for 20 minutes at 350°F. Reduce heat to 300°F. and bake about 15 minutes more, until center is set when tested with a knife. Sprinkle brandy over pie while still warm and serve, warm or cold, topped with whipped cream.

CHOCOLATE ANGEL PIE

SERVES 6–8

4 ounces semisweet chocolate
3 tablespoons hot water
1 cup heavy cream
1 teaspoon vanilla

½ cup chopped pecans
one 8-inch Meringue Shell, in pie
    plate, cooled (page 311)

METHOD:

1. Melt chocolate with the hot water in the top of a double boiler over hot water. Let cool slightly. Whip cream until stiff, add vanilla.

2. Add the pecans to chocolate and fold into whipped cream. Pile lightly into meringue shell.

3. Chill 2 to 3 hours and serve.

CHOCOLATE BUTTERSCOTCH PIE

2½ cups light brown sugar
8 tablespoons (1 stick) unsalted
  butter
3 eggs
1 teaspoon vanilla
½ cup light cream
3 ounces bittersweet chocolate,
  melted and cooled

one 9-inch unbaked, chilled pie shell
  of your choice in pie pan, edges
  fluted high (pages 305–6)
1 cup (½ pint) heavy cream,
  whipped with sugar to taste
semisweet chocolate shavings

METHOD:

1. Preheat oven to 350°F.

2. Beat the sugar and butter together until creamy. Then beat in eggs one at a time and add the vanilla.

3. Beat the light cream with melted chocolate and add to filling, beating until completely mixed. Pour into the pie shell and bake 30 minutes. Reduce the heat to 300° and continue to cook about 45 minutes longer or until set when tested with a knife. Let pie cool, then decorate with whipped cream and chocolate shavings.

Note: The pie puffs up during cooking, then falls as it cools. You may also pour the filling into a partially baked and cooled pie shell. In that case, the cooking time will be slightly less. Test the pie with a knife after about 1 hour. If it comes out clean, the pie is done.

COCONUT CHIFFON PIE

1 tablespoon (1 package)
  unflavored gelatin
¼ cup cold water
3 egg yolks, slightly beaten
½ cup sugar
⅛ teaspoon salt
1½ cups milk, scalded
¾ cup shredded coconut

1 teaspoon vanilla extract
3 egg whites, stiffly beaten
one 9-inch baked pie shell of your
  choice in pie plate, cooled
  (pages 305–6)
whipped cream and toasted coconut
  for garnish

METHOD:

1. Soften gelatin in cold water until dissolved.

2. To beaten egg yolks add ¼ cup sugar and the salt. Slowly stir in the scalded milk. Cook in the top of a double boiler over hot (not boiling) water, stirring constantly until mixture coats spoon.

3. Remove from heat. Add gelatin and stir until dissolved. Refrigerate until mixture is slightly thicker than consistency of unbeaten egg whites.

4. Add shredded coconut and vanilla extract.

5. Gradually beat remaining sugar into beaten egg whites. Fold into gelatin-coconut mixture.

6. Pour filling into baked pie shell. Chill until firm. Garnish with whipped cream and toasted coconut.

ORANGE VELVET COCONUT PIE

SERVES 8–10

FOR THE COCONUT CRUST
  (makes one 9-inch pie crust):
  2 *cups prepared shredded coconut*

FOR THE FILLING:
  4 *teaspoons unflavored gelatin*
  5 *tablespoons water*
  3 *egg yolks, beaten*
  ½ *cup sugar*
  ⅔ *cup water*

pinch of salt
¾ *cup fresh or frozen orange juice*
1 *tablespoon lemon juice*
3 *egg whites*
6 *tablespoons sugar*
1 *cup heavy cream, whipped with*
  sugar to taste

bitter chocolate curls for garnish

METHOD:

1. *Prepare the Coconut Crust:* Preheat oven to 300°F. Press 1½ cups coconut into the bottom of a well-buttered 9-inch pie pan until evenly distributed; then press the remaining ½ cup against the sides to build up to the rim. Bake for 10 minutes (checking the oven frequently as coconut burns quickly) until golden brown. Let crust cool before filling.

2. *Prepare the Filling:* Sprinkle gelatin over 5 tablespoons water and soak for 5 minutes until dissolved.

3. Place egg yolks, ½ cup sugar, water and salt in top of double boiler, add dissolved gelatin and cook over gently boiling water, stirring frequently until it thickens enough to coat a spoon. Remove from heat.

4. Add orange and lemon juices. Let mixture cool.

5. Beat egg whites until frothy, adding the 6 tablespoons of sugar a little at a time. When gelatin mixture is cool and begins to thicken and set, fold in the egg whites.

6. Fill coconut shell and refrigerate until ready to serve. Top with whipped cream and garnish with chocolate curls.

COCONUT VELVET PIE

SERVES 8

FOR THE MERINGUE SHELL:
6 *egg whites at room temperature*
1½ *cups granulated sugar*
pinch of cream of tartar
shredded coconut

FOR THE FILLING:
6 *egg yolks*
¾ *cup sugar*

3 *tablespoons lemon juice, strained*
1½ *teaspoons grated lemon rind*
pinch of salt
3 *cups (1½ pints) heavy cream*

½ *cup toasted coconut and fresh strawberries (or other fruit in season) for garnish*

METHOD:

1. Preheat oven to 275°F.

2. *Prepare the Meringue Shell:* Beat egg whites until fairly stiff, add sugar gradually, then cream of tartar, beating continually until stiff peaks form.

3. Line sides and bottom of a buttered 8-inch pie pan with mixture and sprinkle rim with coconut. Bake until lightly brown and crisp, approximately 1 hour. Let cool.

4. *Prepare the Filling:* Beat egg yolks slightly in top of double boiler over hot water. Stir in sugar, lemon juice and rind and salt. Cook custard until thick, about 8 or 9 minutes.

5. Whip the cream until soft peaks form. When custard is cool, add to whipped cream and pour into meringue shell. Chill for 12 to 24 hours. Garnish pie with strawberries or other seasonal fruit and sprinkle with toasted coconut.

CRANBERRY ICE CREAM PIE

SERVES 8

FOR THE GRAHAM CRACKER CRUST:
1½ cups graham cracker crumbs
¼ cup confectioner's sugar, sifted
6 tablespoons unsalted butter, melted
½ teaspoon ground cinnamon

FOR THE FILLING:
2 seedless (navel) oranges, rinsed and dried

2 cups (about ½ pound) cranberries
½ cup sugar
1 tablespoon lemon juice
1 pint vanilla ice cream, softened

FOR THE GARNISH:
1 cup heavy cream
1 cup cranberries
2 egg whites, beaten until frothy
1 cup sugar or amount needed

METHOD:

1. *Prepare the Graham Cracker Crust:* Preheat oven to 350°F. Combine the graham cracker crumbs with the confectioner's sugar, the melted butter and cinnamon and mix well. Press mixture evenly into a 9-inch pie pan. Bake 10 minutes, then allow to cool completely.

2. *Prepare the Filling:* Peel oranges and remove as much of the white pith as possible. Cut the oranges up roughly, including the peel. Chop coarsely, by hand or in a food processor, together with the cranberries. Stir in the sugar and lemon juice.

3. Fold the cranberry-orange mixture into the softened ice cream until well mixed. Fill the baked and cooled pie shell with this mixture and freeze until firm.

4. *Prepare the Garnish:* About 30 minutes before the pie is to be served, remove it from the freezer to soften slightly. Whip the cream until stiff peaks form, and with a spatula spread the whipped cream over the pie. Dip the cranberries, a few at a time, into the beaten egg whites. Using a slotted spoon, remove the cranberries and roll them in the sugar to coat lightly. Arrange sugared cranberries around the edge of the pie and serve it promptly.

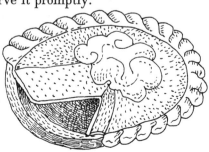

BLACK BOTTOM ICE CREAM PIE

FOR THE CRUST:
  4 *tablespoons (½ stick) unsalted
    butter, melted*
1½ *cups gingersnap crumbs*
  ¼ *cup confestioner's sugar*

FOR THE CHOCOLATE SAUCE:
  6 *ounces semisweet chocolate, in
    pieces*

½ *cup heavy cream, whipped*
½ *teaspoon vanilla extract*
  2 *tablespoons sugar (optional)*

½ *pint chocolate ice cream,
    softened*
  1 *quart vanilla ice cream,* softened

METHOD:

1. *Prepare Crust:* Combine the melted butter with the gingersnap crumbs and sugar. Press against bottom and sides of a 9-inch pie pan (use an 8-inch pan inside the 9-inch to press down firmly). Chill until set.

2. *Prepare the Chocolate Sauce:* Melt chocolate in top of double boiler over hot water, remove from heat and let cool slightly. Thoroughly blend in whipped cream, vanilla and sugar (if you are using it).

3. Spread chocolate ice cream in crust. Spread half the chocolate sauce over the ice cream, then spoon vanilla ice cream on top, building it high in center.

4. Drizzle remaining chocolate sauce over top of pie and freeze until ready to serve.

KENTUCKY LEMON PIE

  6 *eggs*
1½ *cups light corn syrup*
  ¾ *cup sugar*
  1 *teaspoon cornstarch*
  ½ *cup lemon juice, strained*
grated rind of 1 lemon
  1 *tablespoon unsalted butter,
    melted*

*one 10-inch unbaked pie shell of
    your choice, edges fluted high
    (pages 305–6), chilled
    in pie pan*

FOR THE MERINGUE:
  3 *egg whites, at room temperature*
  ¼ *teaspoon cream of tartar*
  3 *tablespoons confectioner's sugar*

METHOD:

1. Preheat oven to 375°F.

2. Beat the eggs with a rotary or electric beater until well mixed. Add the syrup and continue beating till incorporated.

3. Mix the ¾ cup sugar and cornstarch together and beat into the egg mixture.

4. Add lemon juice, rind and butter, continuing to beat until thoroughly mixed.

5. Pour carefully into the chilled pie shell. Bake for 15 minutes, reduce the oven heat to 300°F. and cook 45 minutes longer, or until set. Let cool before covering with meringue.

6. *Meanwhile, prepare the meringue:* Beat the egg whites until frothy. Add the cream of tartar and continue beating until stiff. Add the confectioner's sugar, a tablespoon at a time, beating well between each addition. Do not overbeat.

7. When ready to top pie with meringue, preheat oven to 350°F. Spread meringue over filling so that the meringue touches the pastry edge all around. Leave the surface rough. Bake 10 minutes or until meringue is lightly browned. Cool and refrigerate again before serving.

LEMON TARTS

SERVES 6

12 *tart tins (about 2½ inches wide)*
  lined with unbaked Pastry
  Piecrust (page 305)
2 *egg yolks*
1 *cup sugar*
juice of 1 lemon, strained
grated rind of 1 lemon

4 *tablespoons unsalted butter,*
  melted
2 *tablespoons chopped walnuts or*
  coconut
2 *egg whites, stiffly beaten, but*
  not too dry

METHOD:

1. Preheat oven to 350°F.

2. In large mixing bowl, beat egg yolks well until thick and lemon-colored. Add sugar slowly, then lemon juice and rind.

3. Pour in slightly cooled melted butter and fold in walnuts or coconut and stiffly beaten egg whites.

4. Fill pastry shells and bake for 20 to 25 minutes, or until lightly brown. Serve warm with coffee or tea.

FROSTY LIME PIE

FOR THE GRAHAM CRACKER CRUST:
1¼ cups graham cracker crumbs
¼ cup superfine sugar
4 tablespoons unsalted butter, at
   room temperature

⅔ cup freshly squeezed, strained
   lime juice
2 teaspoons grated lime rind
   (outer layer only)
⅛ teaspoon salt

FOR THE FILLING:
5 eggs, separated
¾ cup superfine sugar

1½ cups heavy cream
thin slices of lime or fresh strawberries and sugar for garnish

METHOD:

1. Preheat oven to 350°F.

2. *Prepare the Graham Cracker Crust:* Put the graham cracker crumbs and ¼ cup of sugar in a bowl. Add the butter and work in with a spoon or your fingers to blend well.

3. Press the mixture evenly into a 9-inch pie pan with your fingertips, then set an 8-inch pie pan over the mixture and press it down to smooth and firm the crust.

4. Bake the crust 10 minutes. Remove and cool to room temperature.

5. *Prepare the Filling:* Using an electric beater or a whisk, beat the egg yolks in the top of a double boiler over hot—not boiling—water until very thick. Gradually beat in ½ cup of the sugar until mixture is very pale and thick and forms a ribbon when the beater is lifted.

6. Stir in the lime juice and rind and continue to cook over simmering water, stirring, until mixture will coat a metal spoon. Do not allow to boil.

7. Turn filling into a large bowl; cool to room temperature.

8. When the yolk mixture is cool, beat the egg whites with the salt until soft peaks form. Gradually beat in the remaining ¼ cup of sugar until the meringue is stiff and shiny.

9. Stir ⅓ of this meringue into the cooled yolk mixture, then gently fold in the remaining meringue.

10. Set oven again at 350°F. Turn filling into cooled pie shell and bake 15 minutes, or until top is lightly tinged with brown. Let pie cool. Refrigerate, then freeze, uncovered. Once it is frozen, enclose in plastic wrap and keep frozen until you plan to serve it.

11. Remove the pie from the freezer 10 minutes before serving. Whip the cream, spoon it over the pie and garnish with lime slices or strawberries dipped in sugar.

Note: This pie will keep, frozen, for 2 to 3 weeks. If a sweeter pie is desired, reduce the lime juice to ½ cup. Leftover pie can be refrozen if not completely defrosted. The pie can also be well chilled and served without freezing.

MACADAMIA NUT PIE

SERVES 6

FOR THE MACADAMIA NUT CRUST:
½ *cup unsalted macadamia nuts*
⅛ *teaspoon salt*
1 *cup all-purpose flour, sifted*
⅓ *cup shortening*
2 *tablespoons ice water*

FOR THE FILLING:
8 *tablespoons (1 stick) unsalted butter*

1 *cup sugar*
4 *eggs, slightly beaten*
1 *cup light corn syrup*
⅛ *teaspoon salt*
1½ *teaspoons vanilla*
1½ *cups unsalted macadamia nuts, chopped*

METHOD:

1. *To prepare the Macadamia Nut Crust:* Place ½ cup macadamia nuts in blender or food processor and pulverize. Combine this with sifted flour, salt and shortening. Using 2 knives or a pastry blender, cut into flour-shortening mixture until it forms coarse lumps about the size of peas. Add ice water and mix lightly. Knead a few times and roll out on board dusted with flour until it is ⅛ inch thick. Arrange dough in 8- or 9-inch pie pan; trim and flute edges. Refrigerate until filling is ready.

2. Preheat oven to 350°F.

3. *Prepare the Filling:* Cream butter and add sugar gradually. When light and lemon-colored, add beaten eggs. Blend in corn syrup. Add salt, vanilla and the 1½ cups chopped nuts. Mix well, then pour into unbaked pie shell. Bake for 35 to 40 minutes.

Note: The piecrust can be made the night before; cover with wax paper and refrigerate until needed.

PLANTATION MOLASSES AND BLACK WALNUT PIE

SERVES 8

3 tablespoons unsalted butter
2 tablespoons all-purpose flour
1 tablespoon cornmeal
1 cup dark molasses
2⅓ tablespoons cider vinegar
pinch of salt
4 eggs, beaten

½ cup black walnuts,
    coarsely chopped
one 9-inch unbaked pie shell of your
    choice (pages 305–6), in
    pie pan
1 cup heavy cream, whipped with
    sugar to taste

METHOD:

1. Preheat oven to 300°F.

2. Cream butter, flour and cornmeal together; add molasses, vinegar and salt and mix. Cook in top of double boiler over hot water until thick, stirring occasionally.

3. Add eggs and cook 3 additional minutes, stirring constantly. Do not boil. Add walnuts. Pour mixture into pastry shell in pie pan. Place on middle shelf of oven and bake until set, about 40 minutes. When tested with a knife, it should come out clean. Let cool. Serve with slightly sweetened whipped cream.

PEACH MALLOW PIE

SERVES 8

1½ tablespoons unflavored gelatin
¼ cup cold water
1 cup sugar
½ cup warm water
½ tablespoon almond extract
2 tablespoons lemon juice,
    strained
6 to 8 large ripe peaches

¾ pound marshmallows, heated
    until soft
1 pint heavy cream, whipped
¼ cup blanched, sliced almonds
1 fully baked 10-inch pie shell of
    your choice (pages 305–6),
    in pie pan

METHOD:

1. Sprinkle gelatin over cold water to soften and set aside.

2. Bring sugar and warm water to a boil in a saucepan, lower heat,

add gelatin and stir until dissolved. Remove from heat; add almond extract and lemon juice.

3. Bring a large pot of water to boil. Plunge peaches briefly into boiling water, peel off skins and slice peaches. Add to hot sugar-gelatin mixture; toss gently until well coated.

4. Remove and reserve 2 peach slices to garnish the top of the pie. Set peach mixture into a bowl of ice water and refrigerate until mixture begins to jell.

5. Whip marshmallows and fold with cream into peach mixture. Pour filling into pie shell, shaping it into a high mound.

6. Sprinkle almonds over entire top. Refrigerate 1 hour. When ready to serve decorate with reserved peach slices.

GRANNY'S SOUTHERN PEANUT PIE

SERVES 6–8

½ cup sugar
1½ cups dark corn syrup
¼ cup shortening
¼ teaspoon salt
3 eggs, beaten
½ teaspoon vanilla

1½ cups roasted peanuts, coarsely
    chopped
one 9-inch unbaked pie shell of your
    choice (pages 305–6), in
    pie pan

METHOD:

1. Preheat oven to 400°F.

2. Combine sugar, corn syrup, shortening and salt in a saucepan. Bring to boil over low heat, remove and let mixture cool 2 or 3 minutes.

3. Pour a little of this hot syrup slowly over the beaten eggs, stirring constantly. Add the rest of the syrup, continuing to stir, until thickened and smooth. Cool.

4. Stir in vanilla and peanuts. Pour into the unbaked pie shell. Bake at 400°F. for 10 minutes, reduce temperature to 375° and bake 35 to 40 minutes longer.

PUMPKIN PIE WITH BOURBON

SERVES 8

2 tablespoons unsalted butter
¾ cup sugar
3 eggs
½ teaspoon salt
¼ teaspoon ground ginger
¼ teaspoon grated nutmeg
½ teaspoon ground cinnamon

1 cup canned pumpkin puree
1 cup undiluted evaporated milk
    or rich cream
¼ cup Bourbon
one 9-inch unbaked pie shell of your
    choice (pages 305–6), in
    pie pan

METHOD:

1. Preheat oven to 450°F.

2. Cream butter and sugar together. Beat in eggs, one at a time, by hand or with electric mixer.

3. Add remaining ingredients, beating after each addition.

4. When well blended, pour into pie shell and bake in 450°F. oven for 10 minutes. Reduce heat to 325°F. and continue baking for about 45 minutes, or until custard filling is firm.

MILE HIGH STRAWBERRY PIE

SERVES 8

The flavor of the small wild strawberry haunts me when my memory takes me back to my childhood in the South. However, today's luscious commercially grown berries are used in this pie.

4 pints ripe strawberries with
    fresh green stems
1 pint heavy cream, whipped

FOR THE STRAWBERRY GLAZE:
1½ cups sugar
½ cup white corn syrup
1½ cups crushed strawberries
1 teaspoon fresh lemon juice,
    strained

1⅓ ounces tapioca flour (not
    granulated tapioca)
2 teaspoons unflavored gelatin,
    softened in 2 tablespoons cold
    water

1 prebaked 10-inch pie shell of
    your choice, edges fluted high
    (pages 305–6), in pie pan

METHOD:

1. Wash berries in a large sieve, shake well and place on paper towels to dry.

2. Remove stems from berries, but reserve 8 large, perfect berries with stems on to garnish pie. Set aside smallest or bruised berries to crush for glaze (enough to make 1½ cups, crushed). Of the berries that are left, cut smaller berries in half and leave the larger ones whole.

3. *Prepare the Strawberry Glaze:* In a saucepan, boil the sugar, corn syrup and crushed berries together for 5 minutes, stirring constantly. Add lemon juice. Beat in the tapioca flour a little at a time and cook, stirring, until thickened. Add softened gelatin. Remove from heat, strain and let mixture cool partially.

4. Brush about 2 tablespoons glaze over bottom and sides of pastry shell.

5. Place large berries stem ends down in bottom of pastry shell, and arrange in mound in center, filling in the spaces between with halved berries. Build the berries high into a pyramid.

6. When all the berries are placed, spoon most of the warm glaze over all the berries and let the pie set in refrigerator for 1 hour before serving.

7. To serve, dip the 8 reserved berries with stems in the remaining glaze and set the berries around the top with the stems up.

8. Using a pastry bag, decorate the pie by building a huge collar around the edge with the whipped cream. When pie is served, let guests help themselves to the rest of the whipped cream as desired.

AUNT ANNIE'S SUGAR PIE

SERVES 8

2 *cups light brown sugar*	1 *teaspoon vanilla*
½ *cup all-purpose flour*	*pinch of salt*
one 9-inch partially baked pie shell	3 *eggs, beaten*
of your choice (pages 305–6),	2 *tablespoons unsalted butter, cut*
in pie pan	*into small pieces*
1½ *cups light cream*	½ *teaspoon freshly grated nutmeg*

METHOD:

1. Preheat oven to 350°F.

2. Mix sugar and flour together in a bowl and place in pie shell.

3. Add cream, vanilla and salt to beaten eggs. Pour over the sugar and flour in the shell. Dot top with butter and dust top with nutmeg.

4. Bake until firm—approximately 45 minutes. Let cool to room temperature before cutting.

SWEET POTATO PIE WITH PINEAPPLE

SERVES 6

3 cups mashed sweet potatoes
2 cups rich milk or light cream
3 tablespoons unsalted butter
4 eggs, separated
¾ cup brown sugar
½ cup light corn syrup
1 teaspoon salt or to taste

1 teaspoon ground ginger
1 teaspoon cinnamon
1 teaspoon allspice
1 cup crushed pineapple, drained
one 8-inch or 9-inch unbaked pie
    shell of your choice (pages
    305–6), in pie pan

METHOD:

1. Preheat oven to 350°F.

2. Mix the mashed sweet potatoes with milk or cream. Add butter, egg yolks, sugar, corn syrup, salt and spices and beat until fluffy, about 2 minutes. Blend in pineapple.

3. Beat the egg whites until stiff and fold into potato mixture.

4. Pour mixture into a pie pan that has been lined with the unbaked pastry.

5. Sprinkle with cinnamon and bake for 45 minutes. Serve warm.

SOUTHERN YAM PIE WITH
CANDIED GINGER TOPPING

SERVES 8

FOR THE FILLING:
*about 3/4 pound fresh yams (2 or 3
    yams)*
3/4 cup light cream or milk
1/3 cup superfine sugar
1/2 cup (packed) light brown sugar
pinch of salt
1 teaspoon ground ginger
1/2 teaspoon ground cinnamon
*1/2 teaspoon nutmeg, freshly grated
    if possible*
pinch of ground cloves
2 large eggs, beaten lightly

*one 9-inch unbaked pie shell of your
    choice, chilled (pages 305–6),
    in pie pan*

FOR THE TOPPING:
4 tablespoons unsalted butter
1/3 cup (packed) light brown sugar
*3/4 cup (about 6 ounces) crystal-
    lized ginger*
*fresh lemon juice to taste (about
    2 tablespoons)*

1 cup heavy cream, whipped

METHOD:

1. *Prepare the Filling:* Preheat oven to 350°F. Scrub the yams and place them in a baking pan. Bake until tender, about 45 minutes. When yams are very soft when pressed with your finger, remove from the oven and raise oven heat to 375°F. Pinch the skins all over without breaking through the skin (this helps release the flesh from the skin). Slash the yams and scoop out the cooked flesh. Puree in a blender, food mill or food processor (or push through a fine sieve) while still hot. Measure 1½ cups of yam puree, reserving any leftover puree for another use. Bring the cream or milk to a simmer in a small saucepan. Place the yam puree in a large mixing bowl (or leave it in the food processor if you have used one) and add the sugar, brown sugar, salt, ginger, cinnamon, nutmeg, cloves and eggs (add half of the beaten eggs at a time), whisking to blend. Stir in the hot cream or milk. Correct all seasonings and let filling cool.

2. When the filling is cooled, remove the pie shell from the refrigerator, pour in the filling, and place on the center shelf of the oven. Bake for 20 to 25 minutes, or until the center is almost set (it will jiggle if you shake the shelf). Remove from the oven and lower heat to 325°F. Cool the pie for a few moments while you prepare the topping.

3. *Prepare the Topping:* Cream butter well with the brown sugar, either in an electric mixer or in a small bowl using a wooden spoon.

Gently rinse excess sugar from the crystallized ginger, pat dry with paper towels and chop coarsely. Add the chopped ginger and lemon juice to the creamed butter-sugar mixture.

4. With a spatula, spread the topping gently and evenly over the pie. Return to the oven and bake for about 25 minutes or until center is set. Check at intervals to prevent burning the topping.

5. Cool. Serve at room temperature, each wedge garnished with a dollop of whipped cream.

YOGURT PIE

SERVES 8–10 (MAKES ONE 10-INCH PIE)

FOR THE GRAHAM CRACKER CRUMB
   SHELL:
24 *graham crackers, finely rolled*
   (about 2 cups)
4 *tablespoons softened butter*
¼ *cup sugar*

FOR THE FILLING:
1 *tablespoon unflavored gelatin*
   (see Note)
¼ *cup cold water*
2 *egg yolks, slightly beaten*
¼ *cup milk*

8 *ounces Neufchâtel cheese at*
   room temperature (see Note)
8 *ounces cream cheese at room*
   temperature
1 *teaspoon vanilla*
1 *teaspoon molasses*
1 *tablespoon clover honey*
2 *cups unflavored yogurt*

½ *cup graham cracker crumbs*
   reserved from Graham Cracker
   Crumb Shell

METHOD:

1. *Prepare the Graham Cracker Crumb Shell:* Preheat oven to 375°F. Blend together crumbs, softened butter and sugar. Set aside ½ cup of crumbs to garnish top of pie. Press the rest firmly against bottom and sides of 10-inch greased pie pan. Bake 8 to 10 minutes. Cool.

2. *Prepare the Filling:* Soften gelatin in cold water and dissolve in the top part of a double boiler over hot water. Add milk to the slightly beaten egg yolks, combine with the gelatin and cook over gently boiling water, stirring occasionally, until it coats a spoon. Set aside to cool.

3. Cream the cheeses, vanilla, molasses and honey together (if mixing machine is used, cream on low speed), add 1 cup yogurt and continue to cream until smooth.

4. Pour the cooled gelatin mixture slowly over the cheese mixture, stirring constantly. Add the second cup of yogurt. Mix well. Pour into

baked Graham Cracker Crumb Shell and chill until firm. When ready to serve, sprinkle top with graham cracker crumbs.

Notes: If a softer filling is desired, use less gelatin. If Neufchâtel cheese is not available, you may substitute an additional 8 ounces of cream cheese.

DESSERT SOUFFLÉS

BRANDIED APPLE SOUFFLÉ
WITH FOAMY SAUCE

SERVES 12

FOR THE SWEETENED APPLESAUCE
  (yield 4–5 cups):
16 *tart apples*
1½ *cups water* (*about*)
 1 *cup sugar* (*or more, if desired*)
 1 *cup raisins*
⅓ *cup apple brandy*
¼ *teaspoon cinnamon*
 1 *tablespoon lemon juice, strained*
 1 *tablespoon grated lemon rind*

FOR THE TOPPING:
 4 *eggs*
 4 *tablespoons unsalted butter*

 1 *cup sugar*
½ *cup all-purpose flour*
 2 *cups hot milk*
2⅛ *tablespoons cinnamon sugar* (*2*
   tablespoons sugar blended with
   ⅛ teaspoon cinnamon)

FOR THE FOAMY SAUCE:
 2 *eggs, separated*
½ *cup sugar*
pinch of salt
 2 *tablespoons apple brandy*
 1 *cup heavy cream, whipped*

METHOD:

1. *Prepare the Sweetened Applesauce:* Wash, cut and remove core and seeds from the apples and cut into quarters. Cook in water to cover until soft. Put through a sieve and add sugar. Keep warm until needed. While the apples are cooking, soak raisins in hot water to cover for 10 minutes. Drain well; add apple brandy and cinnamon and let stand 1 hour. Combine raisin mixture, warm applesauce, lemon juice and rind and blend well.

2. Pour mixture into a buttered 3-quart soufflé dish or heat-proof casserole.

3. Preheat oven to 350°F.

4. *Prepare the Topping:* Separate eggs. Beat egg yolks, butter and sugar together; add flour and slowly blend in the hot milk. Beat egg whites until stiff but not dry, and fold into the yolk mixture until no streaks of white remain. Pour over applesauce mixture in soufflé dish, and sprinkle top with cinnamon sugar.

5. Set dish in pan of hot water and bake for 35 minutes or until top is firm to the touch (bottom will not be firm).

6. *Prepare the Foamy Sauce:* Beat together the egg yolks and sugar until light. Beat egg whites with a pinch of salt until stiff and fold into yolks. Add apple brandy and fold in the whipped cream. Serve the soufflé hot with the sauce spooned over each serving.

HOT APPLE SOUFFLÉ ALEXANDRIA WITH RUM CREAM

SERVES 6

FOR THE APPLESAUCE BASE:
4 *McIntosh apples*
½ *cup water*
1 *tablespoon lemon juice, strained*
½ *cup granulated sugar*
¼ *cup brown sugar*
⅛ *teaspoon cinnamon*
1 *tablespoon unsalted butter*

FOR THE TOPPING:
3 *tablespoons unsalted butter*
1 *cup sugar*
2 *tablespoons lemon juice, strained*
1 *tablespoon grated lemon rind*

3 *egg yolks*
⅛ *teaspoon cinnamon*
¼ *cup all-purpose flour*
¼ *teaspoon salt*
2 *cups milk*
3 *egg whites*
1 *tablespoon cinnamon sugar (1 tablespoon sugar blended with generous pinch cinnamon)*

FOR THE RUM CREAM (makes 2 cups, approximately):
1 *cup heavy cream*
2 *tablespoons powdered sugar*
¼ *cup light rum*

METHOD:

1. *Prepare the Applesauce Base:* Core apples. Slice (do not peel), add water, cover and cook until the apples are soft. Put through a coarse sieve, add lemon juice, sugars, cinnamon and butter and mix. Pour into a buttered 9-by-13-inch baking pan.

2. Preheat oven to 350°F.

3. *Prepare the Topping:* Cream butter and sugar, add lemon juice, lemon rind and egg yolks. Beat until smooth and creamy. Blend cinnamon, flour and salt and fold into butter mixture alternately with milk. Beat egg whites until stiff but not dry and fold in until no streaks of white remain. Pour over applesauce base, and sprinkle the cinnamon sugar over the top.

4. Bake for 50 minutes or until the custard top is set. This soufflé has a firm top and the bottom remains soft.

5. *Meanwhile, prepare the Rum Cream:* Whip the cream with the powdered sugar and then fold in the rum. Serve the soufflé hot with Rum Cream spooned over each serving.

CHERRY SOUFFLÉ

SERVES 6

4 *eggs, separated*
1 *cup sugar*
1 *pound fresh black (Bing)*

cherries, washed, dried, pitted
and coarsely chopped
2–3 *tablespoons cherry brandy*

METHOD:

1. Preheat oven to 325°F.

2. Beat egg yolks, add sugar and continue beating until a thick and creamy consistency.

3. Beat egg whites until stiff but not dry.

4. Mix the chopped cherries and cherry brandy with yolk mixture.

5. Fold in egg whites until mixture is well blended and no streaks of white remain.

6. Pour into a buttered 1½- or 2-quart soufflé dish.

7. Bake until soufflé puffs up and is set, approximately 1 hour. Serve immediately.

MAGIC CHOCOLATE SOUFFLÉ

SERVES 6

5 *ounces dark sweet chocolate*
3 *tablespoons water*
1 *teaspoon instant coffee powder*
½ *cup all-purpose flour*
2 *cups cold milk*

1 *teaspoon vanilla*
½ *cup sugar*
4 *egg yolks*
7 *egg whites*
⅛ *teaspoon salt*

METHOD:

1. Preheat oven to 375°F. Butter a 1½-quart soufflé dish or charlotte mold and dust with sugar.

2. Melt chocolate with the water and instant coffee powder over low heat in a heavy saucepan. Set aside to cool.

3. Mix flour with a small amount of milk to make a smooth, thick paste.

4. Stir in remaining milk gradually to avoid making lumps.

5. Cook over medium heat until mixture is thick and smooth, stirring constantly.

6. Allow to cool slightly, then add chocolate mixture, vanilla and sugar.

7. Add yolks and mix well. Beat whites with salt until very stiff and glossy. Fold into chocolate mixture until no streaks of white remain. Pour soufflé into buttered soufflé dish and bake on center shelf of oven for 40 minutes or until well puffed up and firm. Serve immediately.

CREAM CHEESE SOUFFLÉ

SERVES 6

two 3-ounce packages cream cheese
1 *cup sour cream*
3 *eggs, separated*
6 *tablespoons honey*

pinch of salt
sweetened whipped cream
fresh strawberries

METHOD:

1. Preheat oven to 350°F.

2. Allow cream cheese to soften at room temperature, then beat until smooth and fluffy. Blend in sour cream.

3. Beat egg yolks, add to cream cheese mixture. Stir in honey and salt.

4. Beat egg whites until stiff but not dry. Fold into cream cheese mixture until no streaks of white remain.

5. Pour into a buttered 1½-quart soufflé dish or oven-proof casserole. Bake until top is golden brown—about 45 minutes. Serve hot with sweetened whipped cream and strawberries.

INDIVIDUAL LEMON SOUFFLÉS

SERVES 8

2 *cups sugar*
½ *cup all-purpose flour*
¼ *teaspoon salt*
4 *tablespoons melted butter*

½ *cup lemon juice, strained*
2 *tablespoons grated lemon rind*
6 *eggs, separated*
3 *cups milk*

METHOD:

1. Preheat oven to 350°F.

2. Blend sugar, flour and salt together in a bowl. Add melted butter, lemon juice and rind, and mix well.

3. Beat the egg yolks well and stir into mixture with the milk. Fold in stiffly beaten egg whites until no streaks of white remain.

4. Pour into 8 greased individual soufflé dishes or custard cups. Place in pan of water and bake for 45 minutes, or until the soufflés are puffed. Serve immediately.

QUICK, COOL LEMON SOUFFLÉ

SERVES 6–8

Elegant, cool and creamy, this no-bake soufflé has the lively flavor of fresh lemons. It whips together in only 20 minutes; after that, let your refrigerator take over until you are ready to serve.

2 *envelopes (2 tablespoons)*	2 *cups (1 pint) heavy cream*
unflavored gelatin	1 *tablespoon grated lemon rind*
½ *cup water*	⅔ *cup lemon juice, strained*
6 *eggs*	*candied violets, lemon slices and*
1½ *cups sugar*	*mint leaves for garnish*

METHOD:

1. Prepare 4-cup soufflé dish or other straight-sided baking dish with aluminum foil collar the following way: Measure 2 lengths of foil long enough to encircle dish. Fold in half lengthwise (foil should be about 2 inches higher than the rim of the dish). Fasten collar around dish with tape or paper clips.

2. Sprinkle gelatin over water in a small saucepan. Let stand 10 minutes, until gelatin is softened. Place saucepan over very low heat until gelatin dissolves (mixture will be clear). Remove from heat; cool.

3. Combine eggs and sugar in the large bowl of an electric mixer. Beat at high speed until very thick and light—about 7 minutes.

4. Whip 1½ cups of the cream until soft peaks form; refrigerate.

5. Combine lemon rind and juice with cooled gelatin, then pour into egg-sugar mixture. Beat until well blended.

6. Remove bowl from mixer. Chill briefly for 5 minutes either in refrigerator or by placing bowl in another large bowl partly filled with

ice and water. Stir frequently until mixture is just thick enough to mound.

7. Fold in whipped cream until no streaks of white remain and pour mixture into foil-collared dish. Refrigerate at least 3 hours, or until set. Remove collar gently, freeing soufflé from foil, if necessary, with a small paring knife. Whip remaining cream. Garnish soufflé with whipped cream, candied violets, lemon slices and mint leaves arranged around the violets to resemble the leaves of a flower.

ORANGE SOUFFLÉ WITH RASPBERRY SAUCE

SERVES 6–8

4 *egg yolks*
¾ *cup sugar*
¼ *cup all-purpose flour*
1½ *cups milk, scalded*
1 *orange rind, grated*
½ *cup orange juice*
6 *egg whites*

FOR THE RASPBERRY SAUCE:
2 *cups fresh raspberries, washed and dried thoroughly*
3 *tablespoons red raspberry jelly, melted*
1½ *tablespoons orange-flavored liqueur or to taste*

METHOD:

1. Preheat oven to 375°F.

2. In a heavy saucepan beat together egg yolks and sugar until mixture is thick and creamy. Stir in flour and then, very gradually, stir in the scalded milk.

3. Cook over low heat, stirring constantly with whisk, until it is just below boiling point. Continue cooking (do not let it boil) for 3 minutes.

4. Let mixture cool until lukewarm, then stir in the grated orange rind and juice.

5. In a bowl, whip egg whites until they stand in peaks, fold into orange-flavored base until no white streaks remain.

6. Pour into a 1½- or 2-quart straight-sided soufflé dish which has been buttered and lightly coated with sugar. Bake soufflé on center shelf of the oven for 30 to 35 minutes or until it is well puffed.

7. *Meanwhile, prepare the Raspberry Sauce:* Combine raspberries, jelly and liqueur. Refrigerate until chilled. Serve soufflé immediately with Raspberry Sauce.

MOUSSES AND CREAMS

APRICOT MOUSSE

SERVES 6

This is a very light and refreshing dessert.

1½ cups apricot puree (see Note)
1½ cups sugar
  6 tablespoons Kirsch
  1 cup (½ pint) heavy cream,
    whipped

butter (for sealing cover of mold)
ice
coarse (Kosher) salt

METHOD:

1. Mix apricot puree, sugar and Kirsch very well. Fold in whipped cream gently until no white streaks remain.

2. Pour into a mold (about 1½ quarts) that has been rinsed in ice water.

3. Cover tightly with a piece of foil or parchment paper, and seal the edges with butter.

4. Put the mold into a larger bowl or basin, pack ice and salt around it and leave to set for 2 to 3 hours, or until the mousse is thick and firm. (Make sure mold is well sealed so the salt water will not get in.)

Note: To make apricot puree, cook 1½ pounds of fresh or canned unpeeled apricots with water to cover until tender—about 15 minutes for the fresh. If using canned apricots, simply heat through before pureeing. Drain and puree in blender or food mill.

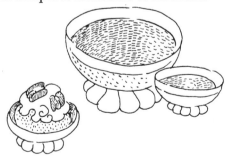

CHOCOLATE MOUSSE

SERVES 6

½ cup milk	1 teaspoon vanilla
¼ cup strong coffee	3 tablespoons brandy (optional)
10 ounces semisweet chocolate	1½ cups heavy cream, whipped
6 egg yolks, beaten	(with sugar to taste, if desired)

METHOD:

1. Heat milk, coffee and chocolate in top of double boiler over hot water until chocolate melts (or see Note below). Remove from heat.

2. Beat melted chocolate into egg yolks, beating until well blended. Beat in vanilla and brandy, mixing until well blended.

3. Fold in 1 cup of the whipped cream, reserving the remaining cream to garnish mousse when served. Serve in a round soufflé dish or a crystal bowl and mound whipped cream over top.

Note: Alternate Method: Chocolate may be left to soften in a warm area (such as on top of the stove) in a dish or mixing bowl for several hours or until soft and then beaten with a wire whisk until creamy, at which point the hot milk and coffee are added. Beat in the egg yolks one at a time, then beat in the vanilla and brandy and fold in 1 cup of the whipped cream (reserving the rest for garnishing the mousse). This method retains the chocolate fragrance very well.

CHOCOLATE-WALNUT BAVARIAN CREAM

SERVES 6

Nuts over chocolate? Chocolate and nuts must have been created for each other, they go together so deliciously.

6-ounces semisweet chocolate bits	¼ cup cognac
½ cup milk	1½ cups heavy cream, whipped
2 teaspoons unflavored gelatin	½ cup chopped toasted walnuts
2 teaspoons cold water	1 square (1 ounce) semisweet
2 eggs, separated	chocolate, melted and cooled,
⅛ teaspoon salt	½ teaspoon instant coffee
¼ teaspoon cream of tartar	powder, and walnut halves for
3 tablespoons sugar	garnish

METHOD:

1. Combine the chocolate bits and milk in a heavy saucepan, or in top of double boiler over water, and cook over very low heat. Stir occasionally until chocolate melts; remove from heat.

2. Sprinkle gelatin over the surface of the cold water and let it soak about 3 minutes until it has absorbed the water and is translucent.

3. Beat egg yolks slightly. Stir in a little of the melted chocolate mixture, then return the rest of chocolate mixture to low heat; add the yolks gradually and cook, stirring, until slightly thickened. Do not allow to boil. Stir gelatin into hot chocolate mixture until dissolved. Cool to room temperature.

4. Beat the egg whites with the salt and cream of tartar until stiff. Gradually beat in the sugar.

5. Stir cognac into the cooled chocolate mixture. Fold in beaten egg whites, 1 cup of the whipped cream (reserve the other ½ cup for the garnish) and the chopped nuts. Turn into a serving bowl and refrigerate overnight or until firm.

6. Fold the ounce of melted chocolate and the coffee into the remaining whipped cream and, using a pastry bag, pipe rosettes to form a garnish on top of the mouse. Decorate with walnut halves and serve.

RED RASPBERRY CREAM

SERVES 6

three 10-ounce packages frozen unsweetened raspberries	*1½ tablespoons cornstarch*
¼ cup sugar	*2 cups (1 pint) heavy cream*

METHOD:

1. Thaw raspberries. Place in a saucepan and simmer slowly over medium heat for 5 minutes.

2. Dissolve the sugar and cornstarch in a little cold water, add to raspberries and cook until mixture thickens. Let cool.

3. Whip cream and gently fold in. Put into an attractive serving bowl or individual dishes and refrigerate until well chilled and firm.

RUSSIAN CREAM

1 *envelope (1 tablespoon)*
   unflavored gelatin
½ *cup cold water*
⅔ *cup light cream*
⅓ *cup honey*

almond extract (optional)
1 *cup sour cream*
strawberries or raspberries for
   garnish

METHOD:

1. Sprinkle gelatin over cold water and let stand about 3 minutes until it has absorbed the water and is translucent.

2. In a saucepan, heat the cream and stir in the honey just until combined. Add gelatin mixture and heat until gelatin is completely dissolved. If desired, add a drop or two of almond extract now. Remove from heat and let cool.

3. When cool, gently stir in the sour cream. Pour into mold or individual sherbet glasses and refrigerate until firm. Do not freeze.

4. Garnish with strawberries or raspberries and serve.

SNOW CREAM WITH RED RASPBERRY SAUCE

2 *cups (1 pint) heavy cream*
2 *teaspoons unflavored gelatin*
⅓ *cup cold water*
1⅓ *cups superfine sugar*
1⅓ *cups sour cream*
one 8-ounce package cream cheese
   2 *teaspoons vanilla*

FOR THE RED RASPBERRY SAUCE:
one 10-ounce package frozen un-
   sweetened raspberries, thawed

1¼ *teaspoons cornstarch dissolved*
   in ⅔ *cup cold water*
⅔ *cup granulated or superfine*
   sugar
3 *tablespoons red wine or orange*
   liqueur

1⅓ *cups heavy cream, whipped*
   (with sugar to taste, if desired)

METHOD:

1. In a heavy-bottomed saucepan, bring the pint of cream to a boil. While cream is cooking, sprinkle gelatin over surface of the water and

let it soak until it is absorbed and translucent—about 3 minutes. Remove pan with the cream from heat and add gelatin, stirring until dissolved and well blended. Add sugar, mix and let cool. When cooled, pour sour cream over, add cream cheese and vanilla, and whip with a wire whisk until smooth. Pour into a serving bowl or individual dishes and refrigerate until firm.

2. *Meanwhile, prepare the Red Raspberry Sauce:* Place raspberries in blender jar, add dissolved cornstarch and ⅔ cup of sugar. Blend and strain. Heat in a saucepan over low flame, stirring constantly until it thickens. Add red wine or orange liqueur and chill.

3. Serve with a tablespoon or two of the Raspberry Sauce spooned over each portion and topped with a dollop of whipped cream.

STRAWBERRY-ORANGE CREAM

SERVES 6

1½ *pints strawberries, washed,* *dried and hulled*	3 *teaspoons grated orange rind*
¾ *cup sugar*	1½ *teaspoons lemon juice*
¾ *cup fresh orange juice*	1½ *cups heavy cream, whipped*

METHOD:

1. Place berries in bowl, sprinkle with 1 tablespoon of the sugar, mix and let stand for 30 minutes.

2. Place remaining sugar, orange juice, rind and lemon juice in a small saucepan. Bring to boil, stir and cook gently for 10 minutes. Remove from heat and let cool.

3. Combine whipped cream and cooled orange syrup, spoon over berries and refrigerate until well chilled.

VELVET CREAM WITH
CHOCOLATE FUDGE SAUCE

SERVES 6

1 envelope (1 tablespoon) unflavored gelatin, plus ½
teaspoon
¼ cup peach juice
1 cup milk
½ cup sugar
⅛ teaspoon salt
2 eggs
2 cups (1 pint) heavy cream,
whipped
1 tablespoon vanilla

FOR THE CHOCOLATE FUDGE SAUCE:
2 ounces unsweetened chocolate
¾ cup sugar
¼ teaspoon salt
½ cup corn syrup
½ cup milk
2 tablespoons unsalted butter
2 teaspoons vanilla

⅓ cup grated coconut toasted in
325°F. oven on baking sheet for
10 minutes, stirring frequently,
to a light golden brown

METHOD:

1. Sprinkle gelatin over the peach juice and let stand until the liquid is absorbed and gelatin is translucent.

2. Bring milk to slow boil in a saucepan and add the softened gelatin, sugar and salt, stirring until dissolved.

3. Beat eggs and add to the milk mixture. Cook on very low heat for about 4 or 5 minutes, stirring until slightly thickened. Remove from heat and let cool.

4. Fold in the whipped cream and vanilla. Turn into a 1½-quart mold and place in refrigerator. Let chill until set and ready to serve.

5. *Prepare the Chocolate Fudge Sauce:* Mix the chocolate, sugar, salt, corn syrup and milk together in a heavy saucepan. Cook over low heat, stirring, until chocolate is melted. Continue cooking until thickened, about 25 minutes, stirring often. Remove from heat, add butter. Cool and stir in vanilla.

6. Serve the Chocolate Fudge Sauce over each serving and sprinkle with the toasted coconut.

DESSERT MOLDS

BLUEBERRY ABSECON

SERVES 6

Absecon is a town in southeastern New Jersey near an area renowned for its cultivation of blueberries. The Absecon, an Indian Tribe, were the original inhabitants of some of the islands just off the Atlantic Ocean there. When the area was later settled by colonists, they called the islands Absecon. One of the islands was later called Atlantic City. Perhaps the "Rocks of Absecon" used in this recipe derive their name from the dangerous shoals along the coast, where many ships, particularly pirate ships, were wrecked.

4 pints (8 cups) blueberries, washed and dried
2 cups sugar
¼ teaspoon freshly grated nutmeg
½ cup Kirsch
1 cup water
2 tablespoons (2 envelopes) unflavored gelatin

½ cup water

FOR THE ROCKS OF ABSECON:
16 slices white bread, crusts removed
½ cup sugar
¼ teaspoon freshly grated nutmeg
6 tablespoons Kirsch

METHOD:

1. Put 2 pints blueberries in a bowl, add 1 cup of sugar, the nutmeg and ½ cup Kirsch.

2. Crush half the berries with a spoon. Cover all and let stand at room temperature for 1 hour.

3. Place the remaining 2 pints of blueberries in a saucepan with the other cup of sugar and 1 cup of water. Cook gently for about 5 minutes.

4. Sprinkle gelatin over ½ cup of cold water and let it soak for 3 minutes until absorbed and translucent; add to hot blueberry mixture. Stir until gelatin dissolves and remove from heat. Add to the uncooked blueberry mixture and let cool; pour into a 2-quart oiled salad mold. Refrigerate until set. When ready to serve, reverse the mold onto a platter and unmold. For easy removal, place a warm damp towel over the mold if it sticks.

5. *Prepare the Rocks of Absecon:* Preheat oven to 350°F. Cut bread into ½-inch cubes, add sugar and nutmeg; toss together and toast in oven until light gold. Remove and sprinkle with the 6 tablespoons Kirsch. When ready to serve the blueberry mold, toss the toasted "Rocks" around the edge of the platter.

SIMCA'S MARQUISE GLACÉ AU CHOCOLAT

SERVES 8

10 *ounces sweet chocolate*
¼ *cup strong coffee*
4 *eggs, separated*
¾ *cup (1½ sticks) sweet butter*
salt

⅔ *cup sugar*
¼ *cup water*
1 *cup (½ pint) heavy cream*
½ *teaspoon vanilla*

METHOD:

1. In the top of double boiler (preferably enamel) set over hot water, slowly melt the chocolate with the coffee, stirring occasionally.

2. Stir in the egg yolks one at a time and continue to cook over hot water until mixture thickens slightly. Do not allow the mixture to boil.

3. Remove pan from the hot water and add the butter cut into small pieces a few at a time. Stir after each addition so that butter melts before adding more. Set aside until needed (see step 7).

4. Beat egg whites with a pinch of salt until they are opaque.

5. Meanwhile, place the sugar and water in a small heavy saucepan. Bring to a boil, stirring until sugar dissolves. Then, bring mixture back to a boil, wihout stirring, until it registers 200° or 225°F. on thermometer. Remove the pan from the heat; let cool slightly.

6. Start beating egg white mixture again and continue beating, while pouring the syrup slowly into the bowl in a steady stream. Use an electric hand beater for this so you can do both simultaneously. Beat this meringue until shiny and firm.

7. Fold the chocolate-butter cream into the meringue and beat well. Turn into a 2-quart stainless steel bowl. Refrigerate until firm.

8. With a flexible spatula or knife, loosen the mold around the edges and sides and gently turn out onto a chilled serving plate (if necessary wrap a warm, damp towel around mold to ease it out). Pour the heavy cream into a chilled bowl, set on ice cubes and beat slowly until mixture is thick. Stir in the vanilla.

9. Using a pastry bag and star tube, decorate the top of the mold

(marquise) with the cream in a lacy design, then make a rim around the bottom with the remaining cream. Serve immediately after decorating.

MAPLE CREAM

SERVES 6

1 cup sifted confectioner's sugar	¼ cup cold water
3 egg yolks	¾ tablespoon maple extract
1⅓ cups milk, scalded	1½ cups heavy cream, whipped
2 teaspoons vanilla extract	shaved chocolate and/or fresh
1½ tablespoons unflavored gelatin	strawberries for garnish

METHOD:

1. Beat sugar and egg yolks together until creamy.

2. Stir in milk and vanilla; cook in top of double boiler over hot (not boiling) water, stirring constantly, for 2 minutes or until mixture coats a spoon. Remove from heat, strain through sieve and set aside.

3. Sprinkle gelatin over surface of cold water to soften until all liquid is absorbed and gelatin translucent, about 3 minutes. Stir into the egg-and-milk mixture. Return to heat, stirring, just until gelatin is dissolved. Strain through sieve into a bowl. Blend in maple extract and allow to cool.

4. When mixture is almost set, fold in whipped cream. Pour mixture into a 1-quart mold which has been moistened with cold water.

5. Refrigerate until firm. Loosen the mold around the edges and down the side with a spatula and gently unmold onto a chilled serving plate (if necessary wrap a warm, damp towel around mold to ease it out). Serve garnished with shaved chocolate and/or fresh strawberries.

RUM CHOCOLATE SOUFFLÉED DESSERT

SERVES 10–12

4½ ounces (squares) sweet chocolate
2 tablespoons very strong coffee
¾ cup sugar
¼ teaspoon salt
4½ tablespoons all-purpose flour
¾ cup (1½ sticks) unsalted butter, melted

¼ cup rum
6 eggs, separated
1 cup heavy cream, whipped
    (with sugar to taste, if desired)
candied violets (or any other
    decorative candy)

METHOD:

1. Preheat oven to 350°F.

2. Line the bottom of a buttered 2½- or 3-quart soufflé dish (or spring-form pan) with wax or parchment paper.

3. Melt chocolate together with coffee in the top of double boiler over hot, but not boiling, water.

4. Mix sugar, salt and flour together and add to the chocolate along with the butter and rum. Mix well.

5. Place egg yolks in a large bowl and beat lightly. Remove double boiler from heat, let cool slightly, and gradually add chocolate mixture to egg yolks, stirring well to mix.

6. Beat egg whites until stiff but not dry and carefully fold into chocolate mixture until no white is visible. Do not overmix. Pour the batter into prepared soufflé dish. Set in a shallow pan of hot water. Bake 1 hour or until set.

7. Allow to cool to room temperature, then refrigerate. (The dessert will shrink as it cools.)

8. If it has been baked in a soufflé dish, loosen the edges and sides of mold with a spatula and unmold the dessert onto a serving platter. Peel off the paper. If it has been cooked in a spring-form pan, remove the sides and, with the help of a spatula, slide the dessert from the base of the pan onto a serving plate.

9. Frost or pipe with whipped cream and decorate with violets or other decorative candy. Refrigerate until served.

STRAWBERRY MOUSSELINE

SERVES 10

3 *pints fresh strawberries*
⅔ *cup sugar*
2 *tablespoons rum*
1 *tablespoon lemon juice*
1 *teaspoon vanilla*
2 *envelopes (2 tablespoons)*
  unflavored gelatin

½ *cup water*
10–12 *ladyfingers*
½ *cup Curaçao liqueur*
1½ *cups heavy cream, whipped*
fresh strawberries for garnish

METHOD:

1. Hull berries and rub them through a sieve into a bowl. Blend with sugar, rum, lemon juice and vanilla; set aside.

2. Sprinkle gelatin over surface of cold water and let soak until all liquid is absorbed and gelatin is translucent, about 3 minutes; then heat gently in saucepan until dissolved. Add to pureed berries. Set bowl into larger bowl filled with cracked ice and stir mixture until it begins to thicken.

3. Rinse a mold, preferably fluted, with cold water. Sprinkle ladyfingers with Curaçao and line sides of mold with them.

4. Fold whipped cream into berry mixture and pour into mold. Refrigerate for several hours or overnight until firm and well chilled. Loosen the edges and sides with a spatula (if necessary wrap a warm, damp towel around mold to ease it out); unmold onto serving dish and garnish with whole berries.

CUSTARDS

CARROT CUSTARD WITH HONEY

SERVES 6

1 cup light cream
1 tablespoon arrowroot
¼ teaspoon freshly grated nutmeg
pinch of salt
4 small eggs, lightly beaten

2 tablespoons juice from carrots
2 cups finely grated raw carrots,
  juice pressed out and reserved
1 tablespoon lemon juice, strained
¼ cup clover honey

METHOD:

1. Preheat oven to 350°F. Butter a 2-quart casserole well.
2. Heat ½ cup cream in saucepan over low heat.
3. Dissolve arrowroot in the remaining cream. Stir into hot cream and cook to thicken, still over low heat. Season with nutmeg and a few grains of salt. Add eggs slowly, beating as you add, and the carrot juice.
4. Add lemon juice to honey and stir into carrots. Fold carrots into egg-cream sauce until well incorporated. Pour into the casserole. Set casserole in a pan half filled with water and bake until set, approximately 30 minutes. Keep checking: If water boils, custard may separate, so lower heat if necessary. Serve either warm or chilled.

CRÈME BRULÉE

SERVES 6

2 cups (1 pint) heavy cream
4 egg yolks
2½ tablespoons granulated sugar

1 teaspoon vanilla
¼ cup sifted light brown sugar

METHOD:

1. Preheat oven to 325°F.
2. Heat cream in top of double boiler over hot water. Beat egg yolks, adding granulated sugar gradually.
3. Remove cream from heat and pour ¼ cup over egg mixture, beat-

ing constantly, then very slowly add remaining cream, stirring continuously. Add vanilla.

4. Pour into a 1½-quart casserole. Place in a pan of hot water and bake uncovered about 45 minutes, or until set.

5. When custard is set, sprinkle with the sifted brown sugar. Place under broiler for 1 or 2 minutes, until sugar melts.

6. Refrigerate and serve very cold.

FRUITED RUM CUSTARD AND BLUEBERRY PARFAIT

SERVES 6

½ cup sugar
2 tablespoons cornstarch
⅛ teaspoon salt
1 cup milk
1½ cups heavy cream
4 egg yolks, well beaten
2 tablespoons unsalted butter

2 tablespoons dark rum
¼ cup chopped mixed candied
    fruits (such as pineapple,
    cherries, apricots, orange peel)
2 cups fresh blueberries, rinsed
    and drained

METHOD:

1. In the top of a double boiler over hot water, mix the sugar, cornstarch and salt together. Stir in milk and 1 cup of the cream. Bring just to a boil, stirring constantly; lower heat, cover and cook slowly over low heat for 10 minutes, stirring occasionally.

2. Beat in egg yolks and butter and continue to cook while stirring until mixture thickens slightly. Cool to lukewarm. Stir in rum and candied fruits. Whip remaining ½ cup cream until stiff, and fold in. Refrigerate until well chilled.

3. Spoon alternate layers of fruited rum custard and blueberries into parfait glasses and serve.

HEAVENLY CUSTARD

SERVES 6

3 cups sugar
1 cup water
3 eggs
6 egg yolks

½ cup milk
½ teaspoon vanilla
few drops of lemon juice
heavy cream, whipped

METHOD:

1. Preheat oven to 350°F.

2. Make a simple syrup in a saucepan: Stir sugar into water until dissolved, bring to a boil, cover and cook until it thickens, about 6 minutes. Cool.

3. While syrup is cooling, lightly beat the eggs and egg yolks together. Add milk, vanilla and a few drops of lemon juice and set aside.

4. Pour the syrup into the bottom of a 1½-quart mold.

5. Pass the egg-milk mixture through a strainer and pour it into the mold on top of the sugar syrup.

6. Place the mold in a pan of water and bake in the oven until done, about 1 hour. Insert a knife around the edge; if it comes out clean, the custard is done. Refrigerate until chilled.

7. When ready to be served, run a knife around the edge and turn the mold upside down on a plate so that the custard will fall on the plate and the syrup will run over it. Serve with whipped cream.

STRAWBERRY CREAM CUSTARD

SERVES 6

4 egg yolks, lightly beaten
2 tablespoons sugar
1½ cups milk
½ teaspoon vanilla
2 cups (1 pint) heavy cream,
    whipped

3 pints (6 cups) strawberries,
    hulled and washed
½ cup superfine sugar
½ cup Kirsch

METHOD:

1. Place egg yolks, 2 tablespoons sugar, milk and vanilla in top of double boiler over barely simmering water. Stir until mixture is smooth

and thick enough to coat a spoon. Remove from heat and let cool. Fold in whipped cream and refrigerate until well chilled and set.

2. Place berries in bowl, sprinkle with sugar and pour Kirsch over them. Mix and refrigerate until chilled.

3. Drain the berries. Combine drained berries and custard, blend gently and refrigerate 1 hour before serving. Spoon a little of the Kirsch-sugar syrup over each serving if desired.

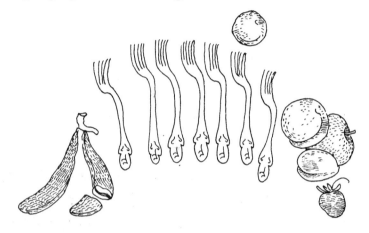

PUDDINGS

GRUNT BERRY

SERVES 6

2 cups (1 pint) berries (blueberries, blackberries, raspberries
or the berry of your choice),
washed and drained
1 cup water
½ cup honey
1 cup whole wheat flour

¼ teaspoon salt
1 tablespoon baking powder
½ cup ground pecans
1 tablespoon unsalted butter
1 cup milk
whipped cream

METHOD:

1. Mix together berries, water and honey and place in a buttered mold with a tightly fitted cover. (The mold should only be ⅔ full when all the batter is added, so choose one of suitable size.)

2. Sift flour, salt and baking powder together; add to ground pecans.

3. With a pastry blender or tips of fingers cut the butter into flour mixture and add the milk, working them together lightly until a soft dough is formed. Drop by spoonfuls on top of the fruit.

4. Place mold on a trivet in a heavy pan and add boiling water so that it comes up to 1 inch from the top of the mold. Cover tightly and steam pudding on high heat until the steam starts to escape; then turn heat to low. Total cooking time is 1 hour. Serve warm with whipped cream.

FRUIT AND NUT PUDDING WITH CREAM

SERVES 8–10

8 *eggs, separated*
2 *cups sugar*
2 *cups whole grain bread crumbs*
  (*such as whole wheat*)
4 *teaspoons vanilla*
1 *tablespoon baking powder*

2 *cups seedless raisins*
2 *cups chopped walnuts*
2 *cups* (*1 pound*) *cooked, pitted*
  and chopped prunes (*see Note*)
whipped cream

METHOD:

1. Preheat oven to 350°F.

2. Beat egg yolks very lightly, adding sugar slowly.

3. Beat whites until very stiff, then stir into yolk-sugar mixture.

4. Add crumbs, vanilla and baking powder and mix well. Then add raisins, walnuts and prunes.

5. Pour batter into a buttered, floured baking dish. Bake for 45 minutes, or until firm. Test with a knife; when it comes out clean, pudding is done.

6. Let cool, cut into squares and serve with whipped cream.

Note: To cook prunes, place in a saucepan with 1½ cups of water. Bring to a boil and let boil for 2 or 3 minutes, then simmer for 10 to 15 minutes. Drain well, remove pits, then chop.

OLD-FASHIONED STEAMED
MOLASSES FRUIT PUDDING
WITH BOURBON HARD SAUCE

SERVES 12

2 cups fine bread crumbs
1 cup Bourbon
4 eggs, beaten
1 cup orange juice
½ cup molasses
8 tablespoons (1 stick) unsalted
  butter, melted
1 teaspoon baking soda
1 cup currants
8 ounces diced candied pineapple
¼ cup all-purpose flour

2 teaspoons cinnamon
¼ teaspoon grated nutmeg
¼ teaspoon ground cloves

FOR THE BOURBON HARD SAUCE:
¾ cup (1½ sticks) unsalted butter
2½ cups confectioner's sugar, sifted
3 tablespoons Bourbon

½ cup Bourbon
sprig of holly for garnish

METHOD:

1. Combine crumbs and 1 cup Bourbon in a large mixing bowl. Mix well, let stand 15 minutes.

2. Add eggs, orange juice, molasses, butter and baking soda; set aside until needed.

3. Combine currants and pineapple. Add spices to flour and sprinkle over combined fruits.

4. Add fruit mixture to crumb-egg-molasses mixture. Mix well. Turn into 2 buttered 1-quart molds, filling each ⅔ full. Place molds on a trivet in a heavy pan, such as a roasting pan, over 1 inch of boiling water. Cover pan tightly. Steam on high heat at first, and then, when the steam starts to escape, on low, for a total of 1½ hours or until pudding tests done when a skewer is inserted and comes out clean. Add more water to the pan to the 1-inch level if it evaporates.

5. *Prepare the Bourbon Hard Sauce:* Cream butter, blend in sifted sugar and add the 3 tablespoons Bourbon. Beat until fluffy.

6. To serve: Turn the puddings onto a large flameproof serving platter. Garnish with sprigs of holly and take to table. Heat the ½ cup Bourbon and pour ¼ cup over each pudding. Ignite Bourbon with a lighted match (stand back and be careful). Serve immediately with a scoop of Bourbon Hard Sauce at the side of each portion.

BAKED INDIAN PUDDING

SERVES 6

6 cups milk
¼ cup honey
¾ cup cornmeal
4 eggs, lightly beaten
1½ teaspoons grated orange peel

⅔ teaspoon cinnamon
1½ teaspoons powdered ginger
1 teaspoon salt
1 cup molasses
vanilla ice cream

METHOD:

1. Preheat oven to 450°F.

2. Heat milk with honey in a saucepan and cook until milk is scalded.

3. Add cornmeal and stir constantly with wire whisk until smooth, well blended and slightly thickened. Remove from stove.

4. Beat a little of the hot milk-cornmeal mixture into the eggs. Then combine egg mixture with the rest of the milk mixture, stirring constantly until well blended.

5. Add orange peel, cinnamon, ginger, salt and molasses. Mix well and pour into buttered baking dish about 2 inches deep.

6. Cover with aluminum foil. Set in a pan of water and bake for 1 hour. Remove foil and bake 10 minutes longer. Remove from oven and serve warm with vanilla ice cream.

HOT LEMON SOUFFLÉ PUDDING WITH LEMON ZEST CREAM

SERVES 6–8

6 tablespoons unsalted butter
2 cups sugar
1 cup fresh lemon juice, strained
3 tablespoons grated lemon rind
4 egg yolks, beaten
7 tablespoons all-purpose flour
2⅔ cups milk

4 egg whites
¼ teaspoon salt

FOR THE LEMON ZEST CREAM:
6 lemons, washed
1½ cups sugar
1½ cups hot water
1½ cups heavy cream

METHOD:

1. Preheat oven to 325°F.
2. Cream butter and add sugar, lemon juice and rind.
3. Add egg yolks and beat to blend.
4. Fold in flour and milk alternately.
5. Beat egg whites with salt until stiff but not dry; fold into mixture.
6. Pour mixture into a low, well-buttered 1½-quart casserole, set in a pan of hot water, and bake until firm (the bottom will be soft), approximately 25 minutes.
7. *Meanwhile, prepare the Lemon Zest Cream:* Cut the zest (the oily outer peel minus the bitter white pith) from the lemons (save lemons for another use), being careful not to cut through to the bitter pith. Dissolve sugar in hot water and boil in a saucepan, stirring, for 5 minutes. Remove syrup from heat and allow to cool. Place in the blender, add the zest and blend: zest should not be too fine. Whip the cream and add the lemon syrup, folding until well mixed.
8. Serve pudding from casserole and top each serving with Lemon Zest Cream.

WILD RICE PUDDING WITH RAISINS

SERVES 6

2½ *cups water*
pinch of salt
  1 *cup wild rice, rinsed and*
    drained
  ½ *cup raisins, washed and drained*
  2 *tablespoons unsalted butter,*
    softened
  3 *tablespoons honey, preferably*
    clover
  ½ *teaspoon freshly grated nutmeg*

  2 *cups milk*
  2 *eggs, lightly beaten*
2–3 *tablespoons orange-flavored*
    liqueur
  1 *cup heavy cream, whipped*
12 *orange sections without rind or*
    seeds, marinated 30 minutes or
    longer in a small amount of
    orange-flavored liqueur for
    garnish

METHOD:

1. Bring 1½ cups of the water to simmering and add salt. Add the wild rice, and cook, covered, until just tender, about 45 minutes. Uncover and toss with a fork to release the steam and to fluff up.
2. Cook the raisins in remaining cup of water until tender, about 15 minutes. Remove from heat and reserve in the cooking liquid.

3. Combine the cooked rice, the raisins and their liquid, butter, honey and nutmeg.

4. Heat milk in the top of a double boiler over simmering water, add rice mixture and stir in the beaten eggs. Cook, stirring, until mixture thickens, but do not let it boil. Remove from the heat and stir in the liqueur. Add more honey and more nutmeg, if desired.

5. Serve warm or cold. Top with the whipped cream and the marinated orange sections.

ICE CREAM AND SHERBET DESSERTS

FLAMING ICE CREAM DESSERT

SERVES 6

Astonish your guests with this dramatic dessert which is prepared and served at tableside in a chafing dish, individual servings prepared one by one. Guests may want to make their own.

3 *cups sugar*	¼ *cup Cointreau*
12 *pats unsalted butter*	¼ *cup Grand Marnier*
juice of 3 lemons or limes, seeds removed	6 *scoops (1½ to 2 pints) vanilla ice cream*
6 *slices fresh pineapple*	6 *tablespoons rum*

METHOD:

Set up a chafing dish over a burner. For each serving:

1. Caramelize ½ cup sugar together with 2 pats butter in the chafing dish.

2. Add the juice of ½ lemon or lime. Let bubble until brown and syrupy.

3. Place a slice of fresh pineapple in syrup to heat.

4. Add 2 teaspoons Cointreau and 2 teaspoons Grand Marnier. Remove from heat.

5. Working quickly, place a small scoop of ice cream in the center of the pineapple; spoon syrup over the ice cream and pineapple.

6. Pour 1 tablespoon of rum over the ice cream. Ignite (stand back and be careful) and serve at once while flaming.

7. Repeat all 6 steps for each serving.

CRÈME DE MENTHE SHERBET
WITH STRAWBERRIES

SERVES 6–8

3 *pints lemon sherbet*
⅓ *cup crème de menthe*

2 *pints fresh strawberries, hulled,*
washed and chilled
superfine sugar (*optional*)

METHOD:

1. Let sherbet soften slightly in refrigerator for about 30 minutes.

2. Turn sherbet into a large bowl and beat with an electric hand mixer, just until smooth and softened—but do not let it melt.

3. Quickly stir in crème de menthe until well combined. Turn into a 6-cup decorative mold.

4. Freeze until very firm, about 24 hours.

5. To serve, invert mold over chilled serving plate. Place hot, damp cloth over mold and shake out sherbet.

6. Dust strawberries with sugar if they are too tart for your taste. Garnish sherbet with some of the strawberries and serve the remaining berries in a bowl on the side.

BRANDIED APPLESAUCE PARFAIT

SERVES 6

FOR THE BRANDIED APPLESAUCE:
   3 *pounds ripe tart apples*
   2 *cups apple cider*
   ¼ *cup brandy*

   1 *pint lemon sherbet*

6 *tablespoons brandy*
1 *cup* (½ *pint*) *heavy cream,*
   whipped (*with sugar to taste,*
   if desired)
24 *pecan halves for garnish*

METHOD:

1. *Prepare the Brandied Applesauce:* Wash (do not peel), core and cut apples in quarters. Place in a 3-quart heavy-bottomed pot, add apple cider, cover and cook until tender. Cool slightly and puree in blender, then put through a fine sieve. There will be approximately 2 cups.

2. Place ½ cup applesauce in each of 6 parfait glasses.

3. Spoon a large ball of the sherbet in the center of each.

4. Pour 1 tablespoon brandy over the sherbet. Top with a large dollop of whipped cream. Place 4 pecan halves around center of the mound of cream in each glass and serve.

FRUIT DESSERTS

BAKED APPLES WITH PORT

SERVES 8

8 *large baking apples, washed*   1 *cup sugar*
   and dried   ¾ *cup water*
8 *teaspoons unsalted butter*   1¼ *cups port wine*

METHOD:
1. Preheat oven to 375°F.
2. Remove cores of apples to ½ inch of bottoms, cut a strip of peel from the hollowed stem ends and place apples in a baking pan.
3. Put a teaspoon of butter in each and sprinkle with 2 tablespoons of the sugar.
4. Pour the water into the pan and bake the apples for 15 minutes, or until about half the water has evaporated.
5. Then add the port and baste frequently for another 20 minutes, or until apples are tender. Serve warm or cold.

BAKED STUFFED APPLES

SERVES 6

6 *large apples (Rome Beauty is a*   ½ *teaspoon cinnamon*
   good variety), washed and dried   1 *cup light corn syrup*
½ *cup raisins*   ½ *cup water*
1 *small apple, cored and chopped*

METHOD:
1. Preheat oven to 375°F.
2. Core the 6 apples to ½ inch of bottom.
3. Pare around stem end to remove about 1 inch of skin.
4. Place apples in a deep baking dish.
5. Mix raisins, chopped apple and cinnamon. Stuff into apples.
6. Blend corn syrup and water together and pour over apples.

7. Cover dish and bake about 40 minutes, or until apples are tender. After apples are done, spoon some of the syrup from baking dish over them. Serve warm.

EVE'S TEMPTATION WITH WHIPPED SYLLABUB

SERVES 6

6 baking apples
3 tablespoons chopped walnuts
3 tablespoons finely cut dates
⅔ cup light brown sugar, firmly
   packed
2 tablespoons superfine sugar
boiling water

⅔ cup light rum, warmed

FOR THE WHIPPED SYLLABUB:
½ cup sugar
2 cups (1 pint) heavy cream
¼ cup sherry
½ teaspoon vanilla

METHOD:

1. Preheat oven to 375°F.

2. Core apples to ½ inch of bottom and peel upper third. Combine nuts, dates and brown sugar and fill centers with mixture.

3. Place in baking dish, and pour in enough boiling water to cover bottom of dish. Cover the dish and bake for 30 to 40 minutes, or until tender.

4. *Prepare the Whipped Syllabub:* Combine sugar with cream and stir to dissolve. Then whip cream until thick. Stir in sherry and vanilla.

5. Remove apples to individual serving plates, pour pan syrup over them, sprinkle lightly with superfine sugar and pour rum over each. Ignite rum with a match (stand back and be careful) and serve apples with a bowl of Whipped Syllabub on the side.

HONEY LIME APPLE WEDGES

SERVES 6

6 apples
9 tablespoons lime juice

¾ cup honey
pinch of cinnamon

METHOD:

1. Wash and dry apples. Core the apples, then peel quickly and sprinkle them at once with lime juice. Cut apples into wedges. Add

honey and cinnamon and toss lightly so that the apple wedges are well coated. Serve at room temperature or refrigerate until chilled.

BANANAS FOSTER

Here is a delightful dessert bearing my name; however the relationship is purely coincidental (it is actually a dish made famous at the popular Brennan's Restaurant in New Orleans).

6 tablespoons unsalted butter
¾ cup brown sugar
6 ripe bananas, peeled and sliced
   lengthwise

½ teaspoon cinnamon
3 ounces (6 tablespoons) banana
   liqueur
6 ounces (¾ cup) light rum

METHOD:

1. Melt butter in chafing dish over burner (or in skillet on top of stove). Blend in brown sugar.

2. Add bananas and sauté. Sprinkle with cinnamon.

3. Heat banana liqueur and rum together until warm and pour over sautéed bananas.

4. Ignite with lighted match on side of chafing dish and baste bananas with flaming liquid, using a long-handled spoon. Be careful to stand back as far as you can. Serve immediately.

BAKED BANANAS AMBROSIA

SERVES 8

8 large medium-ripe yellow
   bananas, peeled and cut in half
   lengthwise
5 tablespoons unsalted butter,
   melted

juice of 1 orange, strained
3 tablespoons honey
¼ cup light brown sugar
¾ cup finely grated coconut
⅔ cup orange liqueur

METHOD:

1. Preheat oven to 400°F.

2. Place bananas on buttered baking sheet or dish and brush with melted butter. Dribble orange juice and honey over bananas.

3. Place in the hot oven and bake 10 minutes. Remove from oven.

4. Mix together the brown sugar and coconut, sprinkle over bananas and bake 5 minutes more.

5. When ready to serve, place under broiler until lightly toasted. Heat liqueur until warm, pour over bananas and flame with lighted match, being careful to stand back. Serve immediately.

BAKED BANANAS WITH VANILLA CREAM

SERVES 6

6 *underripe green-tipped bananas,*
  cut lengthwise
one 12-ounce jar apricot preserves
  ½ *cup orange juice*

¼ *cup golden rum*
½ *cup flaked coconut*
1 *pint vanilla ice cream, softened*

METHOD:

1. Preheat oven to 375°F. Peel bananas; arrange in a shallow baking dish.

2. In a small saucepan, heat preserves until melted; remove from heat. Stir in orange juice and rum.

3. Pour over bananas. Sprinkle with coconut.

4. Bake, uncovered, 20 to 25 minutes, or until bananas are tender and coconut lightly toasted.

5. In a bowl, beat ice cream with a wooden spoon until smooth and of saucelike consistency. Serve over warm bananas.

BLACKBERRY FLUMMERY

SERVES 6–8

3 *pints (6 cups) blackberries,*
  washed and drained
2 *cups sugar*

2 *teaspoons cornstarch*
½ *cup water*
1 *cup heavy cream, whipped*

METHOD:

1. In a saucepan, simmer berries with sugar for 15 minutes, stirring from time to time.

2. Mix cornstarch with water until dissolved and stir into hot berry mixture until it thickens.

3. Let mixture cool. When quite cool, fold in whipped cream and chill until ready to serve.

FRESH FRUIT SALAD IN CHAMPAGNE

SERVES 6

3 *peaches*
6 *apricots*
1½ *pounds raspberries*
10 *ounces strawberries*
8 *ounces fresh red currants*
20 *almonds*

¾ *cup sugar*
½ *bottle chilled champagne*
  (1½ cups)
1 *cup (½ pint) heavy cream,*
  whipped, with sugar to taste

METHOD:

1. Skin the peaches and slice or cut into pieces. Wash the apricots and cut in half or quarters. Do not peel. Hull the strawberries and the raspberries if necessary. Wash and dry berries and currants.

2. Layer fruit (each variety a separate layer) in a glass or china bowl, sprinkling each layer with almonds and sugar.

3. Pour champagne over the fruit just before the salad is brought to the table.

4. Serve whipped cream separately.

Note: An alternative combination is the following: the flesh of a small melon, ½ pound mirabella plums, ½ pound sweet white grapes, 4 peaches and 2 pears (peeled and sliced).

FRUIT CURRY

SERVES 6

1 *large or 2 medium partially*
  ripened mangoes, peeled and
  sliced
2 *fresh peaches, peeled and sliced*
1 *cup diced pineapple*
2 *bananas, peeled and sliced*
2 *cups sauterne*
1½ *cups chicken broth*

1 *tablespoon arrowroot*
cold water
curry powder and salt
3 *tablespoons shelled pistachio*
  nuts
3 *tablespoons seedless raisins*
½ *cup grated coconut*

METHOD:

1. Combine all the fresh fruit. Pour the sauterne over fruit, mix and let stand for 2 hours at room temperature.

2. Drain the sauterne from the fruit and combine it with broth in a saucepan; let simmer for 15 minutes.

3. Dissolve arrowroot in 1½ tablespoons water and add to simmering sauterne-broth mixture, stirring until sauce thickens.

4. Add the curry powder and salt to taste, the fresh fruit, the nuts, raisins and coconut. Simmer for another 5 minutes and serve immediately.

BROILED GRAPEFRUIT WITH CURRIED HONEY

SERVES 6

3 *large grapefruit, cut in half and*
sectioned
2 *tablespoons clover honey*

½ *teaspoon curry powder*
fresh mint leaves for garnish

METHOD:

1. Preheat broiler to medium.

2. Spread 2 teaspoons honey over each grapefruit half; dust curry powder evenly over honey. Let stand at room temperature for 15 minutes.

3. When ready to serve, place grapefruit in a pan under broiler and broil just until bubbling lightly around the edges. Serve garnished with mint leaves.

MELON WITH CHERRIES AND CHAMPAGNE

SERVES 8

2 *large melons (honeydew, cran-*
shaw, casaba or cantaloupe)
½–1 *cup sugar to taste*

½ *pound pitted sweet cherries*
1 *bottle (3 cups) champagne,*
chilled

METHOD:

1. Cut the melon in half, remove the seeds and scoop out the flesh. Reserve the shells and scallop the edges. Cut the melon into small cubes. Put in a bowl, add the sugar and pitted cherries. Mix.

2. Pour in the champagne. Refrigerate for 2 hours. Return the mixture to the halved shells of the melon and serve on crushed ice.

FROSTED ORANGES

SERVES 6

These frosted oranges are refreshing and very pretty. They are nice to serve as a breakfast starter or a luncheon dessert.

6 *large navel oranges*
1 *egg white, unbeaten*
confectioner's sugar

*fresh melon balls, scooped out with
small end of a melon cutter*
sprigs of mint for garnish

METHOD:

1. Cut the tops off the oranges and reserve. With a sharp knife, cut around the inside of the orange along the rind (but not through the skin) and remove the flesh so that only a shell remains. Cut orange pulp into pieces and reserve. If necessary, slice a thin piece of the orange shell on the bottom so that the oranges can stand on a plate.

2. Spread the unbeaten egg white over the shells of the oranges and the cut-off tops.

3. Dust the orange shells and cut-off tops with sugar and allow to dry for a few moments. Mix the reserved orange pieces with melon balls. Fill the shells with the mixed fruit.

4. Replace the tops, use toothpicks if necessary to fasten them on. Garnish each with a sprig of mint. Refrigerate until ready to serve.

ORANGES ORIENTAL

SERVES 6

3 *large navel oranges*
1 *cup water*

2 *cups sugar*
6 *teaspoons Cointreau*

METHOD:

1. Remove outer peel from the oranges and cut the peel into thin julienne strips.

2. Place water in a saucepan with the sugar and the orange strips. Stir until sugar is dissolved and boil 3 to 4 minutes, or until strips are tender.

3. Remove pan from heat and let mixture cool. Cut all the white pith away from the oranges and section them.

4. Place orange sections in a bowl and pour cooled sauce over.

5. When ready to serve, put oranges and sauce in 6 small dishes and spoon 1 teaspoon Cointreau over each portion.

FLAMING PEACHES

SERVES 8

8 *fresh peaches 4 or 5 inches in diameter*
juice of 3 lemons, strained
½ *cup of each: guava, strawberry and raspberry preserves*
½–1 *cup sugar to taste*

2 *teaspoons grated lemon rind*
½ *cup Madeira*
½ *cup Kirsch*
2 *teaspoons vanilla*
12 *ounces slivered almonds*
½ *cup rum*

METHOD:

1. Bring a pot of water to boil. Dip peaches in water for 2 minutes; remove and peel off skins. Cut each peach in half, pit and place in 6 heatproof serving dishes, 2 halves to each dish. Sprinkle with lemon juice.

2. Combine the preserves and strain through a sieve. Mix strained preserves with sugar and lemon rind in a saucepan. Bring to a boil and cook a few minutes until they become a thick syrup.

3. Add Madeira, Kirsch and vanilla and let cool slightly. Pour syrup around the peach halves in each dish.

4. Sprinkle with almond slivers.

5. Warm the rum, pour over the peaches and flame each one by igniting with a match (stand back and be careful). Serve immediately.

PEACHES WITH CHOCOLATE SAUCE

SERVES 6

6 *large, firm peaches*
1½ *cups water*
1½ *cups sugar*
2 *teaspoons vanilla*
½ *teaspoon unsalted butter*
     (optional)

FOR THE CHOCOLATE SAUCE:
1½ *cups milk*

2 *ounces unsweetened chocolate*
2 *egg yolks*
¾ *cup sugar*
⅛ *teaspoon salt*
1 *tablespoon all-purpose flour*
2 *tablespoons unsalted butter*
2 *tablespoons liqueur (Cointreau*
     is a fine one)

METHOD:

1. Bring a pot of water to boil and blanch the peaches by placing them 2 at a time into the boiling water. Let them stand for 2 or 3 minutes. Remove peaches, then peel off the skins and cut in half and remove pit.

2. In a saucepan, combine water and sugar and stir until sugar dissolves. Boil for 5 minutes, add peaches, and then simmer just long enough for peaches to become tender (do not overcook). Remove from heat and add vanilla and the butter, if being used. Let peaches cool.

3. *Prepare the Chocolate Sauce:* Put milk and chocolate in a heavy saucepan or top part of a double boiler. Place pan over a pot of simmering (not boiling) water and simmer long enough for chocolate to melt. Remove from heat and let cool slightly. Meanwhile, whip egg yolks, add sugar and salt and continue to whip while you sift in the flour. When well blended, stir the egg mixture into the chocolate mixture and return to heat for about 5 minutes (do not boil). Add butter, blend in and remove from heat. Let cool and add the liqueur. Should the sauce be too thick, add a little more liqueur or light cream.

4. Serve the peaches in individual dishes, with the Chocolate Sauce in a bowl on the side.

FRESH PEARS DUBONNET

1½ cups red Dubonnet
1½ cups white Dubonnet
1¼ cups sugar
  2 vanilla beans, split, or 1 tea-
    spoon vanilla extract

12 pears, peeled and cored but left
  whole, stems on

FOR THE SAUCE:
  12 egg yolks
  1¼ cups and 1 tablespoon sugar
  1½ cups white Dubonnet

METHOD:

1. Prepare the pears: In saucepan, combine red and white Dubonnet, sugar and vanilla beans or extract. Bring to a boil and add pears. Cover and poach for 20 minutes or until pears are tender, basting frequently with the liquid. Remove pears from heat and let cool in poaching liquid.

2. Mound pears in serving dish with stems up and pour the liquid over them, discarding the vanilla bean. Refrigerate pears, basting occasionally with liquid until chilled.

3. *Prepare the Sauce:* Combine egg yolks and sugar in top of double boiler and heat over simmering water, stirring constantly, until sauce is thickened. Continue stirring while gradually adding Dubonnet. Remove from heat and beat until cool. Serve immediately as a topping for the chilled pears.

RUBY RED PEAR SUPREME

SERVES 6

FOR THE RUBY SAUCE:

2½ cups fresh or frozen (thawed)
  cranberries, washed and stems
  removed
1½ cups water
1 cup sugar
⅓ cup apple brandy
6 pears, peeled, halved and cored,
  or 12 canned pear halves, well
  drained

FOR THE SUPREME TOPPING:

4 egg yolks
1 cup confectioner's sugar
pinch of salt
2 tablespoons apple brandy
1 cup (½ pint) heavy cream,
  whipped
freshly grated nutmeg

¼ cup whole blanched almonds,
  toasted, sprigs of fresh mint and
  nutmeg for garnish

METHOD:

1. *Prepare the Ruby Sauce:* Combine cranberries and water in saucepan; bring to a boil and simmer 15 minutes, stirring occasionally. Remove from heat and puree through a fine sieve. Return pureed cranberries to saucepan and add sugar and apple brandy; stir until sugar is dissolved.

2. Add pears and, if fresh, cook until barely tender; if canned, simply add to the sauce. Remove saucepan from heat and let cool; cover pears and refrigerate until cold.

3. *Prepare the Supreme Topping:* Beat egg yolks; add confectioner's sugar and apple brandy and beat until smooth. Cook in top of double boiler over hot (not boiling) water about 10 minutes or until sauce thickens, stirring constantly. Remove from heat and cool. Fold in the whipped cream.

4. Serve pears with some of the Ruby Sauce in a stemmed glass; spoon Supreme Topping over, dust lightly with nutmeg and garnish with toasted almonds and sprigs of mint.

PINEAPPLE WITH CHAMPAGNE

SERVES 4

1 *fresh ripe medium-size pineapple*
½–1 *cup sugar, depending on tart-*
  ness of pineapple

½ *bottle (1½ cups) champagne,*
  chilled

METHOD:

1. Cut the pineapple in half lengthwise. Insert a long, sharp knife about ½ inch from the outside edge and cut along the rind to loosen the fruit without damaging shell. Remove the fruit from the shell of both halves and reserve the shells. Cut the fruit into small cubes and place in a large bowl.

2. Sprinkle the pineapple cubes with sugar and add the champagne. Stir until sugar is dissolved. Steep for 45 minutes. Spoon half the mixture into each empty pineapple half. Refrigerate until serving time. Serve directly from shells, 1 to a plate.

BRANDIED PRUNES

SERVES 6

Here's a new approach to the prune—a fruit all too often taken for granted.

1 *pound large pitted prunes*
¾ *cup cognac*

12 *ladyfingers*

METHOD:

1. Pour boiling water to cover over prunes to soften. Drain immediately and place prunes in a large jar.

2. Pour cognac over prunes. Cover jar tightly. Shake well and let stand overnight at room temperature.

3. Carefully stuff each pitted prune with another pitted prune by opening end and slipping it in. Refrigerate until well chilled.

4. To serve, divide stuffed prunes among 6 dessert glasses and spoon a little cognac over. Serve 2 ladyfingers with each portion.

RASPBERRIES WITH SABAYON

SERVES 8

2 *pints fresh raspberries, rinsed
and drained*

½ *cup sugar*
½ *cup dry white wine*
2 *tablespoons raspberry brandy*

FOR THE SABAYON:
8 *egg yolks, at room temperature*

METHOD:

1. Beat egg yolks and sugar in electric mixer on high speed until mixture is pale lemon-colored and forms a ribbon when lifted with beater. Gradually beat in wine and brandy.

2. Pour mixture into top part of double boiler. Cook over low heat, whisking constantly, until mixture thickens into a fluffy custard, about 5 minutes. Remove from heat immediately.

3. Divide raspberries among 8 dessert bowls. Spoon Sabayon over berries immediately and serve.

STRAWBERRIES IMBROVNEV

SERVES 2 OR 3

After you have placed one of these strawberries in your mouth, you'll taste the special flavor of each ingredient, then they will all mellow into a singular taste sensation—the incomparable taste of Strawberries Imbrovnev.

1½ *pints fresh strawberries (stems
on, if possible), washed and
patted dry.*
¾ *cup Grand Marnier (or any
other orange-flavored liqueur)*

¾ *cup confectioner's sugar*
¾ *cup sour cream*
¾ *cup brown sugar*

METHOD:

1. Pile the strawberries in a small decorative basket and place in the middle of a large flat tray, silver if you have one.

2. Surround the container with four small silver or china bowls, one

filled with the liqueur, the second with confectioner's sugar, the third with sour cream and the fourth with brown sugar.

3. To eat: Holding a strawberry by the stem, dip it first into the liqueur, then in the confectioner's sugar, then in the sour cream, and finally in the brown sugar.

STRAWBERRIES OR RASPBERRIES WITH CHAMPAGNE

SERVES 6

1 *pound strawberries or raspberries*
½ *cup sugar*

¼ *bottle (¾ cup) champagne, chilled*
1 *cup (½ pint) heavy cream, whipped*

METHOD:

1. Wash the berries and drain well. Put them in a glass bowl, sprinkle with the sugar, mix gently to coat and refrigerate until chilled. See that the champagne is well chilled when ready to serve the berries.

2. Pour the champagne over the fruit just before serving. Serve whipped cream separately.

FLAMBÉED STRAWBERRY OMELET

SERVES 6

2 *cups crushed strawberries*
¼ *cup sugar or 2 tablespoons honey*
¼ *cup sherry*
2 *tablespoons Kirsch or other liqueur*
4 *eggs, separated*

½ *teaspoon salt*
pinch of pepper and salt
½ *cup heavy cream*
1 *tablespoon unsalted butter*
superfine sugar
¼ *cup light rum, warmed*

METHOD:

1. Combine berries, the ¼ cup sugar or honey, sherry and Kirsch (or other liqueur) and let stand 1 hour.

2. When ready to make the omelet, preheat oven to 350°F.

3. Beat egg yolks, adding salt, pepper and cream.

4. Beat egg whites until stiff but not dry. Fold into egg yolk mixture.

5. Melt butter in a 9-inch oven-proof skillet and when hot, pour in egg mixture and cook over low heat 3 to 5 minutes or until omelet puffs and is browned on the bottom. Place in oven for 10 to 15 minutes, until top springs back when touched with your finger.

6. Slip omelet onto a hot platter when ready to serve. Meanwhile, in a saucepan, heat berry mixture but do not boil. Pour over and around omelet, sprinkle with superfine sugar. Pour rum over berries, ignite with a lighted match (stand back and be careful) and serve flaming.

CHAPTER ELEVEN
BEVERAGES

SIR CECIL BEATON'S
ELDER FLOWER CHAMPAGNE

MAKES 2 QUARTS

The flowers of the elder tree, which are creamy white and grow in large clusters, produce a honeylike, strongly flavored and slightly bitter wine—actually an old-fashioned herbal remedy or tisane. The black or red elderberries are also used to make wine and jelly.

8 *cups water*
3/4 *pound light brown sugar*
2 *clusters elder flowers*

1 *tablespoon white wine vinegar*
juice of 1/2 lemon
grated peel of 1/2 lemon

METHOD:

1. Place water, sugar, flowers, vinegar, lemon juice and grated lemon peel in a large earthenware crock. Mix and let stand 24 hours at room temperature.

2. Strain into sterilized screw-top bottles and close tightly. The champagne will be ready to drink in 14 days, but it tastes better if left longer. Chill well before serving.

CRANBERRY CURAÇAO

SERVES 8

1 *cup Curaçao*
1½ *cups sugar*
2 *cups orange sections, seeded and diced*

6 *cups fresh or frozen (thawed) cranberries*

METHOD:

1. Put the Curaçao, sugar and diced oranges in blender jar and cover. Turn on high speed and blend about 3 seconds.

2. Add the cranberries and blend until well crushed.

3. Pour liquid mixture from blender into a bowl and refrigerate until ready to serve.

MONTEGO BAY PUNCH

SERVES 8 (2 DRINKS A PERSON)

1½ cups sugar
1¼ cups boiling water
1 cup fresh lime juice
2½ cups Jamaica rum
1 egg white

1 or 2 drops of green food coloring
(optional)
1 cup very finely crushed ice
4 slices lime, cut in half, and
grated nutmeg for garnish

METHOD:

1. Place the sugar in a medium-size saucepan, add boiling water and boil for about 10 minutes to make a thick syrup. Remove from heat and cool.

2. Add lime juice to syrup and mix; add the rum. Put in freezer for about 4 hours to chill very well.

3. When ready to serve, add egg white and optional green coloring. Add the crushed ice, pour into blender in batches and blend for a few seconds until very frothy. Serve in chilled glasses garnished with a half slice of lime and a pinch of grated nutmeg on top.

OLD SOUTH EGGNOG

MAKES ABOUT 24 SIX-OUNCE DRINKS

12 eggs, separated
1 pound sugar
1 quart milk

1 quart cream
1 pint Bourbon
freshly grated nutmeg

METHOD:

1. Beat the egg whites very stiff with ½ pound of sugar. Set aside.

2. Beat the egg yolks with the remaining sugar. Stir milk and cream into the egg yolks.

3. Now here's the real secret of successful eggnog: Dribble the Bourbon into the mixture drop by drop.

4. Fold the beaten egg whites in gently and refrigerate until chilled. Serve eggnog topped with freshly grated nutmeg.

COFFEE ALEXANDER

SERVES 8

1½ cups crème de cacao
8 cups strong ice-cold coffee

¾ pint heavy cream, lightly
   whipped

METHOD:

1. Pour 3 tablespoons of crème de cacao in the bottom of 8 tall, slim glasses. Fill each almost to the top with the cold coffee. Mix.

2. Spoon a dollop of the lightly whipped cream to float over the top and serve.

SUMMER ICED COFFEE

SERVES 6

½ cup instant coffee
¾ teaspoon cinnamon
⅛ teaspoon ground cloves
1 cup boiling water

3 cups cold water
2 trays of ice cubes
sugar (optional)
cream (optional)

METHOD:

1. Combine coffee, cinnamon and cloves in a 1½ quart pitcher. Add boiling water; stir until coffee is dissolved.

2. Add cold water and refrigerate, covered, until ready to serve.

3. To serve: Put several ice cubes in each of 6 tall glasses. Place a lemon twist in each and fill with chilled coffee. Serve with sugar and cream if desired.

SPICED ICED TEA

SERVES 6

6 cups cold water
1 stick cinnamon
5 whole cloves
3 tablespoons tea leaves

¼ cup fresh lemon juice, strained
sugar or honey to taste
6 lemon slices for garnish

METHOD:

1. Combine water, cinnamon and cloves in a saucepan. Bring water and spices to a rolling boil.

2. Remove from heat. Add tea. Brew 5 or 6 minutes; stir and strain into a large pitcher. Add lemon juice and sugar or honey to taste.

3. Cool to room temperature. To serve, pour into ice-filled glasses and garnish with a slice of lemon.

BRUNCH FRUIT PUNCH

SERVES 6–8

3 *cups orange juice, fresh, if*
possible
2 *cups apple juice*
2½ *cups peach juice*

¼ *cup lime juice, strained*
¼ *cup honey*
lime slices for garnish

METHOD:

1. Blend all ingredients together.

2. Serve well chilled, or over very finely crushed ice, with a slice of lime slightly slit on one side and stuck on the rim of each glass for garnish.

PART II
THE MENUS

BOUNTIFUL BRUNCHES

A NOTE ON THE MENUS: *The menus that follow have all been planned to achieve a harmonious blend of taste and appearance. For recipe directions, consult the Index beginning on page 389. You will, of course, adjust quantities to the number of persons being served.*

Baked Apples with Port
Mock Cheese Soufflé
Orange Muffins

❧

Baked Stuffed Apples
Cheese Fondue on Toast
Hot Potato Scones

❧

Cranberry Curaçao
Cheese and Eggs
Banana Bran Muffins

❧

Sliced Mango or Papaya with
Lime Wedges
Southern Crab Cakes
Brunch Berry Muffins

❧

Honey-Lime Apple Wedges
Baked Tomatoes and Cheese
Cornflake Muffins

❧

Apricot Juice or Slice of Cantaloupe
Baked Ham Hash and Tomatoes
Sally Lunn Bread

LUXURIOUS LUNCHEONS

The flavors and spices in some of these dishes may evoke memories of different countries you have visited.

Chicken Curry Soup
Shrimp and Vegetable Scampi
Orange Velvet Coconut Pie

❧

Fish Stew Américaine
Raw Broccoli Salad
Orange Soufflé with Raspberry Sauce

❧

Lamb and Vegetable Pot Pie
Radish and Jerusalem Artichoke
Relish
Basic Sponge Cake Roulade
Spiced Iced Tea

❧

Crusted Onion Soup
Baked Chicken Hash
Acorn Squash with Pineapple
Baked Bananas with Vanilla Cream

❧

Provençale Bean Soup
Tomato Cheese Pie
Cole Slaw with Sour Cream Dressing
Melon with Cherries in Champagne

❧

Cream of Sorrel Soup
Shrimp Kebabs
Kentucky Bourbon Cake

❧

Garden Soup
or
Lobster Stew
Spider Corn Bread
Hot Apple Soufflé Alexandria
with Rum Cream

SPECIAL OCCASION LUNCHEONS

Chicken Gumbo Soup
Onion Pie
Endive, Heart of Romaine and
Watercress Salad
Old-Fashioned 1–2–3–4 Cake

❧

Montego Bay Punch
Maryland Crab Tartar Rolled in
Virginia Ham
Tomato, Mushroom, Avocado and
Endive Salad
Simca's Marquise Glacée au Chocolat

❧

Cheese Balls
Cream of Asparagus Soup
Baked Herbed Salmon
Hostess Peas
Chocolate Cheese Cake
Coffee Alexander

❧

Chilled Cucumber Soup
Salmon Seviche
Marinated Vegetables
Blackberry Flummery

❧

Duck Liver Pâté with Pistachio Nuts
Smoked Breast of Turkey with
Broccoli
Herbed Bread
Seasoned Spinach
Macadamia Nut Pie

❧

Boston Clam Chowder
Steak and Kidney Pie
Lettuce and Watercress with Spicy
Dressing
Peaches with Chocolate Sauce

❧

Crunchy Vegetable Salad with
Ginger Lime Dressing
Sweetbreads with Pears
Golden Dandelion Blossoms Sauté
Brown Derby Grapefruit Cake

❧

Virginia Peanut Soup
Fried Pig's Trotters
Sour Cream Biscuits with
Smoked Ham Butter
Spinach Salad Bowl
Plantation Molasses and Black
Walnut Pie

VEGETARIAN LUNCHEON

Baked Potatoes Topped with
Creamed Leeks
Baked Creamy Beets on a Bed of
Steamed Honey-Flavored Beet Tops
Celery Root with Creole Mustard

Butter
Radish and Jerusalem Artichoke
Relish
Carrot Custard with Honey

DIVINE DINNERS

Potato Leek Soup
Flank Steak in Wine with
Egg Noodles
Creamed Green Beans
Gale Beets
Eve's Temptation with Whipped
Syllabub

Fresh Tomato Bouillon
Lamb Stew
Brussels Sprouts on a bed of
Toasted Bread Cubes
Jellied Beet Salad
Southern Potato Buns
Fruited Rum Custard Blueberry
Parfait

Fried Frog's Legs
Roast Chicken with Vegetables
Blushing Rice
Hot Lemon Soufflé Pudding with
Lemon Zest Cream

Cream of Fresh Mushroom Soup
Roasted Guinea Hen
Sweet Potato Pie with Pineapple
Crème de Menthe Sherbet with
Strawberries

Chilled Orange Soup
Scallops with Champagne
Smothered Quail
Caribbean Rice
Beet and Horseradish Relish
Peach Mallow Pie

Oyster Stew
Pheasant with Marsala
Hot Puffs Filled with Butter
Zucchini with Sliced Toasted
Almonds
Yogurt Pie

Oxtail-Barley Soup
Lobster-Stuffed Sole
Hot Potato Salad
Picadillo-Stuffed Onions
Strawberry-Orange Cream

❧❦

Golden Cheese and Beer Soup
Baked Flounder Filets in Marguéry
Sauce
Pommes Soufflés
Garlic-Seasoned Broccoli
Russian Cream

❧❦

Fresh Mushroom Consommé
Baked Jumbo Shrimp Stuffed with
Dilled Maryland Backfin Crab Meat
Creamy Cheese Potatoes
Vegetable Spaghetti
Brandied Prunes

❧❦

Broiled Grapefruit with Curried
Honey
Deviled Halibut Steaks
Fresh Corn Pudding
Onion Hush Puppies
Brandied Applesauce Parfait

❧❦

Orange Carrot Soup
Deviled Oysters
Venison Pot Roast
Stuffed Artichoke Petals
Heavenly Custard

❧❦

Veal Cordon Bleu
Pink Beans with Herbs
Steamed Cauliflower with
Hollandaise Sauce
Kentucky Lemon Pie

❧❦

Crab Meat Dewey
Pumpkin Soup
Fennel Pork Roast
Steamed Rice
Herbed Scalloped Tomatoes
Coconut Chiffon Pie

❧❦

Veal Chops Orloff
Mixed Greens Sauté
Raw Beet, Peanut and Tomato Salad
Pumpkin Pie with Bourbon

❧❦

Roast Pigeon
Hominy Grits Soufflé
Tomato Relish
Fruit Curry

❧❦

Filet of Salmon with Champagne
Baked Curried Tomato
Pureed Lima Beans
Mile High Strawberry Pie

❧❦

Chicken Creole Soup with
Brown Rice
Ham Patties with Orange Celery
Sauce
Butterfly Squash on Tomato Rings
Cream Cheese Soufflé

❧❦

Mousse of Avocado on Herbed Toast
Braised Trout Wrapped in Lettuce
"Magic Wheat" Gourmet
Stuffed Mushrooms with
Spinach Sauce
Flambéed Strawberry Omelet

❧❦

Gumbo
Roast Veal with Orange Sauce
Glazed Onions
Julienne Carrots and Snow Peas
Flaming Peaches

❧❦

Button Mushrooms with Dilled
Sour Cream on Toast
Squash Soup Spiked with Apple

Southern Corn Sticks
Roast East Hampton Golden Goose
Green Bean with Pimento Butter
Endive and Heart of Romaine Salad
with Mango Wedges and Cheddar
Cheese Fingers
Frosty Lime Pie

❦

Chicken Liver and California
Walnut Pâté
Roast Golden Boneless Chicken
with Curried Chutney Glaze
Corn and Cheese "Pie"
Green Beans with Tomatoes
Turnip-Radish Relish
Wild Rice Pudding with Raisins

❦

Oysters Provençale
Golden Apple Soup
Venison Rump Roast
Savory Wild Rice
California Relish
Chocolate Almond Dream Cake

❦

Baked Imperial Crab Snug Harbor
Spinach, Egg and Parmesan
Cheese Soup
Filets of Sole with Champagne
Potato Puffs
Apricot Sour Cream Pie

❦

Lobster Saramba
Stuffed Roast Squab
Steamed Carrots with Lemon
Butter Glaze
Strawberries Imbrovnev

❦

Potted Deviled Crab
Bourbon Beef and Oyster Pot
Double Baked Potatoes
Brussels Sprouts with Peanuts

Snow Cream with Red Raspberry
Sauce

❦

Carrot Blini with Red Caviar
Jerusalem Artichoke-and-
Celery Soup
Cajun Turtle Stew
Orange-Flavored Rice
Baked Tomatoes Stuffed with Leeks
Avocado Supreme
Coconut Velvet Pie

❦

Sea Food Chowder
Bass Stewed in Champagne
Southern Baked Beans
Guacamole-Filled Tomatoes
Strawberry Mousseline

❦

Cheese Anchovy Spread
Mushroom Soup
Quail with Champagne
Oyster Pancakes—Eastern Shore
Butterfly Squash on Tomato Rings
Baked Onions Stuffed with
Pecans or Peanuts
Cherry Soufflé

❦

Medallion (Rock Lobster Tail)
Cocktail
Happy Duckling in Burgundy
Green Beans with Pimento Butter
Spinach, Mushrooms, Jerusalem
Artichokes and Endive Salad with
Ginger Wine Dressing
Bananas Foster

❦

Roast Crown of Mutton Stuffed with
Prunes and Rice
Red Cabbage and Chestnuts
in Red Wine
Apple Cake

A DINNER FROM THE GOOD EARTH:
A VEGETARIAN TREAT

Root vegetables, which grow down deep in the topsoil layer, may possibly absorb more of the vital elements than vegetables that grow on vines and stems above the surface. So it is important for us to eat as many of these vegetables as possible—especially raw or in a partially cooked state with their well-scrubbed skins left on. Remember, the carrot yellow, the beet red, the onion green and the turnip white are nature's own good earth colors. Even though the vegetables listed in the following menu are all from the good earth, it is often necessary to add a bit of garnish or seasoning to enhance the flavors a little. It is also important that the vegetables never be overcooked.

Celery Root Vinaigrette with
Roasted Garlic Cloves
Iced Jerusalem Artichoke Slices
Radish Roses with Mustard Butter

Cream of Leek Soup with Puffed
Potato Skins and Roasted Peanuts

Platter of:
Baked Whole Baby Beets with
Creamed Fresh Horseradish
Purple Top Turnips with

Candied Ginger Root
Roasted Whole Honey Glazed
Onions with Toasted Curried
Walnut Halves
Braised Parsnips Rolled in
Chive Crumbs
Steamed Whole Carrots Rolled
in Parsley Butter

Southern Yam Pie with Crunchy
Pecan Topping
Elder Flower Champagne

HOLIDAY FEASTS

New Year's Eve

Chilled Apple Soup
Marinated Rump of Beef
Savory Brown Rice
Creamed Silver Onions

Dressed Spinach
Individual Lemon Soufflés
Coffee Alexander

Easter

Tomato Consommé
Prague Ham en Croûte with
Champagne
Baked Creamed Potatoes

Asparagus with Lemon Butter
Carob Almond Torte with Butter
Cream Frosting and Orange Zest

Fourth of July

Chilled Cucumber Soup
Soy-Honey Glazed Barbecued
Spareribs

Zucchini Gratin
Cauliflower Salad
Black Bottom Ice Cream Pie

There's Something About a Turkey
at Thanksgiving

Since the first Thanksgiving, this big bird has ruled supreme. Other feathered aristocrats have tried to fill the Thanksgiving niche but they've never really made much headway. The turkey just refuses to step aside, no matter what the competition. And these days more turkey is being served on all menus everywhere throughout the year.

And so it should be, for the bird really has what it takes. The turkey is economical and comparatively low in calories and fat. Leftovers yield those delicious slices of white meat, ideal for so many uses, cold plates and sandwiches included. The dark meat combines with white for delicious salads, and the bones make a rich, hearty soup. The possibilities are endless.

So, on this November holiday, make the most of our traditional American bird, unrivaled as a true symbol of Thanksgiving.

Chafing Dish Oysters	Stewed Creamy Chestnuts
Onion Soup	Baked Tomatoes Stuffed with Rice
Boneless Stuffed Turkey	Carob Cheesecake

Thanksgiving Without the Turkey

Baked Silver Onion Soup with White Wine	Puree of Green Peas with Capers
Toasted Cheese Fingers	Tossed Green Salad with Shredded Beets, with Red Wine Vinaigrette Dressing
Chutney-Glazed Roast Chicken with Pecan Stuffing	Icy Fresh Cranberry Pie
Corn Fritters	

Christmas

Old South Eggnog	Double Baked Sweet Potatoes
Consommé of Fresh Lemon Soup	Red Cabbage and Chestnuts in Wine
Roast Goose with Savory Fruit Stuffing	Coconut and Cherry Torte with Burgundy Wine Sauce

BEDAZZLING BUFFETS AND PERFECT PARTIES

Sherried Crab Bake
Cheese Soup
Filet of Beef Burgundy
with Bordelaise Sauce
Baked Stuffed Artichokes
Pureed Ginger Carrots
Fresh Pears Dubonnet

❧

Leek and Watercress Soup with
Southern Corn Sticks
Baked Salmon in Rhine Wine
Mousseline Potatoes
Guacamole Salad
Walnut Glory Cake

❧

Lobster Bisque
Roast Hip of Beef
French Potato Soufflé
Cauliflowerets with Mushrooms and
Sweet Pepper Strips
Old-Fashioned Steamed Molasses
Fruit Pudding with Bourbon
Hard Sauce

❧

Quick Beet Consommé
Savory Scallops
Baked Lamb Hash au Gratin
Candied Parsnips with Pineapple
Chocolate Cheese Cake I

❧

Puree of Black Bean Soup
Mushroom Shrimp Hot Pot
Black Walnut, Apple and
Watercress with Sesame-Vermouth
Dressing
Brandied Apple Soufflé with
Foamy Sauce

❧

Celery Root Soup
Herbed Mixed Grill
Radish and Carrot Salad with
Eggless "Mayonnaise"
Mother's Fudge Cake

❧

Baked Lamb Hash au Gratin
Curried Mushrooms
Asparagus Tips, Zucchini, Red
Pepper and Watercress Salad with
French Dressing with Horseradish
Delightful Chocolate Cake

❧

Crown Roast of Pork
Wild and White Rice
Green Peas with Red Sweet
Pepper Strips and Onion Rings
Rum Chocolate Souffléed Dessert

INDEX

INDEX